PERL
HACKS™

Other Perl resources from O'Reilly

Related titles
Perl Best Practices

Perl Testing: A Developer's Notebook™

Advanced Perl Programming

Programming Perl

Intermediate Perl

Perl Cookbook

Hacks Series Home
hacks.oreilly.com is a community site for developers and power users of all stripes. Readers learn from each other as they share their favorite tips and tools for Mac OS X, Linux, Google, Windows XP, and more.

Perl Books Resource Center
perl.oreilly.com is a complete catalog of O'Reilly's books on Perl and related technologies, including sample chapters and code examples.

Perl.com is the central web site for the Perl community. It is the perfect starting place for finding out everything there is to know about Perl.

Conferences
O'Reilly brings diverse innovators together to nurture the ideas that spark revolutionary industries. We specialize in documenting the latest tools and systems, translating the innovator's knowledge into useful skills for those in the trenches. Visit *conferences.oreilly.com* for our upcoming events.

Safari Bookshelf (*safari.oreilly.com*) is the premier online reference library for programmers and IT professionals. Conduct searches across more than 1,000 books. Subscribers can zero in on answers to time-critical questions in a matter of seconds. Read the books on your Bookshelf from cover to cover or simply flip to the page you need. Try it today for free.

PERL
HACKS™

chromatic with Damian Conway
and Curtis "Ovid" Poe

O'REILLY®

Beijing · Cambridge · Farnham · Köln · Paris · Sebastopol · Taipei · Tokyo

Perl Hacks™

by chromatic with Damian Conway and Curtis "Ovid" Poe

Editors: Allison Randal and Tatiana Apandi

Production Editor: Darren Kelly

Copyeditor: Nancy Reinhardt

Proofreader: Darren Kelly

Indexer: Johnna VanHoose Dinse

Cover Designer: Linda Palo

Interior Designer: David Futato

Illustrators: Robert Romano and Jessamyn Read

Printing History:

May 2006:   First Edition.

 This book uses RepKover™, a durable and flexible lay-flat binding.

ISBN: 0-596-52674-1
[M]

Contents

Credits

About the Authors

chromatic works for O'Reilly Media, where he edits the free and open source web sites of the O'Reilly Network. In his spare time, he writes books such as this one. In the remaining minutes, he contributes to the CPAN, Perl 5, Perl 6, Parrot, and even Pugs. He lives just west of Portland, Oregon by a park and a creek and would like to finish more projects someday, including writing a novel, a comic book, a television show, and sleeping. Catch up on his hobbies at *http://wgz.org/chromatic*.

Dr. Damian Conway is a professional Perl boffin. As the author of numerous popular CPAN modules (*http://search.cpan.org/~dconway*) and two highly regarded books on Perl, he is also a widely sought-after conference speaker and runs an international IT training company—Thoughtstream (*http://damian.conway.org*)—which provides Perl training from beginner to masterclass level throughout Europe, North America, and Australasia. He spends most of his less-than-copious free time working with Larry Wall on the design of Perl 6. [Hack #5], [Hack #13], [Hack #14], [Hack #34], [Hack #54], [Hack #86], [Hack #90], [Hack #92], [Hack #93], [Hack #94], [Hack #95], [Hack #99], [Hack #100]

Earlier this century, displaying his usual stellar sense of timing, Curtis "Ovid" Poe switched from mainframes to web programming in Perl and promptly watched the dot-com industry implode. Despite this minor setback and working for several currently non-existent companies, Ovid stuck with Perl and actually discovered he liked it. A frequent speaker at user groups and author of numerous CPAN modules and a popular Perl CGI course, Ovid is a Perl Foundation Steering Committee member and also heads the TPF grant committee. [Hack #10], [Hack #31], [Hack #50], [Hack #56], [Hack #57], [Hack #58], [Hack #60]

About the Contributors

Perl is also a language with a rich and varied community of experts, wizards, gurus, goofs, and ne'er-do-wells. A few of the most colorful characters* contributed to this book.

Adrian Howard still hopes that Lisp and Smalltalk will take over the world, but in the meantime gets paid for playing with Perl and Ruby amongst other things. Agile fanatic. Testing bigot. Usability zealot. Recently guilt tripped into being a Perl Grant Manager by Ovid. Saving up for a small castle to share with his beloved Kathryn and a small band of loyal Yorkshire Terriers. [Hack #15], [Hack #63]

Chris Dolan is a software developer living in Madison, Wisconsin. With a Ph.D. in Astronomy, he has a very strong math and science background. He started programming professionally as a teenager in the late 1980s. During his free time, he is an active participant in several online software development communities and is an avid bicyclist. [Hack #40]

David Landgren started using Perl 4.019 when awk was no longer sufficient to cope with the things he was trying to do. In 1999 he founded the Paris Perl Mongers and helped organize the YAPC::Europe 2003 conference. He currently works at a large French human resources firm, where he likes to go by the title of IT Operations Manager, using Perl everywhere. He spends what little spare time he has left writing summaries for the perl5-porters mailing list. Contact him at *david@landgren.net*. [Hack #98]

David Wheeler, a longtime Perl hacker, made a name for himself as the lead developer of the Bricolage content management system, and as President and founder of Kineticode (*http://www.kineticode.com*), a web software company. His work on Bricolage led him over the last year to develop the Kinetic Platform, a next-generation enterprise web services application platform. He lives in Portland, Oregon. [Hack #7], [Hack #28]

Guillaume Cottenceau is a software developer. He's been interested in computers for too long to remember, enjoys programming with various tools and languages, and found himself lucky enough to be the catalyst for a game written in Perl called "Frozen-Bubble" which is regularly cited as the favorite game of the Linux community. [Hack #16]

H. Merijn Brand is a Perl 5 porter, the Configure pumpking, and an Amsterdam Perl Monger. He was born on December 30, 1961, is married, and has two kids. He has worked as a data analyst for PROCURA B.V. in

---

* Pun strongly intended.

The Netherlands since June 1991. Visit his home page at *http://mirrors.develooper.com/hpux*. [Hack #21]

Jesse Vincent doesn't drink that often, but does find that a drink or two tends to improve the CPAN remarkably. [Hack #37]

Joe McMahon is a test automation architect at Yahoo! whose background includes extensive development experience: 25 years of work at NASA, with everything from spacecraft ground communications systems to Web development. He has contributed to core Perl test support, supplied the debuggers internal documentation, and supports several CPAN modules, from `App::SimpleScan` and `WWW::Mechanize::Pluggable` to `Date::PeriodParser` and `GraphViz::Data::Structure`. [Hack #59]

Joshua ben Jore came to Perl because he had to write a CGI app for a political campaign and he'd heard that Perl was best for that sort of thing. He stayed when he found out for himself how wonderful CPAN was. His latest projects have been working toward getting Lispy macros and lazy evaluation in Perl and learning what Prolog has to offer. He is well-known at perlmonks.org under the handle diotalevi and admits to being a Morris dancer. [Hack #83]

Michael Graham is a Perl programmer who lives in Toronto where he writes web applications with `CGI::Application` and its rich suite of plug-ins. He works at Wilder & Associates (*http://www.wilder.ca*). He likes music, long walks on the beach, and test-driven development. [Hack #68], [Hack #69]

Philippe "BooK" Bruhat, author of `HTTP::Proxy` and `Net::Proxy`, lives in Lyon, France with his wife and cat and is an active member of the French and European Perl communities. He worked on the translations of *Programming Perl*, 3rd Edition and *Perl Best Practices* for O'Reilly France, and publishes Perl articles in *GNU/Linux Magazine France*. As the co-developper of Act (A Conference Toolkit) and a member of the YAPC Europe Foundation, he helps organize European Perl workshops and conferences, at which he is also a regular speaker. He would love it if you tried his `Acme::MetaSyntactic` module (updated weekly). [Hack #18], [Hack #97]

Ricardo Signes trained for a career in philosophy, but the sudden onset of the Industrial Revolution forced him to work with baser forms of logic. He lives in Bethlehem, Pennsylvania and writes Perl for Pobox.com. [Hack #8]

Sean M. Burke is a perfectly normal human being, based on organic molecules, and exhibiting bilateral symmetry. He is typical. He has written two O'Reilly books, *Perl and LWP* and *RTF Pocket Guide*, has contributed dozens of modules to CPAN, and was a regular columnist for *The Perl Journal* for about five years. (His articles appear in the various O'Reilly *Best of the*

Perl Journal books, notably the *Games, Diversions & Perl Culture* volume.) Trained as a linguist, he now lives on an island in southeast Alaska, where he develops tools for Native language preservation. Wild rumors place his web site at *http://interglacial.com*. [Hack #3], [Hack #6], [Hack #11]

Simon Wistow currently herds London.pm—the largest and most rowdy of all the Perl Monger groups. In his spare time he writes rather too many CPAN modules of dubious usefulness. [Hack #39]

Stephen B. Jenkins (a.k.a. Erudil) is the senior programmer/analyst at the Aerodynamics Laboratory of the Institute for Aerospace Research, National Research Council of Canada. He has written for *Dr. Dobb's Journal, Linux Journal, The Perl Journal*, the USENIX Association, the American Institute of Aeronautics and Astronautics, the Aerospace and Electronics Systems Society of the IEEE, and the Association for Computing Machinery. For more info, see *http://www.Erudil.com*. [Hack #101]

Tim Allwine is a Senior Software Engineer at O'Reilly Media, Inc. He develops software for the Market Research group, writes various spidering tools that collect data from disparate sites, and is involved in the development of web services at O'Reilly. [Hack #71]

Tom Moertel is a regular contributor to the Pittsburgh Perl Mongers. He created Test::LectroTest, a specification-based testing system for Perl, and PXSL ("pixel"), a convenient shorthand for writing markup-heavy XML documents. He also wrote *The Coder's Guide to Coffee*, a concise guide to the programmer's most misunderstood utility beverage. He lives in Pittsburgh, Pennsylvania, where he runs a consulting practice specializing in solving difficult software problems. Read more about his projects and interests, which include espresso and functional programming, at *http://blog.moertel.com*. [Hack #61]

Brett Warden, BSEE, specializes in Perl programming and embedded/telco systems. He lives in the Northwest U.S. with his wife and son. You can find a collection of odd projects at *http://www.wgz.com/bwarden*. His Perl Monks username is isotope. [Hack #42]

Acknowledgments

The authors wish to thank their editor, Allison Randal, for shepherding the process and smoothing out all of the non-writing details, as well as the production and marketing and business departments at O'Reilly Media for turning this book from plain text into the lovely printed form you hold in your hands.

Thanks also to Nathan Torkington for helping to start this process.

chromatic

Thanks go primarily to my co-authors, two fine programmers it is my privilege to know as colleagues and friends, as well as to all of the contributors, without whom this book would be much shorter, much less interesting, and much less fun. Thanks also go to my friends, family, and commiserators, especially the U of P crew and Aleatha, Esther, Eva, Kate, Katie, Laura, and Mel. Thanks and respect go to my work and hobby colleagues, including all of the programmers who have invented and refined these tools which allow us to work and play.

Finally, I dedicate this book to my family, Brett, Danielle, Jacob, Jack, and Brad in the hope that I am a worthy brother, brother-in-law, uncle, and cat caretaker.

Damian Conway

To chromatic, Allison, and Nat, for inviting me to help them build this wonderful new Perl jungle gym. To Larry Wall, who invented the extraordinary playground upon which it is constructed. And to my many, many friends throughout the worldwide Perl community, whose encouragement and support has allowed me to play here for the past decade.

Above all, to my beloved Linda, whose love, beauty, and grace illuminate every day of my life.

Curtis "Ovid" Poe

There's no way I could have participated in this without the Perl community having patiently answered so many of my silly questions when I started learning Perl years ago. They didn't just teach me Perl, they taught me how to be a programmer. Many thanks to chromatic and Allison for shrink-wrapping my monkey. I'll never forgive you. Mostly, though, I want to thank Sean and Lil, two people without whom the world would be a sadder place for me.

Technical Reviewers

The authors extend tremendous thanks to the technical reviewers who found many errors, suggested many rephrasings, and argued over important formatting details to make this book clear, accurate, and interesting. They are Ann Barcomb, Daniel Bosold, Brad Bowman, Philippe "BooK" Bruhat, the #cgiapp IRC channel, Chris Dolan, Michael Graham, Garick Hamlin, Joshua ben Jore, Yves Orton, Ricardo Signes, and David Wheeler.

Preface

Perl is a language with a rich and expressive vocabulary. Since its original release in 1987, it's moved from quick-and-dirty extraction and reporting to web programming, data munging, GUI building, automation gluing, and full-blown application development. It's the duct tape of the Internet and a Swiss-Army chainsaw.

Like duct tape and multitools, Perl can do just about anything you can imagine and really want to do.

If you just want to get your job done quickly, you can write the simplest, easiest Perl you know and go on to other things. If you want to build big applications, you can do that—with some experience and a little discipline. If you want to solve your problem and don't mind a little help, the CPAN is there to give you a hand.

That's all very productive, and being productive can be fulfilling…but Perl can also be fun.

Imagine a litter of kittens, tumbling across the floor in a ball of teeth and claws and fur and tiny little growls. They're playing, sure, but they're also practicing the skills they need to survive in the scary wild world. They're careful not to hurt each other, but the tactics and surprises of one clever kitten can teach the others valuable lessons.

What makes a Perl guru? It's knowledge, partly, but it's mostly the curiosity to play with the language, discover surprises, and even invent a few of your own. That's why this book was so much fun to write. Here are 101 tips, tricks, and techniques from some of the best Perl programmers in the world. Some are immediately productive. Some are sneak attacks that you might only use when you have no other choice. Most of them have two parts: the immediate problem you need to solve right now and a deeper, subtler technique that you can adapt to other situations. All of them are worth studying.

It's good to be productive. That's why you program in Perl. Add in the fun of learning—especially lessons it took these Perl gurus *years* to learn—and you'll be ready for anything. Amaze your friends. Astound your coworkers. Walk into the jungle of code and specifications and customer requests with the confidence that you can take down any problem that jumps out at you.

You will.

Why Perl Hacks?

The term *hacking* has an unfortunate reputation in the popular press, where it often refers to someone who breaks into systems or wreaks havoc with computers. Among enthusiasts, on the other hand, the term *hack* refers to a "quick-n-dirty" solution to a problem or a clever way to do something. The term *hacker* is very much a compliment, praising someone for being *creative* and having the technical chops to get things done. O'Reilly's Hacks series is an attempt to reclaim the word, document the ways people are hacking (in a good way), and pass the hacker ethic of creative participation on to a new generation of hackers. Seeing how others approach systems and problems is often the quickest way to learn about a new technology.

It's also fun.

Of course, no single book could possibly document all of the interesting and creative and mind-expanding things people can and do achieve with Perl... but we hope this book will put you in the right mindset to hack your own crazy ideas.

How To Use This Book

We've divided this book along various topics, not according to any sense of relative difficulty. Skip around and flip through the book; if you see an interesting title or some paragraph catches your eye, read it! Where possible, we've added cross references to related hacks in the text. For example, if you and your coworkers are right now celebrating beer-thirty on a lazy Friday afternoon, start with "Drink to the CPAN" [Hack #37].

How This Book Is Organized

Chapter 1, *Productivity Hacks*

Admit it. When you sit down to code, something annoys you. It may be repetitive commands, looking up documentation, or the fact that your coworkers just can't align their equals signs. Getting rid of those interruptions and annoyances will make your life easier and your coding sessions more enjoyable. This chapter suggests a few ideas.

Chapter 2, *User Interaction*

Menus, graphics, beeps, and command lines: these are all ways your programs grab user attention. Do it kindly. Do it with style. Do it with convenience. This chapter is all about working with other people.

Chapter 3, *Data Munging*

What does Perl love to extract and report? Data! Hook it up to databases and set it loose on files. It's so easy you might not realize that your code is, well, slow and kludgy. That's okay. Take the tips in this chapter to heart and you can polish your Perl to slice and dice data again.

Chapter 4, *Working with Modules*

Perl 5's unit of reusable code is the module. When you unleash the power of modules—whether your own or those written by other people—you're on track to becoming a real guru. To do that, you need to go beyond the idea "one file, one namespace, one module." You need to understand what makes them work and how to exploit all of the clever possibilities they provide. This chapter leads the way.

Chapter 5, *Object Hacks*

Abstraction, encapsulation, and genericity are the keys to designing large, maintainable systems. Objects are one way to go. Sure, some people claim that Perl doesn't really do OO, but they're wrong and you can prove it. Go beyond the blessed hashes and find ways to build powerful abstractions in this chapter.

Chapter 6, *Debugging*

Of course your code works, but someday you'll have to dig through a pile of Perl left by an obnoxious coworker (even if that was you before you read this book). Don't go in unarmed. Prepare yourself for the worst with a toolkit full of tips and techniques to disarm the hairiest, weirdest code you can imagine. This chapter will shine light on those lurking monsters (and they're not so bad once you get to know them).

Chapter 7, *Developer Tricks*

Maintaining a program is different from maintaining an entire system. This is doubly true if you work with other people. If anything, discipline and consistency are more important than ever. Of course, so are clever ways to convince other people to do the right thing. Need some leverage to get your shop in shape? This chapter has answers.

Chapter 8, *Know Thy Code*

"Know thyself," the inscription said. This is the oracle of Perl, not Delphi, so the admonition is a little different. If you *really* want to take advantage of the deeper mysteries of Perl, you have to be able to look deeply into the language, the libraries, and the interpreter itself—as well as your own code—and understand what's happening. This chapter will take you from programmer to guru. Hang on.

Chapter 9, *Expand Your Perl Foo*

When the phrase "Perl Fu" just isn't metasyntactic enough, it's time to move on to "Perl Foo." Almost no one has explored every corner of Perl. There's just too much to learn. Until now there have been no maps. This chapter will fill your head with a few of the odder ideas in the world of Perl. Then you'll be ready to discover your own.

Conventions Used in This Book

This book uses the following typographical conventions:

Plain text

Indicates menu titles, menu options, and menu buttons.

Italic

Indicates new terms, URLs, email addresses, filenames, file extensions, pathnames, and directories.

Constant width

Indicates commands, options, switches, variables, attributes, keys, functions, the contents of files, and the output from commands.

Constant width bold

Shows commands or other text that you should type literally.

Constant width italic

Shows text that you should replace with user-supplied values.

Gray type

Used to indicate a cross-reference within the text.

This icon signifies a tip, suggestion, or general note.

This icon indicates a warning or caution.

The thermometer icons, found next to each hack, indicate the relative complexity of the hack:

beginner   moderate   expert

Using Code Examples

This book is here to help you get your job done. In general, you may use the code in this book in your programs and documentation. You do not need to contact us for permission unless you're reproducing a significant portion of the code. For example, writing a program that uses several chunks of code from this book does not require permission. Selling or distributing a CD-ROM of examples from O'Reilly books does require permission. Answering a question by citing this book and quoting example code does not require permission. Incorporating a significant amount of example code from this book into your product's documentation does require permission.

We appreciate, but do not require, attribution. An attribution usually includes the title, author, publisher, and ISBN. For example: "*Perl Hacks* by chromatic with Damian Conway and Curtis 'Ovid' Poe. Copyright 2006 O'Reilly Media, Inc., 0-596-52674-1."

If you feel your use of code examples falls outside fair use or the permission given above, feel free to contact us at *permissions@oreilly.com*.

Safari® Enabled

 When you see a Safari® Enabled icon on the cover of your favorite technology book, that means the book is available online through the O'Reilly Network Safari Bookshelf.

Safari offers a solution that's better than e-books. It's a virtual library that lets you easily search thousands of top tech books, cut and paste code samples, download chapters, and find quick answers when you need the most accurate, current information. Try it for free at *http://safari.oreilly.com*.

We'd Like to Hear from You

Please address comments and questions concerning this book to the publisher:

O'Reilly Media, Inc.
1005 Gravenstein Highway North
Sebastopol, CA 95472
800-998-9938 (in the U.S. or Canada)
707-829-0515 (international/local)
707-829-0104 (fax)

We have a web page for this book, where we list errata, examples, and any additional information. You can access this page at:

http://www.oreilly.com/catalog/perlhks

To comment or ask technical questions about this book, send email to:

bookquestions@oreilly.com

For more information about our books, conferences, Resource Centers, and the O'Reilly Network, see our web site at:

http://www.oreilly.com/

## CHAPTER ONE

Productivity Hacks

Hacks 1–11

Everyone wants to be more productive. That's probably why you use Perl: to get more work done in less time with less work.

Productivity isn't all about saving time, though. Saving effort is even more important, whether you mean finding the information you want, automating away repeated tasks, or finding ways not to have to think about things that you do all the time. In some ways, this is the notion of *relentless automation*—finding every little niggling task that always interrupts your current project by being so annoying, difficult, cumbersome, or different and then hiding it behind an alias, a shell script, a process, or whatever.

Here are a few ideas for ways to make your programming life easier and more productive. Try them, enjoy your new sense of free time, and let yourself notice the new points of friction in your life. Then solve them, too!

HACK #1

Add CPAN Shortcuts to Firefox

Keep module documentation and distributions mere keystrokes away.

If Perl has only one advantage over other programming languages, it's the number of modules on the CPAN (*http://www.cpan.org/*) that solve so many problems effectively. That brings up a smaller problem, though—choosing an appropriate module for the job.

http://search.cpan.org/ helps, but if you visit the site many times a day, the steps to start a search through the web interface can become annoying. Fortunately, the Mozilla family of web browsers, including Mozilla Firefox, let you set up shortcuts that make browsing much easier. These shortcuts are just bookmarked URLs with substitutable sections and keywords, but they're very powerful and useful—almost command-line aliases ("Make the Most of Shell Aliases" [Hack #4]) for your browser.

Here are three of the most useful.

Search for a Module

The first technique is to find the module you want. Normally, you could visit the CPAN search site, type the appropriate words in the box, submit the form, and browse through the results. That's too much work though!

Open the bookmark menu in your browser; this is Bookmarks → Manage Bookmarks in Mozilla Firefox. Create a new bookmark. For name, put **Search CPAN** and for Keyword enter **cpan**. In the Location box, type:

```
http://search.cpan.org/search?mode=module;query=%s
```

Figure 1-1 shows the completed dialog box. Press OK, then go back to the browser. Clear the location bar, then type **cpan Acme** and hit Enter. This will take you immediately to the first page of search results for modules with Acme in their names.

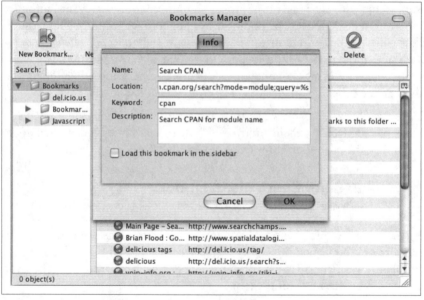

Figure 1-1. Creating a new keyword bookmark search

Read Module Documentation

If you know exactly the name of the module you want, it's more convenient to jump straight to information about that module. Create a new bookmark named **Show Module Documentation**, with the keyword of **cpod** and the location:

```
http://search.cpan.org/perldoc/%s
```

Press OK, then type **cpod `Test::Builder`** and press Enter. You'll see the latest version of the Test::Builder documentation.

> This doesn't seem to work for POD-only modules, such as Test::Tutorial. Also, beware that the case must match exactly.

Find Module Comments

Sometimes it's more valuable to find advice from other people about a module, especially when you may have uncovered a bug or something inexplicable in the documentation. The AnnoCPAN project (*http://www.annocpan.org/*) is a public site that allows users to annotate the documentation of any CPAN module. This is a good way to share your hard-won knowledge about a module with the world.

Create a new bookmark yet again, with a name of **AnnoCPAN Module Documentation** and a keyword of **apod**. Set the location to:

```
http://www.annocpan.org/?mode=search;field=Module;latest=1;name=%s
```

Save the bookmark, then type **apod `GraphViz`** in the browser's location bar and press Enter. Scroll down a few pages and you should see notes on various paragraphs of the documentation.

Hacking the Hack

The keyword search feature of Firefox turns your browser's address bar into a command line. It's simple to write your own CGI script or mod_perl handler to add a new command to the browser—all it has to do is take a query string and return information. You could easily write code to implement a single command that aggregates different documentation sources (for example, you can search JavaScript and HTML and Perl documentation with a single query).

The URL of the bookmark can be a javascript: URL that runs code in the browser. In essence you're creating a bookmarklet that you trigger on the command line. You could use JavaScript to open the search results in a new window or tab or search for the currently selected text.

Put Perldoc to Work
Do more than just read the documentation.

Perl has a huge amount of documentation available through the perldoc utility—and not just from the command line. These docs cover everything from

the core language and tutorials through the standard library and any additional modules you install or even write. perldoc can do more, though.

Here are a few switches and options to increase your productivity.

Find Operator Documentation

The perlfunc document lists every built-in operator in the language in alpha-
betical order. If you need to know the order of arguments to substr( ), you
could type **perldoc perlfunc**, and then search for the correct occurrence of
substr.

> In a decent pager, such as less on a Unix-like system, use the
> forward slash (/) to begin a search. Type the rest of the name
> and hit Enter to begin searching. Press n to find the next
> occurrence and N to find the previous one.

Why search yourself, though? perldoc's -f switch searches perlfunc for you,
presenting only the documentation for the named operator. Type instead:

```
$ perldoc -f substr
```

The program will launch your favorite pager, showing only the documentation for substr. Handy.

Answer a FAQ

The Perl FAQ is a very useful piece of the core documentation, with a table
of contents in perlfaq and nine other documents (perlfaq1 through
perlfaq9) full of frequently asked questions and their answers.

Searching every document for your question, however, is more tedious than
searching perlfunc. (Do skim perlfaq once in a while to see what questions
there are, though.) Fortunately, the -q switch allows you to specify a search
pattern for FAQ keywords.

If you remember that somewhere the FAQ explains how to shuffle an array,
but you can't remember where, try:

```
$ perldoc -q shuffle
```

As with the -f switch, this will launch your favorite pager to view every
question with the term shuffle in the title.

-q also handles regular expressions, so if you want to search for every mention of Perl 6, with or without that blessed space, try:

```
$ perldoc -q "Perl ?6"
```

The quotes prevent the shell from interpreting the space as an argument separator.

Webify It

Maybe the command line isn't your thing. Maybe you work in a group of programmers who won't leave their comfortable IDEs long enough to type a few commands—and who certainly won't read documentation from anywhere but the IDE or a web page.

That's okay. perldoc can produce HTML (or any other type of output for which you have a POD translator installed), too. Use the -o switch with your preferred output format. To turn perltoc into HTML, use the command:

```
$ perldoc -oHTML -dperltoc.html perltoc
```

The -d switch specifies the destination filename.

Valid HTML formatters include any of Pod::Perldoc::HTML, Pod::Simple:: HTML, and Pod::HTML. If you have another formatter of the appropriate name installed, you can use it.

If you have multiple potential formatters for a type installed, use -M*full_module_name* instead of -o to disambiguate.

Find that Module!

Maybe you already know how to find, slice, and dice the documentation. Have you ever run a program that picked up the wrong version of a module? Sure, you can modify the program to print %INC and @INC and crawl through the output to see what went wrong—but perldoc has to be able to figure out where the module lives to show its documentation. Exploit it!

The -l switch tells perldoc to find the named module (or document) and print its location instead of formatting and displaying the text. Here's where Test::Tutorial and perlunintro live on my system:

```
$ perldoc -l Test::Tutorial
/usr/lib/perl5/vendor_perl/5.8.7/Test/Tutorial.pod

$ perldoc -l perluniintro
/usr/lib/perl5/5.8.7/pod/perluniintro.pod
```

> If you have multiple versions of Perl installed, be sure you
> use the *correct* version of perldoc; it uses the @INC path in its
> own version of Perl.

This can be much faster than doing a locate or find and grep from the command line.

Browse the Code

perldoc -l is pretty useful, especially if you want to know where a module is, so that you can look inside it. One more switch makes that even more useful, however. The -m option shows the plain, unrendered text of the named module or document in your favorite pager.

If you suspect that the author of Test::MockObject has hidden some useful methods from you,* browse the source of the module with:

```
$ perldoc -m Test::MockObject
```

You can't *edit* the text of the module from here, but being able to read it—or being able to read the raw POD of a module with POD errors that cause its formatting to fail—can be very helpful.

> Likewise, the -u option shows only the unformatted POD
> source, without the code.

HACK #3 Browse Perl Docs Online

Host your own HTML documentation.

perldoc is a fine way to view the documentation for Perl and all your installed modules and to output them in the file format of your choice ("Put Perldoc to Work" [Hack #2]). perldoc's little brother, podwebserver, is an even handier way to browse documentation—and bookmark it, and search it, and sometimes even hardcopy it, all through whatever web browser you're using this week.

The Hack

podwebserver provides basically perldoc-as-HTML over HTTP. Sure, you could always just browse the documentation at *http://search.cpan.org/*—but

---

* He hasn't.

using podwebserver means that you'll be seeing the documentation for exactly *your* system's Perl version and module versions.

podwebserver's HTML is compatible with fancy browsers as well as with more lightweight tools such as lynx, elinks, or even the w3m browser in Emacs. In fact, there have been persistent rumors of some users adventurously accessing podwebserver via cell phones, or even using something called "the Micro-Soft Internet Explorer." O'Reilly Media, Inc. can neither confirm nor deny these rumors.

If podwebserver isn't on your system, install the Pod::Webserver module from CPAN.

Running the Hack

To run podwebserver, just start it from the command line. You don't need root access:

```
$ podwebserver
```

Then start a web browser and browse to *http://localhost:8020/*. You'll see the index of the installed documentation (Figure 1-2).

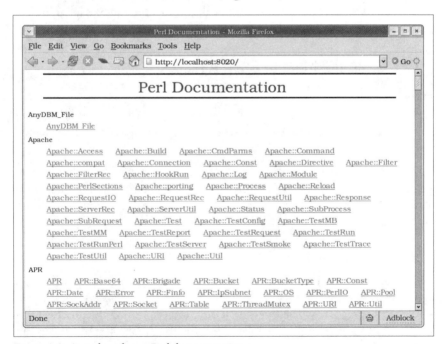

Figure 1-2. An index of your Perl documentation

If you don't want to bind the web server to localhost, or if you have something already running on port 8020, use the -H and -p arguments to change the host and port.

```
$ podwebserver -H windwheel -p 8080
```

Hacking the Hack

Running a program and switching to your web browser to view a bookmark is too much work when you just want to check some documentation. Make your life easier with a little shell script ("Make the Most of Shell Aliases" [Hack #4]):

```
#!/bin/sh

podwebserver &
sleep 2
firefox -remote 'openurl( http://localhost:8020/, new-tab)'
```

Save the program as ~/bin/podweb, make it executable (chmod +x ~/bin/podweb), make sure ~/bin/podweb is in your $PATH, then run it:

```
$ podweb
```

If you have Mozilla Firefox open, this will pop up the index page in a new tab. Other web browsers have similar invocation schemes.

Make the Most of Shell Aliases
HACK #4   Make programming easier by programming your shell.

Perl is a language for people who type. It grew up from the shell to write all kinds of programs, but it still rewards people who don't mind launching programs from the command line.

If you spend your time writing Perl from the command line (whether you write short scripts or full-blown programs), spending a few minutes automating common tasks can save you lots of development time—and even more trouble.

Configuring Your Shell

The single most useful shell trick is the realias command. Normally creating a persistent alias means adding something to your .bashrc (or equivalent) file, starting a new shell, testing it, and then repeating the process until you get it right. Wouldn't it be nice to be able to edit and test a new alias in a single process?

Edit your .bashrc file and add a single line:

```
source ~/.aliases
```

Then create the file ~/.aliases, containing:

```
alias realias='$EDITOR ~/.aliases; source ~/.aliases'
```

 If you prefer tcsh, edit your .cshrc file. Then replace the = sign with a single space in all of the alias declarations.

Launch a new shell. Type the command realias and your favorite editor (assuming you have the EDITOR environment variable set, and if you don't something is *weird*) will open with your ~/.aliases file. Add a line and save and quit:

```
alias reperl='perl -de0'
```

Now type reperl* at the command line:

```
$ reperl

Loading DB routines from perl5db.pl version 1.28
Editor support available.

Enter h or 'h h' for help, or 'man perldebug' for more help.

main::(-e:1):   0
  DB<1> q
```

Within a single shell session you've identified a useful command that may be difficult to remember, automated it, and have started to use it productively. Nifty.

Useful Shell Aliases

What makes a good shell alias for Perl programming? Obviously a command that's difficult to remember, such as the one to put the Perl debugger into pseudo-interactive mode. Another good approach is to alias commands that are lengthy or otherwise difficult to type. One final category is a series of chained commands you find yourself typing often.

Here are a few examples. Change the paths as necessary, of course, but have fun removing a little more of the tedium from your life every time you notice yourself repeating something you could automate away. That's the Perl way.

Juggle multiple Perl versions. Suppose you're in the midst of upgrading Perl versions while you still have to maintain an older installation. You might have multiple versions of Perl installed. Instead of typing different paths all

---

* A pronounceable version of REPL—Read, Evaluate, Print, and Loop.

the time and instead of relying on tab completion to differentiate between perl5.8.8 and perl5.6.2 and so on, make the names different at the start:

```
alias newperl='/usr/local/bin/perl5.8.8'
alias oldperl='/usr/local/bin/perl5.6.2'
```

This is especially handy if you have a system Perl installed and don't want to break things by overwriting it.

Juggle multiple module versions. Suppose that you also must test your code against multiple versions of a module or library. For example, you need to know if your code works against version 4.x *and* 5.x of a database. Alias away the different library paths:

```
alias newdbperl='perl -M/home/dev/newlib/'
alias olddbperl='perl -M/home/dev/oldlib/'
```

Don't forget multipart commands. If you're a rigorous tester, you've likely encountered Devel::Cover. Though it's easy to use, it takes multiple steps to write a new report. Alias that away!

```
alias testcover='cover -delete; ./Build testcover; cover'
```

Remember configuration options. Suppose that you decide to test the Pugs project (*http://www.pugscode.org/*) and want to embed both Perl 5 and Parrot. Because Pugs undergoes such rapid development, you might have to run its *Makefile.PL* several times a week. Why make yourself remember how to configure it with the correct options every time? Alias it!

```
alias makepugs='PARROT_PATH="/home/chromatic/dev/parrot" \
    PUGS_EMBED="perl 5 parrot" \
    perl Makefile.PL && make'
```

Find a module's version. Sometimes you really need to know the version of a module—especially when you're tracking down a bug across multiple machines or pondering an upgrade. Typing out:

```
$ perl -MCGI::Application -le 'print CGI::Application->VERSION'
4.03
```

every time is too much work. Stick a function instead in your *.bashrc*:

```
function pmver () { perl -M$1 -le "print $1->VERSION"; }
```

You can also add more error checking and turn it into an alias:

```
alias pmver="perl -le '\$m = shift; eval qq(require \$m)
    or die qq(module \"\$m\" is not installed\\n); print \$m->VERSION'"
```

Either way, run it as pmver:

```
$ pmver CGI::Application
4.03
```

Change Unix paths to Windows paths and back. These aliases work on Windows under Cygwin too. Even though it's still Windows on one side and Unix on the other, there's no reason you can't make it work correctly. Here's an alias that translates a Unix path to a Windows path and executes the Windows version of gvim on the file:

```
alias gvim='perl -we "exec q{/cygdrive/c/Progra~1/Vim/vim63/gvim.exe},
   map { s/^(.*)$/(-f \$1)?qx{cygpath -aw \"\$1\"}:\$1/e; chomp; \$_; }
   (@ARGV); "'
```

Launching general Windows programs from bash requires a similar hack:

```
alias winrun='exec 'cmd', "/c", ((split '/',$0)[-1], map {
   s/^(.*)$/(-f $1)?qx{cygpath -w "$1"}:$1/e;chomp;$_; } (@ARGV));'
```

Now you can launch non-Cygwin programs with arguments.

HACK #5 Autocomplete Perl Identifiers in Vim

Why type a full identifier if your editor can do it for you?

Good variable and function names are a great boon to productivity and maintainability, but brevity and clarity are often at odds. Instead of wearing out your keys, fingertips, and memory, consider making your text editor do the typing for you.

The Hack

If you use Vim, you have access to a handy autocompletion mechanism. In insert mode, type one or more letters of an identifier, then hit CTRL-N. The editor will complete your identifier using the first identifier in the same file that starts with the same letter(s). Hitting CTRL-N again gives you the second matching identifier, and so on.

This can be a real timesaver if you use long variable or subroutine names. As long as you've already typed an identifier once in a file, you can autocomplete it ever after, just by typing the first few letters and then CTRL-Ning to the right name:

```
sub find_the_factorial_of
{
    my ($the_number_whose_factorial_I_want) = @_;

    return 1 if $the_n<CTRL-N> <= 1;

    return $the_n<CTRL-N> * find<CTRL-N>($the_n<CTRL-N> - 1);
}
```

Unfortunately, Vim's idea of an identifier (in Vim-speak, a "keyword") isn't as broad as Perl's. Specifically, the editor doesn't recognize the colon character as a valid part of an identifier, which is annoying if you happen to like multipart class names, or qualified package variables.

However, it's easy to teach Vim that those intervening double-colons are valid parts of the identifiers. Add them to the editor's list of keyword characters by adding the line to your *.vimrc* file:

```
set iskeyword+=:
```

Then the following works too:

```
use Sub::Normal;

my $sub = Sub<CTRL-N>->new( );   # Expands to: Sub::Normal->new( )
```

Finding Identifiers Automatically

Of course, you still have to type the full name of Sub::Normal once, as part of the initial use statement. That really isn't as Lazy as it could be. It would be much better if Vim just magically knew about all the Perl modules you have installed and could cleverly autocomplete their names from the very first time you used them.

As it happens, that's easy to arrange as well. You just need a file that lists every module you have installed. Then tell Vim (in *.vimrc* again) to use all the identifiers in that file as a second source of keyword completions:

```
set complete+=k~/.vim_extras/file_that_lists_every_installed_Perl_module
```

The complete+=k tells Vim you're adding to the existing sources of completions for keywords. The path name that follows specifies the file containing the additional completions.

All you need is a simple Perl script to generate that file for you:

```
use File::Find 'find';

# Where to create this list...
my $LIST_DIR  = "$ENV{HOME}/.vim_extras/"
my $LIST_FILE = "file_that_lists_every_installed_Perl_module";

# Make sure the directory is available...
unless (-e $LIST_DIR )
{
    mkdir $LIST_DIR
        or die "Couldn't create directory $LIST_DIR ($!)\n";
}

# (Re)create the file...
open my $fh, '>', "$LIST_DIR$LIST_FILE"
    or die "Couldn't create file '$LIST_FILE' ($!)\n";
```

```
# Only report each module once (the first time it's seen)...
my %already_seen;

# Walk through the module include directories, finding .pm files...
for my $incl_dir (@INC)
{
    find
    {
        wanted => sub
        {
            my $file = $_;

            # They have to end in .pm...
            return unless $file =~ /\.pm\z/;

            # Convert the path name to a module name...
            $file =~ s{^\Q$incl_dir/\E}{ };
            $file =~ s{/}{::}g;
            $file =~ s{\.pm\z}{ };

            # Handle standard subdirectories (like site_perl/ or 5.8.6/)...
            $file =~ s{^.*\b[a-z_0-9]+::}{ };
            $file =~ s{^\d+\.\d+\.\d+::(?:[a-z_][a-z_0-9]*::)?}{ };
            return if $file =~ m{^::};

            # Print the module's name (once)...
            print {$fh} $file, "\n" unless $already_seen{$file}++;
        },
        no_chdir => 1,
    }, $incl_dir;
}
```

Of course, you don't have to call the file *.vim_extras/file_that_lists_every_installed_Perl_module*. Just change the $LIST_DIR and $LIST_FILE variables to something saner.

Hacking the Hack

It's a natural next step to automate the generation of this file via cron. Beyond that, though, consider using Vim auto-commands to update the module list when you load and save files. To get information on auto-commands, type :help autocmd-intro within Vim. You could also check in and check out these module lists from a central repository to ensure that your editor knows about the class your coworker just added.

For a final coup-de-grace, consider extracting variable and subroutine names from the files as well. This will let you complete method names and exported variables. You could do this with regular expressions as heuristics, or through modules such as Parse::Perl.

Emacs users take heart. You can usually find equivalents by searching the web for *taskname* cperl-mode. Here's an auto-completion minor mode to add to your ~/.emacs file:

```
(defadvice cperl-indent-command

    (around cperl-indent-or-complete)

    "Changes \\[cperl-indent-command] so it
autocompletes when at the end of a word."

    (if (looking-at "\\>")

        (dabbrev-expand nil)

      ad-do-it))

  (eval-after-load "cperl-mode"

    '(progn (require 'dabbrev) (ad-activate 'cperl-
indent-command)))
```

HACK #6 Use the Best Emacs Mode for Perl

Configure Emacs for easy Perl coding.

While perl-mode is the classic Perl-editing mode that Emacs uses for Perl files by default, most Perl programmers prefer the newer cperl-mode. (The "c" in the name is because its early versions borrowed code from c-mode. It's not actually written in C, nor meant for C.) Enabling it is easy.

The Hack

cperl-mode is probably already included in your version of Emacs, but you can get an up-to-date version from *http://math.berkeley.edu/~ilya/software/ emacs/*. Save it to an Emacs library directory. Then enable it for *.pl* and *.pm* files by adding nine lines to your ~/.emacs file:

```
(load-library "cperl-mode")
  (add-to-list 'auto-mode-alist '("\\.[Pp][LlMm][Cc]?$" . cperl-mode))
  (while (let ((orig (rassoc 'perl-mode auto-mode-alist)))
            (if orig (setcdr orig 'cperl-mode))))
  (while (let ((orig (rassoc 'perl-mode interpreter-mode-alist)))
          (if orig (setcdr orig 'cperl-mode))))
  (dolist (interpreter '("perl" "perl5" "miniperl" "pugs"))
    (unless (assoc interpreter interpreter-mode-alist)
      (add-to-list 'interpreter-mode-alist (cons interpreter 'cperl-mode))))
```

What can you do with it?

Put Perldoc at your fingertips. cperl-mode provides a handy function for calling perldoc, but does not associate it with any key by default. To put it at your fingertips, add one line to your *.emacs* file:

```
(global-set-key "\M-p" 'cperl-perldoc) ; alt-p
```

If you want to use `Pod::Webserver` **[Hack #3]**, use one of the various in-Emacs web browsers:

```
(global-set-key "\M-p" '(lambda () (interactive)
  (require 'w3m)
  (w3m-goto-url "http://localhost:8020/")
))
```

If you prefer your normal web browser, just set some particular key to start it up on the `Pod::Webserver` page:

```
(global-set-key "\M-p"
  '(lambda () (interactive) (start-process "" nil
  "firefox" "http://localhost:8020/"
  ; Or however you launch your favorite browser, like:
  ;   "gnome-terminal" "-e" "lynx http://localhost:8020/"
  ;   "xterm" "-e" "elinks http://localhost:8020/"
)))
```

Use a special mode just for Pod. One problem with both cperl-mode and perl-mode is that they both treat Pod the same: they just ignore it. To get better syntax highlighting for Pod, switch to the pod-mode. It probably isn't part of your Emacs distribution, so you download the latest version from *http://www.cpan.org/authors/id/S/SC/SCHWIGON/pod-mode/*.

Once installed, enable it in your *.emacs* file with:

```
(require 'pod-mode)
(add-to-list 'auto-mode-alist
  '("\\.pod$" . pod-mode))

; You might appreciate turning on these
;   features by default for Pod:

(add-hook 'pod-mode-hook '(lambda () (progn
  (font-lock-mode)    ; =syntax highlighting
  (auto-fill-mode 1) ; =wordwrap
  (flyspell-mode 1)  ; =spellchecking
)))
```

HACK #7 Enforce Local Style

Keep your code clean without editing it by hand.

One of the first barriers to understanding code written by others is that their formatting style may not match yours. This is especially true if you find yourself maintaining code that, at best, has grown with little direction over the years. Whether you work with other developers and want to maintain a consistent set of coding guidelines, or you want to find *some* structure in a big ball of mud, perltidy can help untangle and bring consistency to even the scariest code.

Enforce Local Style

The Hack

Install the CPAN module `Perl::Tidy`. This will also install the `perltidy` utility. Now you can use it!

From the command line. Run `perltidy` on a Perl program or module and it
will write out a tidied version of that file with a *.tdy* suffix. For example,
given *poorly_written_script.pl*, `perltidy` will, if possible, reformat the code
and write the new version to *poorly_written_script.pl.tdy*. You can then run
tests against the new code to verify that it performs just as did the previous
version (even if it is much easier to read).

This command reformats the contents of *some_ugly_code.pl* so that it's no
longer, well, *ugly*. How effective is it? The Perltidy docs offer an example.
Before:

```
$_ = <<'EOL';
   $url = URI::URL->new( "http://www/" );   die if $url eq "xXx";
EOL
LOOP:{print(" digits"),redo LOOP if/\G\d+\b[,.;]?\s*/gc;print(" lowercase"),
redo LOOP if/\G[a-z]+\b[,.;]?\s*/gc;print(" UPPERCASE"),redo LOOP
if/\G[A-Z]+\b[,.;]?\s*/gc;print(" Capitalized"),
redo LOOP if/\G[A-Z][a-z]+\b[,.;]?\s*/gc;
print(" MiXeD"),redo LOOP if/\G[A-Za-z]+\b[,.;]?\s*/gc;print(
" alphanumeric"),redo LOOP if/\G[A-Za-z0-9]+\b[,.;]?\s*/gc;print(" line-
noise"
),redo LOOP if/\G[^A-Za-z0-9]+/gc;print". That's all!\n";}
```

After:

```
$_ = <<'EOL';
   $url = URI::URL->new( "http://www/" );   die if $url eq "xXx";
EOL
LOOP: {
    print(" digits"),        redo LOOP if /\G\d+\b[,.;]?\s*/gc;
    print(" lowercase"),     redo LOOP if /\G[a-z]+\b[,.;]?\s*/gc;
    print(" UPPERCASE"),     redo LOOP if /\G[A-Z]+\b[,.;]?\s*/gc;
    print(" Capitalized"),   redo LOOP if /\G[A-Z][a-z]+\b[,.;]?\s*/gc;
    print(" MiXeD"),         redo LOOP if /\G[A-Za-z]+\b[,.;]?\s*/gc;
    print(" alphanumeric"),  redo LOOP if /\G[A-Za-z0-9]+\b[,.;]?\s*/gc;
    print(" line-noise"),    redo LOOP if /\G[^A-Za-z0-9]+/gc;
    print ". That's all!\n";
}
```

Big difference!

Perltidy is of course great for enforcing a particular coding style as you work,
but it's also a lifesaver when the task of maintaining someone else's spaghetti code suddenly falls on you.

The default is good for the paranoid. For the adventurous, use the -b flag,
which modifies the files in place and writes the originals to backup files. For

example running `perltidy -b scary_script.pl` will produce a tidied *scary_script.pl*, if possible, and a *scary_script.pl.bak*.

> This operation is not idempotent—perltidy *will* overwrite an existing backup file of the same name, if it exists.

The default formatting options may be inappropriate for your use. `Perl::Tidy` looks for a *.perltidyrc* file, first in your current directory, next in your home directory, and then in system-wide directories. The contents of this file are simple; they're the same command line switches that `perltidy` uses. For example, the author's preferred *.perltidyrc* file contains:

```
-ci=4 # indent 4 spaces when breaking a long line
-et=4 # replace 4 leading spaces with a tab
-bl   # place opening braces on newlines
```

See `man perltidy` for a complete list of formatting options.

Within Vim. The `perltidy` program is also useful from within text editors that can call external programs. This makes it possible to tidy code within an editor, without saving and opening external files—it's great for figuring out what poorly indented code does. From Vim, run it on the entirety of the current buffer with the ex command `%! perltidy`. It also makes a great Vim map—add to your *.vimrc* file something like:

```
map ,pt  <Esc>:%! perltidy<CR>
map ,ptv <Esc>:'<,'>! perltidy<CR>
```

Then in edit mode, type **,pt** and `perltidy` will reformat the contents of the current buffer. Select a region and **,ptv** will format its contents.

> If you have a coding style that differs from the default values, add the command-line options to the maps.

Within Emacs. If you use Emacs to edit your Perl code, you can be virtuously lazy when it comes to reformatting your code. Just drop a bit of code into your *~/.emacs* file and restart Emacs:

```
(defmacro mark-active ()
    "Xemacs/emacs compatibility macro"
    (if (boundp 'mark-active)
        'mark-active
      '(mark)))
(defun perltidy ()
  "Run perltidy on the current region or buffer."
  (interactive)
```

```
; Inexplicably, save-excursion doesn't work here.
(let ((orig-point (point)))
  (unless (mark-active) (mark-defun))
  (shell-command-on-region (point) (mark) "perltidy -q" nil t)
  (goto-char orig-point)))
(global-set-key "\C-ct" 'perltidy)
```

Then the next time you open up a file full of spaghetti Perl, just hit **C-c t**
and watch as the "paragraph" of nearby code magically becomes legible!
Better yet, if you want to reformat the entire file, hit **M-x mark-whole-buffer**
and then **C-c t**.

To make Emacs tidy your code automatically when you save it, add this
snippet of code:

```
(defvar perltidy-mode nil
    "Automatically 'perltidy' when saving.")
(make-variable-buffer-local 'perltidy-mode)
(defun perltidy-write-hook ()
  "Perltidys a buffer during 'write-file-hooks' for 'perltidy-mode'"
  (if perltidy-mode
      (save-excursion
        (widen)
        (mark-whole-buffer)
        (not (perltidy)))
    nil))
(defun perltidy-mode (&optional arg)
  "Perltidy minor mode."
  (interactive "P")
  (setq perltidy-mode
        (if (null arg)
            (not perltidy-mode)
          (> (prefix-numeric-value arg) 0)))
  (make-local-hook 'write-file-hooks)
  (if perltidy-mode
      (add-hook 'write-file-hooks 'perltidy-write-hook)
    (remove-hook 'write-file-hooks 'perltidy-write-hook)))
(if (not (assq 'perltidy-mode minor-mode-alist))
    (setq minor-mode-alist
          (cons '(perltidy-mode " Perltidy")
                minor-mode-alist)))
(eval-after-load "cperl-mode"
  '(add-hook 'cperl-mode-hook 'perltidy-mode))
```

Run M-x perltidy-mode to disable or re-enable the automatic code tidying.

HACK #8 Don't Save Bad Perl

Don't even write out your file if the Perl isn't valid!

Perl tests tend to start by checking that your code compiles. Even if the tests
don't check, you'll know it pretty quickly as all your code collapses in a

string of compiler errors. Then you have to fire up your editor again and track down the problem. It's simple, though, to tell Vim that if your Perl code won't compile, it shouldn't even write it to disk.

Even better, you can load Perl's error messages back into Vim to jump right to the problem spots.

The Hack

Vim supports filetype plug-ins that alter its behavior based on the type of file being edited. Enable these by adding a line to your *.vimrc*:

```
filetype plugin on
```

Now you can put files in *~/.vim/ftplugin* (*My Documents_vimfiles\ftplugin* on Windows) and Vim will load them when it needs them. Perl plug-ins start with *perl_*, so save the following file as *perl_synwrite.vim*:

```
" perl_synwrite.vim: check syntax of Perl before writing
" latest version at: http://www.vim.org/scripts/script.php?script_id=896

"" abort if b:did_perl_synwrite is true: already loaded or user pref
if exists("b:did_perl_synwrite")
  finish
endif
let b:did_perl_synwrite = 1

"" set buffer :au pref: if defined globally, inherit; otherwise, false
if (exists("perl_synwrite_au") && !exists("b:perl_synwrite_au"))
  let b:perl_synwrite_au = perl_synwrite_au
elseif !exists("b:perl_synwrite_au")
  let b:perl_synwrite_au = 0
endif

"" set buffer quickfix pref: if defined globally, inherit; otherwise, false
if (exists("perl_synwrite_qf") && !exists("b:perl_synwrite_qf"))
  let b:perl_synwrite_qf = perl_synwrite_qf
elseif !exists("b:perl_synwrite_qf")
  let b:perl_synwrite_qf = 0
endif

"" execute the given do_command if the buffer is syntactically correct perl
"" -- or if do_anyway is true
function! s:PerlSynDo(do_anyway,do_command)
  let command = "!perl -c"

  if (b:perl_synwrite_qf)
    " this env var tells Vi::QuickFix to replace "-" with actual filename
    let $VI_QUICKFIX_SOURCEFILE=expand("%")
    let command = command . " -MVi::QuickFix"
  endif
```

```
" respect taint checking
if (match(getline(1), "^#!.\\+perl.\\+-T") == 0)
  let command = command . " -T"
endif

exec "write" command

silent! cgetfile " try to read the error file
if !v:shell_error || a:do_anyway
  exec a:do_command
  set nomod
endif
endfunction

"" set up the autocommand, if b:perl_synwrite_au is true
if (b:perl_synwrite_au > 0)
  let b:undo_ftplugin = "au! perl_synwrite * " . expand("%")

  augroup perl_synwrite
    exec "au BufWriteCmd,FileWriteCmd " . expand("%") .
        " call s:PerlSynDo(0,\"write <afile>\")"
  augroup END
endif

"" the :Write command
command -buffer -nargs=* -complete=file -range=% -bang Write call \
    s:PerlSynDo("<bang>"=="!","<line1>,<line2>write<bang> <args>")
```

Running the Hack

When you edit a Perl file, use :W instead of :w to write the file. If the file fails to compile with perl -c, Vim will refuse to write the file to disk. You can always fall back to :w, or use :W! to check, but write out the file even if it has bad syntax.

Hacking the Hack

The plug-in has two configurable options that you can set in your *.vimrc*. The first is perl_synwrite_au, which hooks the :W command's logic onto an autocommand that fires when you use :w. This will let you use :w for any sort of file, but still enjoy the syntax error catching of the plug-in. It's a little twitchy, though, when you start passing arguments to :w, so you're probably best off just using :W.

The second is perl_synwrite_qf, which lets the plug-in use the Vi::QuickFix module to parse perl's errors into a format that Vim can use to jump to problems. With this option set, perl will write errors to *error.err*, which Vim will read when you use its QuickFix commands. :help quickfix lists all of the commands, but the two most useful are :cf to jump to the first syntax error and :copen to open a new window listing all your errors. In that new window, you can move to the error that interests you, hit Enter, and jump to the error in your buffer.

Vi::QuickFix relies on tying the standard error stream, which isn't possible in Perl 5.6, so if you use *perl_synwrite.vim* in more than one development environment, you might want to set the perl_synwrite_qf option dynamically:

```
silent call system("perl -e0 -MVi::QuickFix")
let perl_synwrite_qf = ! v:shell_error
```

In other words, if Perl can't use the Vi::QuickFix module, don't try using it for the plug-in.

 By default, Vim thinks that *.t files are Tads, or maybe Nroff, files. It's easy to fix; create a file in *~/.vim/ftdetect* containing:

```
au BufRead,BufNewFile *.t
    set ft=perl
```

Now when you edit 00-load.t, Vim will know it's Perl and not your latest interactive fiction masterpiece.

Emacs users, you can use a minor mode to run a Perl syntax check before saving the file. Whenever perl -c fails, Emacs will not save your file. To save files anyway, toggle the mode off with M-x perl-syntax-mode. See "Enforce Local Style" [Hack #7] for a related tip on automatically tidying your code when saving.

```
(defvar perl-syntax-bin "perl"
    "The perl binary used to check syntax.")
  (defun perl-syntax-check-only ()
    "Returns a either nil or t depending on whether \
     the current buffer passes perl's syntax check."
    (interactive)
    (let ((buf (get-buffer-create "*Perl syntax check*")))
      (let ((syntax-ok (= 0 (save-excursion
                              (widen)
                              (call-process-region
                               (point-min) (point-max) perl-syntax-bin nil
buf nil "-c"))) ))
        (if syntax-ok (kill-buffer buf)
          (display-buffer buf))
        syntax-ok)))
  (defvar perl-syntax-mode nil
    "Check perl syntax before saving.")
  (make-variable-buffer-local 'perl-syntax-mode)
  (defun perl-syntax-write-hook ()
    "Check perl syntax during `write-file-hooks' for 'perl-syntax-mode'"
    (if perl-syntax-mode
        (save-excursion
```

```
          (widen)
          (mark-whole-buffer)
          (not (perl-syntax-check-only)))
     nil))
  (defun perl-syntax-mode (&optional arg)
    "Perl syntax checking minor mode."
    (interactive "P")
    (setq perl-syntax-mode
          (if (null arg)
              (not perl-syntax-mode)
            (> (prefix-numeric-value arg) 0)))
    (make-local-hook 'write-file-hooks)
    (if perl-syntax-mode
        (add-hook 'write-file-hooks 'perl-syntax-write-hook)
      (remove-hook 'write-file-hooks 'perl-syntax-write-hook)))
  (if (not (assq 'perl-syntax-mode minor-mode-alist))
      (setq minor-mode-alist
            (cons '(perl-syntax-mode " Perl Syntax")
                  minor-mode-alist)))
  (eval-after-load "cperl-mode"
    '(add-hook 'cperl-mode-hook 'perl-syntax-mode))
```

 HACK
#9

Automate Checkin Code Reviews

Let `Perl::Tidy` be your first code review—on every Subversion checkin!

In a multideveloper project, relying on developers to follow the coding standards without fail and to run perltidy against all of their code ("Enforce Local Style" [Hack #7]) before every checkin is unrealistic, especially because this is tedious work. Fortunately, this is an automatable process. If you use Subversion (or Svk), it's easy to write a hook that checks code for tidiness, however you define it.

The Hack

For various reasons, it's not possible to manipulate the committed files with a pre-commit hook in Subversion. That's why this is a hack.

Within your Subversion repository, copy the *hooks/post-commit.tmpl* file to *hooks/post-commit*—unless you already have the file. Remove all code that runs other commands (again, unless you're already using it). Add a single line:

```
perl /usr/local/bin/check_tidy_file.pl "$REPOS" "$REV"
```

Adjust the file path appropriately. Make the *hooks/post-commit* file executable with chmod +x on Unix.

Finally, save the *check_tidy_file.pl* program to the path you used in the file.
The program is:

```perl
#!/usr/bin/perl

use strict;
use warnings;

use Perl::Tidy;
use File::Temp;
use File::Spec::Functions;

my $svnlook     = '/usr/bin/svnlook';
my $diff        = '/usr/bin/diff -u';

# eat the arguments so as not to confuse Perl::Tidy
my ($repo, $rev) = @ARGV;
@ARGV            = ();

my @diffs;

for my $changed_file (get_changed_perl_files( $repo, $rev ))
{
    my $source = get_revision( $repo, $rev, $changed_file );
    Perl::Tidy::perltidy( source => \$source, destination => \(my $dest) );
    push @diffs, get_diff( $changed_file, $source, $dest );
}

report_diffs( @diffs );

sub get_changed_perl_files
{
    my ($repo, $rev) = @_;

    my @files;

    for my $change (`$svnlook changed $repo -r $rev`)
    {
        my ($status, $file) =  split( /\s+/, $change );
        next unless $file    =~ /\.p[lm]\z/;
        push @files, $file;
    }

    return @files;
}

sub get_revision
{
    my ($repo, $rev, $file) = @_;
    return scalar `$svnlook cat $repo -r $rev $file`;
}

sub get_diff
{
```

```
    my $filename       = shift;
    return if $_[0] eq $_[1];

    my $dir   = File::Temp::tempdir( );
    my @files = map { catdir( $dir, $filename . $_ ) } qw( .orig .tidy );

    for my $file (@files)
    {
        open( my $out, '>', $file ) or die "Couldn't write $file: $!\n";
        print $out shift;
        close $out;
    }

    return scalar `$diff @files`;
}

sub report_diffs
{
    for my $diff (@_)
    {
        warn "Error:\n$diff\n";
    }
}
```

When Subversion finishes committing a checkin to the repository, it calls the *hooks/post-commit* script, which itself launches other programs, passing the repository path and the number of the just-committed revision. This program uses the svnlook command to find the modified files, skipping everything that's not a Perl program or module (files ending in *.pl* or *.pm*).

For each of these files, it grabs the entire contents from the just-completed revision and runs it through Perl::Tidy (the actual engine of the perltidy utility). If the resulting file is the same as the revision, everything is fine. Otherwise, it runs a diff utility to see the changes necessary to make the file tidy. From there, report_diffs( ) receives a list of these differences.

Hacking the Hack

As it is now, the program is only useful when run directly with the path to the repository and a revision number. It *could* instead write the differences to a file, automatically check in the revised versions in a new checkin, or e-mail the diffs to a list of programmers.

To use a *.perltidyrc* file with the tidier program, add the perltidy => $rcfile_path arguments to the perltidy( ) call, where $rcfile_path contains the path to the *.perltidyrc* file to use.

HACK #10

Run Tests from Within Vim

Run your tests from your editor.

One of the nice things about Perl is the "tweak, run, tweak, run" development cycle. There's no separate compile phase to slow you down. However, you likely find yourself frequently writing tests and madly switching back and forth between the tests and the code. When you run the tests, you may exit the editor or type something like !perl -Ilib/ t/test_program.t in vi's command mode. This breaks the "tweak, run" rhythm.

The Hack

Perl programmers don't like to slow things down. Instead, consider binding keys in your editor to the chicken-bone voodoo you use to run your test suite.

Binding keys. By running the tests from within the editor, you no longer have to remember how to execute the tests or edit the editor. Just tweak and run. Add the following line to your *.vimrc* file to run the currently edited test file by typing **,t** (comma, tee):

```
map ,t <Esc>:!prove -vl %<CR>
```

This technique uses the prove program to run your tests. prove is a handy little program distributed with and designed to run your tests through Test:: Harness. The switches are v (vee), which tells prove to run in "verbose" mode and show all of the test output, and l (ell), which tells prove to add *lib/* to @INC.

If *lib/* is not where you typically do your development, use the I switch to add a different path to @INC.

```
map ,t <Esc>:!prove -Iwork/ -v %<CR>
```

Seeing failures. If it's a long test and you get a few failures, it can be difficult to see where the failures were. If that's the case, use ,T (comma capital tee) to pipe the results through your favorite pager.

```
map ,T <Esc>:!prove -lv % \| less<CR>
```

 Of course, make sure your editor does not have those keys already mapped to something else. This hack does not recommend breaking existing mappings in your editor.

Managing paths. These techniques do tend to require that you edit your tests in the "standard" way. If you have your tests organized in subdirectories, switching to the *t/customer/* directory and editing *save.t* may cause problems when trying to tell prove which directories to use. If you habitually do this, don't tell prove which paths to add to @INC.

```
map ,t  <Esc>:!prove -v %<CR>
```

Instead, have your *tests* add paths to @INC:

```
use lib '../../lib';
```

That can get a bit clumsy and it can make it rather tough to reorganize your tests, but it works.

> Here's a little alisp for Emacs users to put into your *~/.emacs* file to get the same thing. It binds to C-c t, but you can change to whatever you prefer:
>
> ```
> (eval-after-load "cperl-mode"
>    '(add-hook 'cperl-mode-hook
>        (lambda () (local-set-key "\C-ct" 'cperl-
> prove))))
>   (defun cperl-prove ()
>    "Run the current test."
>    (interactive)
>    (shell-command (concat "prove -v "
>      (shell-quote-argument (buffer-file-name)))))
> ```

HACK #11 Run Perl from Emacs

Make Perl and Elisp play nicely together.

Emacs's long and varied history happens to embody much of Perl's "There's More Than One Way To Do It" approach to things. This is especially evident when you run a small bit of Perl code from within Emacs. Here's how to do just that.

The Hack

Suppose you really need to know the higher bits of the current value of time( ). In Perl, that's print time() 8>>;. You could use the shell-command command (normally on Control-Alt-One), and enter:

```
perl -e 'print time( ) >> 8;'
```

Emacs will dutifully run that command line and then show the output. Note though that you have to remember to quote and/or backslash-escape the Perl expression according to the rules of your default shell. This quickly becomes maddening if the expression itself contains quotes and/or backslashes or even is several lines long.

An alternative is to start an "Emacs shell" in an Emacs subwindow, then start the Perl debugger in that shell. That is, type **alt-x "shell"** Enter, and then **perl -de1** Enter, and then enter the expression just as if you were running the debugger in a normal terminal window:

```
% perl -de1

Loading DB routines from perl5db.pl version 1.27
Editor support available.

Enter h or `h h' for help, or `man perldebug' for more help.

main::(-e:1):    1
  DB<1> p time( ) >> 8
4448317
  DB<2>
```

This means you don't have to escape the Perl expression as you would if you were sending it through a command line, but it does require you to know at least a bit about the Perl debugger and the Emacs shell. It also becomes troublesome in its own way when your expression is several lines long.

A simpler alternative is to save your snippet to a file named *delme123.pl* and to run that via a command line, but this is a very effective way to fill every directory in reach with files named with the same variant of *delme*.

I prefer defining a new function just for running Perl code in the Region (what you have selected in Emacs, between the Point and the Mark):

```
(defun perl-eval (beg end)
  "Run selected region as Perl code"
  (interactive "r")
  (shell-command-on-region beg end "perl")
  ; feeds the region to perl on STDIN
)
```

I bind it to my CTRL-Alt-p key:

```
(global-set-key "\M-\C-p" 'perl-eval)
```

Then when I want to run some Perl expression in whatever buffer I happen to be in, I just set the mark, type the expression, and hit CTRL-Alt-p. It requires no special escaping, nor are there any problems when the Perl code spans several lines.

CHAPTER TWO

User Interaction
Hacks 12–18

Without users, there'd be few reasons to write programs. Without users—and this includes *you*—there'd be few bugs reported for weird error messages, strange behaviors, and classic "What were you thinking and why did it do that?" moments.

Your programs don't have to be that way. You can make your users happy, make your code work where it has to work, and even make pretty graphics with Perl, all by mastering a few tricks and tips. When your program has to interact with a real person somewhere, do it with style. People may not notice when your code just stays out of their way, but you'll know by their happy glows of productivity.

HACK #12 Use $EDITOR As Your UI

Nothing beats your favorite editor for editing text.

If you live on the command line and have a reputation for turning your favorite beverage* into code, you're likely pretty handy on the keyboard. If you're a relentless automator, you probably have dozens of little programs and aliases to make your life easier.

Sometimes they need arguments. Yet beyond a certain point, prompting for arguments every time or inventing more and more command-line options just doesn't work anymore. Before you resign yourself to the fate of writing a little GUI or a web frontend, consider using a more comfortable user interface instead—your preferred text editor.

---

* Your author recommends peppermint tea.

The Hack

Suppose you have a series of little programs for updating your web site. Your workflow is to create a small YAML file with a new posting, then run that data through a template, update the index, and copy those pages to your server. Instead of copying a blank YAML file (or trying to recreate the necessary fields and formatting by hand), just launch an editor.

For example, a simple news site might have entries that need only a title, the date of posting, and a multiline block of text to run through some formatter. Easy:

```
use YAML 'DumpFile';
use POSIX 'strftime';

local $YAML::UseBlock = 1;

exit 1 unless -d 'posts';

my @posts = <posts/*.yaml>;
my $file  = 'posts/' . ( @posts + 1 ) . '.yaml';

my $fields =
{
    title => '',
    date  => strftime( '%d %B %Y', localtime() ),
    text  => "\n\n",
};

DumpFile( $file, $fields );

system( $ENV{EDITOR}, $file ) == 0
    or die "Error launching $ENV{EDITOR}: $!\n";
```

Assuming you have the EDITOR environment variable set to your preferred editor, this program creates a new blank post in the *posts/* subdirectory with the appropriate id (monotonically increasing, of course), then drops you in your editor to edit the YAML file. It has already populated the date field with the current date in the proper format. Additionally, setting $YAML:: UseBlock to a true value makes YAML treat the multiline text string as a YAML heredoc, making it much easier to edit.

Running the Hack

From the proper directory, just run the program. It will launch a new editor on the file. When you've finished editing, save and quit, and the program will continue.

This may work very differently on non-Unix systems.

Hacking the Hack

You don't have to give up on error checking even without a formal GUI. If you can't read in the YAML file or don't have all of the right fields filled in, you can rewrite the file with as much or as little information as you like, prompting the user to try again. You can even add comments or special fields to the file explaining the error.

To read in the file, just call LoadFile with the filename—then continue as normal, as if the user hadn't had to create the file.

HACK #13   Interact Correctly on the Command Line

Be kind to other programs.

Command-line programs that expect input from the keyboard are easy, right? Certainly they're easier than writing good GUI applications, right? Not necessarily. The Unix command line is flexible and powerful, but that flexibility can break naively written programs.

Prompting for interactive input in Perl typically looks like:

```
print "> ";
while (my $next_cmd = <>)
{
    chomp $next_cmd;
    process($next_cmd);
    print "> ";
}
```

If your program needs to handle noninteractive situations as well, things get a whole lot more complicated. The usual solution is something like:

```
print "> " if -t *ARGV && -t select;
while (my $next_cmd = <>)
{
    chomp $next_cmd;
    process($next_cmd);
    print "> " if -t *ARGV && -t select;
}
```

The -t test checks whether its filehandle argument is connected to a terminal. To handle interactive cases correctly, you need to check both that you're reading from a terminal (-t *ARGV) and that you're writing to one (-t select). It's a common mistake to mess those tests up, and write instead:

```
print "> " if -t *STDIN && -t *STDOUT;
```

The problem is that the <> operator doesn't read from STDIN; it reads from ARGV. If there are filenames specified on the command line, those two file-handles aren't the same. Likewise, although print usually writes to STDOUT, it won't if you've explicitly select-ed some other destination. You need to call select with no arguments to get the filehandle which each print will currently target.

Worse, still, even the correct version:

```
print "> " if -t *ARGV && -t select;
```

doesn't always work correctly. That's because the ARGV filehandle is magically self-opening, but only magically self-opens during the first read operation on it. If you haven't already done at least one <> before you start prompting for input, then the ARGV handle won't be open yet, so the first -t *ARGV test (the one before the while loop) won't be true, and the first prompt won't print.

To accurately test if an application is running interactively in all possible circumstances, you need an elaborate nightmare:

```
use Scalar::Util qw( openhandle );

sub is_interactive
{
    # Not interactive if output is not to terminal...
    return 0 if not -t select;

    # If *ARGV is opened, we're interactive if...
    if (openhandle *ARGV)
    {
        # ...it's currently opened to the magic '-' file
        #    and the standard input is interactive...
        return -t *STDIN if defined $ARGV && $ARGV eq '-';

        # ...or it's at end-of-file and the next file
        #    is the magic '-' file...
        return @ARGV>0 && $ARGV[0] eq '-' && -t *STDIN if eof *ARGV;

        # ...or it's directly attached to the terminal
        return -t *ARGV;
    }

    # If *ARGV isn't opened, it will be interactive if *STDIN is
    # attached to a terminal and either there are no files specified
    # on the command line or if there are files and the first is the
    # magic '-' file...
    else
    {
        return -t *STDIN && (@ARGV==0 || $ARGV[0] eq '-');
    }
}
```

The Hack

Of course, no one wants to reinvent *that* for each project, so there's a CPAN module that does it for you:

```
use IO::Interactive qw( is_interactive );

print "> " if is_interactive;
while (my $next_cmd = <>)
{
    chomp $next_cmd;
    process($next_cmd);
    print "> " if is_interactive;
}
```

The Hack

The module has a second interface that's even Lazier. Instead of an explicit interactivity test, it can provide you with a writable filehandle that implicitly tests for interactivity:

```
use IO::Interactive qw( interactive );

print {interactive} "> ";
while (my $next_cmd = <>)
{
    chomp $next_cmd;
    process($next_cmd);
    print {interactive} "> ";
}
```

HACK #14 Simplify Your Terminal Interactions

Read data from users correctly, effectively, and without thinking about it.

Even when you know the right way to handle interactive I/O [Hack #13], the resulting code can still be frustratingly messy:

```
my $offset;
print "Enter an offset: " if is_interactive;
GET_OFFSET:
while (<>)
{
    chomp;
    if (m/\A [+-] \d+ \z/x)
    {
        $offset = $_;
        last GET_OFFSET;
    }
    print "Enter an offset (please enter an integer): "
        if is_interactive;
}
```

You can achieve exactly the same effect (and much more) with the prompt( ) subroutine provided by the IO::Prompt CPAN module. Instead of all the above infrastructure code, just write:

```
use IO::Prompt;

my $offset = prompt( "Enter an offset: ", -integer );
```

prompt( ) prints the string you give it, reads a line from standard input, chomps it, and then tests the input value against any constraint you specify (for example, -integer). If the constraint is not satisfied, the prompt repeats, along with a clarification of what was wrong. When the user finally enters an acceptable value, prompt( ) returns it.

Most importantly, prompt( ) is smart enough not to bother writing out any prompts if the application isn't running interactively, so you don't have to code explicitly for that case.

> Infrastructure code is code that doesn't actually contribute to solving your problem, but merely exists to hold your program together. Typically this kind of code implements standard low-level tasks that probably ought to have built-ins dedicated to them. Many modules in the standard library and on CPAN exist solely to provide cleaner alternatives to continually rewriting your own infrastructure code. Discovering and using them can significantly decrease both the size and cruftiness of your code.

Train -req

prompt( ) has a general mechanism for telling it what kind of input you need and how to ask for that input. For example:

```
my $hex_num = prompt( "Enter a hex number> ",
        -req => { "A *hex* number please!> " => qr/^[0-9A-F]+$/i }
        );

print "That's ", hex($hex_num), " in base 10\n";
```

When this code executes, you will see something like:

```
Enter a hex number> 2B|!2B
A *hex* number please!> C3PO
A *hex* number please!> 124C1
That's 74945 in base 10
```

The -req argument takes a hash reference, in which each value is something to test the input against, and each key is a secondary prompt to print when the test fails. The tests can be regexes (which the input must match) or subroutines (which receive the input as $_ and should return true if that input satisfies the constraint). For example:

```
my $factor = prompt( "Enter a prime: ",
                        -req => { "Try again: " => sub { is_prime($_) } }
                    );
```

Yea or Nay

One particularly useful constraint that prompt( ) supports is a mode that accepts only the letters y or n as input:

```
if (prompt -YESNO, "Quit? ")
{
    save_changes($changes)
        if $changes && prompt -yes, "Save changes? ";
    print "Changes: $changes\n";
    exit;
}
```

The first call to prompt( ) requires the user to type a word beginning with Y or N. It will ignore anything else and return the prompt with an explanation. If the input is Y, the call will return true; if N, it will return false. On the other hand, the second call (with the -yes argument) actually accepts any input. If that string starts with a y or Y, prompt( ) returns true; for any other input, it returns false. For example:

```
Quit? q
Quit? (Please enter 'Y' or 'N') Y
Save changes? n
Changes: not saved
```

These different combinations of -YES/-yes/-no/-NO allow for varying degrees of punctiliousness in obtaining the user's consent. In particular, using -YESNO forces users to hit Shift and one of only two possible keys, which often provides enough of a pause to prevent unthinking responses that they'll deeply regret about 0.1 seconds after hitting Enter.

At the Touch of a Button

On the other hand, sometimes it's immensely annoying to have to press Enter at all. Sometimes you want to hit a single key and just let the application get on with things. Thus prompt( ) provides a single character mode:

```
for my $file (@matching_files)
{
    next unless prompt -one_char, -yes, "Copy $file? ";
    copy($file, "$backup_dir/$file");
}
```

With -one_char in effect, the first typed character completes the entire input operation. In this case, prompt( ) returns true only if that character was y or Y.

Of course, single character mode can accept more than just y and n. For example, the following call allows the user to select a drive instantly, simply by typing its single character name (in upper- or lowercase):

```
my $drive = uc prompt "Select a drive: ",
                      -one_char,
                      -req => { "Please select A-F: " => qr/[A-F]/i };
```

Engage Cloaking Device

You can tell prompt( ) not to echo input (good for passwords):

```
my $passwd = prompt( "First password: ", -echo=>"" );
```

or to echo something different in place of what you actually type (also good for passwords):

```
my $passwd = prompt( "Second password: ", -echo=>"*" );
```

This allows you to produce interfaces like:

```
First password:
Second password: ********
```

What's On the Menu?

Often you can't rely on users to type in the right responses; it's easier to list them and ask the user to choose. This is menu-driven interaction, and prompt( ) supports various forms of it. The simplest is just to give the subroutine a list of possible responses in an array:

```
my $device = prompt 'Activate which device?',
                    -menu =>
                    [
                        'Sharks with "laser" beams',
                        'Disinhibiter gas grenades',
                        'Death ray',
                        'Mirror ball',
                    ];

print "Activating $device in 10:00 and counting...\n";
```

This produces the request:

```
Activate which device?
  a. Sharks with "laser" beams
  b. Disinhibiter gas grenades
  c. Death ray
  d. Mirror ball
> q
(Please enter a-d) > d
Activating Mirror ball in 10:00 and counting...
```

The menu call to prompt only accepts characters in the range displayed, and returns the value corresponding to the character entered.

You can also pass the -menu option a hash reference:

```
my $device = prompt 'Initiate which master plan?',
                -menu =>
                {
                    Cousteau => 'Sharks with "laser" beams',
                    Libido  => 'Disinhibiter gas grenades',
                    Friar   => 'Death ray',
                    Shiny   => 'Mirror ball',
                };

print "Activating $device in 10:00 and counting...\n";
```

in which case it will show the list of keys and return the value corresponding to the key selected:

```
Initiate which master plan?
 a. Cousteau
 b. Friar
 c. Libido
 d. Shiny
> d
Activating Mirror ball in 10:00 and counting...
```

You can even nest hashes and arrays:

```
my $device = prompt 'Select your platform:',
                -menu =>
                {
                    Windows => [ 'WinCE', 'WinME', 'WinNT' ],
                    MacOS   => {
                                'MacOS 9' => 'Mac (Classic)',
                                'MacOS X' => 'Mac (New Age)',
                               },
                    Linux   => 'Linux',
                };
```

to create hierarchical menus:

```
Select your platform:
 a. Linux
 b. MacOS
 c. Windows
> b

MacOS:
 a. MacOS 9
 b. Mac OS X
> b

Compiling for Mac (New Age)...
```

HACK **#15**

Alert Your Mac

Schedule GUI alerts from the command line.

Growl (*http://www.growl.info/*) is a small utility for Mac OS X that allows any application to send notifications to the user. The notifications pop up as a small box in a corner of the screen, overlayed on the current active window (as shown in Figure 2-1).

Figure 2-1. A simple Growl notification

The Hack

You can send Growl notifications from Perl, thanks to Chris Nandor's Mac::Growl. The first thing you have to do is tell Growl that your script wants to send notifications. The following code registers a script named growlalert and tells Growl that it sends alert notifications:

```
use Mac::Growl;

Mac::Growl::RegisterNotifications(
    'growlalert', # application name
    [ 'alert' ],  # notifications this app sends
    [ 'alert' ],  # enable these notifications
);
```

Growl displays a notification to let you know the script has registered successfully (Figure 2-2). You need only register an application once on each machine that uses it.

Figure 2-2. A newly registered application

When you want to send a notification, call PostNotification( ), passing the name of the script, the kind of notification to send, a title, and a description:

```
Mac::Growl::PostNotification(
    'growlalert', # application name
    'alert',      # type of notification
    "This is a title",
    "This is a description.",
);
```

This will pop up a notification window (Figure 2-3) and fade it out again after a few seconds.

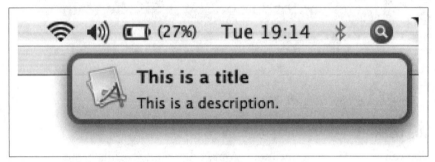

Figure 2-3. Notification with title and description

Running the Hack

You might want a small script that sends you an alert after a time delay. The following command-line utility takes a time period to delay and a message to display in the alert. It calculates the time when the alert should appear, then forks to return control of the terminal window to the user. The forked child sleeps the requested amount of time, and then posts a Growl notification with the message as the title and no description.

```
my %seconds_per =
(
    's'   => 1,
    'm'   => 60,
    'h'   => 60*60,
);

my ( $period, @message ) = @ARGV;
my ( $number, $unit )    = ( $period =~ m/^([\.\d]+)(.*)$/ )
        or die "usage: ga number[smh] message\n";
$unit ||= 's';

my $growl_time = $number * $seconds_per{$unit};

my $pid        = fork;
die "fork failed ($!)\n" unless defined $pid;
```

```
unless ( $pid )
{
    require Mac::Growl;
    sleep $growl_time;

    Mac::Growl::PostNotification(
        'growlalert', # application name
        'alert',      # type of notification
        "@message",   # title
        "",           # no description
        1,            # notification is sticky
    );
}
```

The additional argument passed to PostNotification tells Growl that the notification should stay on the screen until the user clicks it, instead of fading after a few seconds.

Some common uses of this program are:

```
$ ga 5m coffee
$ ga 2.5h 'oxford soon - get off the train'
```

Hacking the Hack

For Unix systems running the X Window system, use the xmessage command instead of Mac::Growl:

```
unless ( $pid )
{
    sleep $growl_time;
    system( 'xmessage', @message );
}
```

You can get creative there, popping up the window near the cursor or automatically fading out after a specified period of time.

On Windows systems running the messenger service, the proper invocation is something like:

```
unless ( $pid )
{
    sleep $growl_time;
    system( qw( cmd net send localhost ), @message );
}
```

HACK #16   Interactive Graphical Apps

Paint pretty pictures with Perl.

People often see Perl as a general-purpose language: you start by using it to write short scripts, do administrative tasks, or text processing. If you happen to appreciate it, you end up enjoying its flexibility and power to perform almost anything that doesn't require the speed of compiled binaries.

Consider instead the number one requirement of games. Unless you're exclusively a fan of card games, you'd say "CPU power." Fortunately a crazy guy named David J. Goehrig had the mysterious idea to bind the functions of the C low-level graphical library SDL for the Perl language. The result is an object-oriented approach to SDL called *sdlperl*.

Blitting with SDL Perl

With SDL you will manipulate *surfaces*. These are rectangular images, and the most common operation is to copy one onto another; this is *blitting*.* To implement a basic image loader with SDL Perl in just four non-comment lines of code, write:

```
use SDL::App;

# open a 640x480 window for your application
our $app = SDL::App->new(-width => 640, -height => 480);

# create a surface out of an image file specified on the command-line
our $img = SDL::Surface->new( -name => $ARGV[0] );

# blit the surface onto the window of your application
$img->blit( undef, $app, undef );

# flush all pending screen updates
$app->flip( );

# sleep for 3 seconds to let the user view the image
sleep 3;
```

You might wonder how to perform positioning and cropping during a blit. In the previous code, replace the two undef parameter values with instances of SDL::Rect, the first one specifying the *rectangle* to copy from the source *surface*, and the second specifying the *rectangle* where to blit on the destination *surface*. When you use undef instead, SDL uses top-left positioning and full sizing. Here's a blit replacement that specifies a 100×100 area in the source *surface* at a horizontal offset of 200 pixels:

```
$img->blit( SDL::Rect->new(
    -width => 100, -height => 100, -x => 200, -y => 0
), $app, undef);
```

---

* A blit is the action of copying a series of bits between memory addresses. The main goal of this operation is to perform the copy as fast as possible.

Animating with SDL Perl

You're already closer than you think to being able to write a full-fledged game with SDL Perl. The previous example opened the application, created a *surface* from an image file, and showed it onscreen. Add sound and input handling, and you're (mostly) done! Sound is too easy to use to show here; input handling requires the proper monitoring of *events* reported by an instance of SDL::Event.

The simplest option for input handling is to loop waiting for new events. This is fine if you have no animated sprites on screen (movement will block while you wait on the loop), but if you need to handle animations, you need a main loop that performs more steps:

- Erase all sprites at their current position.
- Check *events* to see if user interaction changes anything in the game.
- Move sprites and update game states.
- Draw all sprites at their new position.
- Tell SDL Perl to display any changes on screen.
- Synchronize the animation by sleeping for a short amount of time, corresponding to the target animation speed.

Iterate forever through these steps, and you have the core of a game engine.

You might wonder if any visual artifacts (*flickers*) are visible between the moment you erase all sprites and the moment you draw them at their new positions. This will not happen, because windowing systems use back buffers, synchronizing them only when the program explicitly asks for a screen update.

A Working Animation

To illustrate everything, here's a short example program animating a colored rectangle and its fading tail (as shown in Figure 2-4). It first creates the needed series of *surfaces*, with a fading color and transparency, then implements the above main loop, animating the sprites along a periodic path. Monitoring events allows the user to temporarily stop the animation by pressing any key and to exit by hitting the escape key or by closing the application window. Read through this example for extensive details about its implementation.

```
use SDL;
use SDL::App;
use strict;
```

Figure 2-4. An animation with SDL Perl

```perl
# specify the target animation speed here, in milliseconds between two
# frames; for 50 frames per second, this is 20 ms
our $TARGET_ANIM_SPEED = 20;

# define an array where to store all the rectangles changed between two
# frames; this allows faster screen updates than using SDL::App#flip
our @update_rects;

# initialize the background surface to an image file if user specified one
# on the commandline, to blank otherwise

our $background = SDL::Surface->new(-f $ARGV[0] ? (-name   => $ARGV[0])
                                                : (-width  => 640,
                                                   -height => 480      ));
# open a 640x480 window for the application
our $app = SDL::App->new(-width => 640, -height => 480);

# copy the whole background surface to the application window
$background->blit(undef, $app, undef);

# update the application window
$app->flip;

# define an array where to store all the surfaces representing
# the colored sprites with all the levels of color and transparency
our @imgs = map
{
    # create a 30x20 surface for one sprite
    my $surface = SDL::Surface->new(
        -width => 30, -height => 20, -depth => 32
    );

    # fill the surface with a solid color; let it fade from
    # blue to white while the mapped int value is iterated over
```

```
    $surface->fill(undef,
        SDL::Color->new(-r => 128+$_*255/45, -g => 128+$_*255/45, -b => 255)
    );

    # set the transparency of the surface (more and more transparent)
    $surface->set_alpha(SDL_SRCALPHA, (15-$_)*255/15);

    # convert the surface to the display format, to allow faster blits
    # to the application window
    $surface->display_format();

} (1..15);

# define a helper function to blit a surface at a given position on the
# application window, adding the rectangle involved to the array of needed
# updates

sub blit_at
{
    my ($surface, $x, $y) = @_;
    my $dest_rect = SDL::Rect->new(
        -width => $surface->width(), -height => $surface->height(),
        -x => $x, '-y' => $y
    );
    $surface->blit(undef, $app, $dest_rect);
    push @update_rects, $dest_rect;
}

# define a helper function to blit the portion of background similar to the
# area of a surface at a given position on the application window, adding
# the rectangle involved to the array of needed updates; this actually
# "erases" the surface previously blitted there
sub erase_at
{
    my ($surface, $x, $y) = @_;
    my $dest_rect = SDL::Rect->new(
        -width => $surface->width(), -height => $surface->height(),
        -x => $x, '-y' => $y
    );
    $background->blit($dest_rect, $app, $dest_rect);
    push @update_rects, $dest_rect;
}

# define an array to store the positions of the sprites, a counter to
# calculate new positions of the sprite while it's animated, and a boolean
# to know if the animation has stopped or not
our (@pos, $counter, $stopped);

# define an instance of SDL::Event for event monitoring
our $event = SDL::Event->new();

# start the main loop here
while (1)
{
```

```perl
# store the current value of the sdlperl milliseconds counter; the end
# of the mainloop uses it for animation synchronization
my $synchro_ticks = $app->ticks();

# erase all sprites at their current positions (stored by @pos)
for (my $i = 0; $i < @pos; $i++)
{
    erase_at($imgs[$i], $pos[$i]{'x'}, $pos[$i]{'y'});
}

# ask for new events
$event->pump();

if ($event->poll != 0)
{
    # if the event is a key press, stop the animation
    if ($event->type() == SDL_KEYDOWN)
    {
        $stopped = 1;
    }

    # if the event is a key release, resume the animation
    if ($event->type() == SDL_KEYUP)
    {
        $stopped = 0;
    }

    # if we receive a "QUIT" event (user clicked the "close" icon of the
    # application window) or the user hit the Escape key, exit program
    if ($event->type == SDL_QUIT ||
        $event->type == SDL_KEYDOWN && $event->key_sym == SDLK_ESCAPE)
    {
        die "quit\n";
    }
}

# if the animation is not stopped, increase the counter
$stopped or $counter++;

# insert a new position in top of @pos; let positions be a sine-based
# smooth curve
unshift @pos,
{
    'x' => 320 + 200 * sin($counter/30),
    'y' => 240 +  80 * cos($counter/25),
};

# remove the superfluous positions
@pos > 15 and pop @pos;

# draw all sprites at their new positions
for (my $i = @pos - 1; $i >= 0; $i--)
{
```

```
        blit_at($imgs[$i], $pos[$i]{'x'}, $pos[$i]{'y'});
    }

    # tell sdlperl to flush all updates in the specified rectangles
    $app->update(@update_rects);

    # empty the array of rectangles needing an update
    @update_rects = ( );

    # wait the time necessary for this frame to last the target number of
    # milliseconds of a frame.  This allows the animation to look smooth
    my $to_wait = $TARGET_ANIM_SPEED - ($app->ticks - $synchro_ticks);
    $to_wait > 0 and $app->delay($to_wait);
}
```

HACK #17 Collect Configuration Information

Save and re-use configuration information.

Some code you write needs configuration information when you build and install it. For example, consider a program that can use any of several optional and conflicting plug-ins. The user must decide what to use when she builds the module, especially if some of the dependencies themselves have dependencies.

When you run your tests and the code in general, having this information available in one spot is very valuable—you can avoid expensive and tricky checks if you hide everything behind a single, consistent interface.

How do you collect and store this information? Ask the user, and then write it into a simple configuration module!

The Hack

Both Module::Build and ExtUtils::MakeMaker provide user prompting features to ask questions and get answers. The benefit of this is that they silently accept the defaults during automated installations. Users at the keyboard can still answer a prompt, while users who just want the software to install won't launch the installer, turn away, and return an hour later to find that another prompt has halted the process in the meantime.

Module::Build is easier to extend, so here's a simple subclass that allows you to specify questions, default values, and configuration keys before writing out a standard module containing this information:

```
package Module::Build::Configurator;

use strict;
use warnings;
```

```perl
use base 'Module::Build';

use SUPER;
use File::Path;
use Data::Dumper;
use File::Spec::Functions;

sub new
{
    my ($class, %args) = @_;
    my $self           = super();
    my $config         = $self->notes( 'config_data' ) || {};

    for my $question ( @{ $args{config_questions} } )
    {
        my ($q, $name, $default) = map { defined $_ ? $_ : '' } @$question;
        $config->{$name}         = $self->prompt( $q, $default );
    }

    $self->notes( 'config_module', $args{config_module} );
    $self->notes( 'config_data',   $config );
    return $self;
}

sub ACTION_build
{
    $_[0]->write_config();
    super();
}

sub write_config
{
    my $self      = shift;
    my $file      = $self->notes( 'config_module' );
    my $data      = $self->notes( 'config_data' );
    my $dump      = Data::Dumper->new( [ $data ], [ 'config_data' ] )->Dump;
    my $file_path = catfile( 'lib', split( /::/, $file . '.pm' ) );

    my $path      = ( splitpath( $file_path ) )[1];
    mkpath( $path ) unless -d $path;

    my $package   = <<END_MODULE;
package $file;

my $dump

sub get_value
{
    my (\$class, \$key) = \@_;

    return unless exists \$config_data->{ \$key };
    return                \$config_data->{ \$key };
}
```

```
      1;
END_MODULE

    $package =~ s/^\t//gm;

    open( my $fh, '>', $file_path )
        or die "Cannot write config file '$path': $!\n";
    print $fh $package;
    close $fh;
}

    1;
```

The module itself is a straightforward subclass of Module::Build. It overrides new( ) to collect the config_module argument (containing the name of
the configuration module to write) and to loop over every configuration
question (specified with config_questions). The latter argument is an array
reference of array references containing the name of the question to ask, the
name of the value as stored in the configuration module, and the default
value of the question, if any. In an unattended installation, the prompt( )
method will return the default value rather than interrupt the process.

The module also overrides ACTION_build( ), the method that perl ./Build
runs, to write the configuration file. The write_config( ) method takes the
hash of configuration data created in new( ) (and stored with Module::Build's
handy notes( ) mechanism), serializes it with Data::Dumper, and writes it and
a module skeleton to the necessary path under *lib/*.

> Note the use of File::Spec::Functions and File::Path to
> improve file handling and to make sure that the destination
> directory exists for the configuration module.

Using the Hack

To use the hack, write a *Build.PL* file as normal:

```
use Module::Build::Configurator;

my $build = Module::Build::Configurator->new(
    module_name     => 'User::IrisScan',
    config_module   => 'User::IrisScan::Config',
    config_questions =>
    [
        [ 'What is your name?',                        'name', 'Anouska' ],
        [ 'Rate yourself as a spy from 1 to 10.',   'rating', '10'      ],
        [ 'What is your eye color?',             'eye_color', 'blue'    ],
    ],
);

$build->create_build_script( );
```

This file builds a distribution for the User::IrisScan module. Run it to see the prompts:

```
$ perl Build.PL
What is your name? [Anouska] Faye
Rate yourself as a spy from 1 to 10. [10] 8
What is your eye color? [blue] blue
Deleting Build
Removed previous script 'Build'
Creating new 'Build' script for 'User-IrisScan' version '1.28'
$
```

Now look at *lib/User/IrisScan/Config.pm*:

```
package User::IrisScan::Config;

my $config_data = {
                'eye_color' => 'blue',
                'name' => 'Faye',
                'rating' => '8'
            };


sub get_value
{
    my ($class, $key) = @_;

    return unless exists $config_data->{ $key };
    return            $config_data->{ $key };
}

1;
```

You can use this configuration module within your tests or within the program now as normal. If you're clever, you can even check for this module when *upgrading* your software. If it exists, use the configured values there for the defaults. Your users will love you.

Rewrite the Web
HACK #18
Use the power of Perl to rewrite the web.

The Greasemonkey extension for Mozilla Firefox and related browsers is a powerful way to modify web pages to your liking. In fact, the Mozilla family projects are customizable in many ways—as long as you like writing C++, JavaScript, or XUL.

If your network doesn't run only Firefox, or if you just prefer to customize the Web with Perl instead of any other language, HTTP::Proxy can help.

The Hack

For whatever reason (registrar greed, mostly), plenty of useful sites such as Perl Monks have *.com* and *.org* domain names. One visitor might use *http://www.perlmonks.com/*, while the truly blessed saints prefer *http://perlmonks.org/*. That's all well and good except for the cases where you have logged in to the site through one domain name but not the others. Your HTTP cookie uses the specific domain name for identification.

Thus you may follow a link from somewhere that leads to the correct site with the incorrect domain name. How annoying!

Fixing this with HTTP::Proxy is easy though:

```perl
use strict;
use warnings;

use HTTP::Proxy ':log';
use HTTP::Proxy::HeaderFilter::simple;

# start the proxy with the given command-line parameters
my $proxy = HTTP::Proxy->new( @ARGV );

for my $redirect (<DATA>)
{
    chomp $redirect;

    my ($pattern, $destination) = split( /\|/, $redirect );
    my $filter                  = get_filter( $destination );

    $proxy->push_filter( host => $pattern, request => $filter );
}

$proxy->start();

my %filters;

sub get_filter
{
    my $site = shift;

    return $filters{ $site } ||= HTTP::Proxy::HeaderFilter::simple->new(
        sub
        {
            my ( $self, $headers, $message ) = @_;

            # modify the host part of the request only
            $message->uri()->host( $site );

            # create a new redirect response
            my $res = HTTP::Response->new(
                301,
                "Moved to $site",
```

```
                    [ Location => $message->uri( ) ]
            );

            # and make the proxy send it back to the client
            $self->proxy( )->response( $res );
        }
    );
}

__DATA__
perlmonks.com|perlmonks.org
www.perlmonks.org|perlmonks.org
```

The program creates a new HTTP::Proxy object, then reads all of the data at the end of the program to create header filters. When a request comes in, the proxy runs all header filters that match the request. These filters can manipulate the request as appropriate.

In this example, if the host of a request matches perlmonks.com, the filter sends back an HTTP 301 status code redirecting the request to perlmonks. org. A well-behaved client will repeat the request with the new host (this time, sending along the proper cookie).

The use of the %filters lexical is the Orcish Maneuver. Read the line in get_filter( ) as "return the cached object or cache a new one".

Running the Hack

Run the program from the command line. If necessary, pass in arguments, perhaps to run on a different port:

```
$ perl memoryproxy.pl port 5000
```

Configure your browser to use this proxy and try to visit *http://perlmonks. com/*). You'll end up at *http://perlmonks.org/*.

Hacking the Hack

There are countless uses for HTTP::Proxy, even beyond rewriting both request and response headers and bodies. Try:

- Restricting a browsing session to no more than ten minutes at a time during working hours.
- Maintaining a list (or graph or tree) of relationships between sites.
- Forbidding yourself from wasting time reading certain sites during working hours.
- Creating shortcuts for URLs **[Hack #1]** across multiple browsers without manipulating local DNS records.

## CHAPTER THREE

Data Munging
Hacks 19–27

Perl has always been in love with data. No matter where you find it, Perl happily processes and extracts and reports on files, databases, web pages, spreadsheets, other programs, and anything that produces data. Perl's so happy to do this that it even overlooks brute-force, rough manipulations. Hey, pragmatism works!

Perl can be gentle, too. A little subtlety, a little style and finesse, and you can write maintainable, easy-to-understand code that's just as powerful as the wild-eyed forge-ahead-at-all-costs just-do-the-job code. Why? It's often faster and more correct—as well as more secure, more powerful, and shorter.

Sure, slinging data between sources sounds about as glamorous as slinging hash at the local diner, but it doesn't have to be that way. Here are several ideas to munge that yummy data with all of the elegance and style and power and clarity that you know you have.

HACK
#19

Treat a File As an Array

Pretend a big stream of data on disk is a nice, malleable Perl data structure.

One of the big disappointments in programming is realizing that, although you can think of a text file as a long list of properly terminated lines, to the computer, it's just a big blob of ones and zeroes. If all you need to do is read the lines of a file and process them in order, you're fine. If you have a big file that you can't load into memory and can't process each line in order...well, good luck.

Fortunately, Mark Jason Dominus's Tie::File module exists, and is even in the core as of Perl 5.8.0. What good is it?

The Hack

Imagine you have a million-line CSV file of inventory data from a customer that's just not quite right. You can't import it into a spreadsheet, because that's too much data. You need to do some processing, inserting some lines and rearranging others. Importing the data into a little SQLite database won't work either because trying to get the queries right is too troublesome.

Tie::File won't help you write the rules for transforming lines, but it will take the pain out of manipulating the lines of a file. Just:

```
use Tie::File;

tie my @csv_lines, 'Tie::File', 'big_file.csv'
    or die "Cannot open big_file.csv: !$\n";
```

Running the Hack

Suppose that your big CSV file contains a list of products and operations. That is, each line is either a list of product data (product id, name, price, supplier, et cetera) or some operation to perform on the previous *n* products. Operations take the form opname:number. Obviously the file would be easier to process if the operations appeared *before* the data on which to operate, but you can't always change customer data formats to something sane. In fact, this might be the easiest way to clean the data for other processes.

Tie::File makes this almost trivial:

```
for my $i ( 0 .. $#csv_lines )
{
    next unless my ($op, $num) = $csv_lines[ $i ] =~ /^(\w+):(\d+)/;
    next unless my $op_sub     = __PACKAGE__->can( 'op_' . $op );

    my $start                  = $i - $num;
    my $end                    = $i - 1;
    my @lines                  = @csv_lines[ $start .. $end ];
    my @newlines               = $op_sub->( @lines );

    splice @csv_lines, $start, $num + 1, @newlines;
}
```

Okay, there *is* a bit of cleverness in finding the right range of lines to modify, but consider how much trickier the code would have to be to do this *while* looping through the file a line at a time.

Of course, you can use all of the standard array manipulation operations (push, pop, shift, unshift, and splice) as necessary.

Read Files Backwards

#20 Process the most recent lines of a file first.

Perl's position in system administration is stable and secure, due in no small part to its fast and flexible text-processing abilities. If you need to slice and dice log files, monitor services, and send out messages, you *could* glue together the perfect combination of shell and command-line utilities, or you could have Perl do it.

Of course, Perl is a general-purpose language and doesn't always provide every tool you might need by default. For example, if you find yourself processing system logs often, you might wish for a way to read files in reverse order, the most recent line first. Sure, you *could* slurp all of the lines into an array and read the last one, but on a busy system with lots of huge logs, that can be slow and memory-consuming.

Fortunately, there's more than one way to do it.

The Hack

Yes, you *could* look up perldoc -F -X and find a file's size and read backwards until you find the appropriate newline and then read forward...but just install File::ReadBackwards from the CPAN instead.

Suppose you have a server process that continually writes its status to a file. You only care about its current status (at least for now), not its historical data. If its status is up, everything is happy. If its status is down, you need to panic and notify everyone, especially if it's 3 a.m. on Boxing Day.

Simulate the program that writes its logs with:

```perl
#!/usr/bin/perl

use strict;
use warnings;

use Time::HiRes 'sleep';

local $| = 1;

for ( 1 .. 10000 )
{
    my $status = $_ % 10 ? 'up' : 'down';
    print "$status\n";
    sleep( 0.1 );
}
```

This program writes a status message to STDOUT ten times a second; nine of those are up and the last is down. Run it and redirect it to a file such as *status.log*. In bash, this is:

```
$ perl write_fake_log.pl > status.log &
```

Running the Hack

With *status.log* continually growing with newer information, finding the most recent status is easy with File::ReadBackwards:

```
use FileReadBackwards;

my $bw = File::ReadBackwards->new( 'status.log' )
    or die "Cannot read 'status.log': $!\n";

exit( 0 ) if $bw->readline( ) =~ /up/;

# panic( ) ...
```

The program is straightforward. Create a File::ReadBackwards object by passing the name of the file you want to read. Then, every time you call readline( ) on the object, you'll receive the previous line of the file, starting with the last line and working backwards to the first line.

Hacking the Hack

Note that the current version of the module (1.04) does not flock the file it reads, so you may read a partial line. Also, you may get a partial line, depending on how large your filesystem's buffers are and how much the process has written to it. If either is important to you, the source code is short, full of good comments, and easy to modify—but if you just need the last *n* lines of a file, this is the easy way.

HACK
#21
Use Any Spreadsheet As a Data Source
Make your data analysis independent of the spreadsheet program.

Spreadsheets are useful for holding structured data, usually based on columns and rows. Most often part of the data is calculated data from other cells in the same spreadsheet.

If you want to work with that data, you face the problem of too many standards and programs. Writing a script that has to read the data from the spreadsheet is more writing an interface to the spreadsheet than actually working with the interesting data.

Accessing Cell Data

The `Spreadsheet::Read` module gives you a single interface to the data of most spreadsheet formats available, hiding all the troublesome work that deals with the parsers and the portability stuff, yet being flexible enough to get to the guts of the spreadsheet.

It's easy to use:

```
use Spreadsheet::Read;

my $ref  = ReadData( 'test.xls' );
my $fval = $ref->[1]{A3};
my $uval = $ref->[1]{cell}[1][3];
```

Here $ref is a reference to a structure that represents the *data* from the spreadsheet (*test.xls*). The reference points to a list (the worksheets) of hashes (the data).

Every cell has two representations: either access it by its name (A3), in which case the interface gives you the formatted value, or the `cell` hash, in which case you get the unformatted value of the cell.

Do I need Spreadsheet::Read for that? No you don't, but it makes life easier. Setting aside all the good things of the various user interfaces for the available spreadsheets (95% probably Excel or OpenOffice.org), coding access to the cell data in the available native parsers is not always as easy as it should be. These interfaces try to give you full control, but you have no easy way to access the data.

Some examples for native equivalences of the previous code snippet are:

* Microsoft Excel
* OpenOffice.org
* Comma Separated Values

They all show you the contents of cell A3, where you can interpret the CSV file as a collection of rows (the lines) and columns (the fields).

`Spreadsheet::Read` gives the same interface to all of these, but uses the native parser in the background. The only thing you have to alter if you change spreadsheet formats is the `ReadData( )` call:

```
my $ref = ReadData( 'test.xls' );

# or
my $ref = ReadData( 'test.sxc' );

# or
my $ref = ReadData( 'test.csv' );
```

which will make your code much more readable, maintainable, and portable. Your code won't depend on the spreadsheet format used by the people shipping you the data.

Accessing a data column. Accessing a single field is good if you know the field you need to access, but quite often, your script has to analyze the data (structure) itself. For that you need a full set of data. Spreadsheet user interfaces always refer to the data location as a (column, row) pair, where (Perl) programmers more often use the (row, column) way of indexing. Perl starts indexing at 0, where spreadsheets usually start with 1. Spreadsheet::Read starts with 1 for the data and uses the zeroth field for internal control data. To fetch a complete column:

```
# Fetch me column "B"
my @colB = @{ $ref->[1]{cell}[2] };
shift @colB;
```

or:

```
my @colB = @{$ref->[1]{cell}[2]}[1..$#{$ref->[1]{cell}[2]}];
```

Accessing a row of data. Likewise for fetching a complete row:

```
# Fetch me row 4
my @row4 = map { $ref->[1]{cell}[$_][4] } 1..$ref->[1]{maxcol};
```

Using programmer-style indexing. If you need to go over and through the complete set of data and prefer to have the data in a list of rows, instead of a list of columns, indexed from 0 not 1, Spreadsheet::Read offers a function to convert that for you:

```
use Spreadsheet::Read qw( rows );

# Get all data in a row oriented list
my @rows = rows( $ref->[1] );

# A3 is now in $rows[2][0]
```

Showing all data in a spreadsheet. Want to show all of the data in a spreadsheet?

```
use Spreadsheet::Read;

my $file        = 'test.xls';
my $spreadsheet = ReadData( $file )         or die "Cannot read $file\n";
my $sheet_count = $spreadsheet->[0]{sheets} or die "No sheets in $file\n";

for my $sheet_index (1 .. $sheet_count)
{
```

```
# Skip empty worksheets
my $sheet = $spreadsheet->[$sheet_index] or next;

printf( "%s - %02d: [ %-12s ] %3d Cols, %5d Rows\n", $file,
    $sheet_index, $sheet->{label}, $sheet->{maxcol}, $sheet->{maxrow} );

for my $row ( 1 .. $sheet->{maxrow} )
{
    print join "\t" => map {
    $sheet->{cell}[$_][$row] // "-" } 1 .. $sheet->{maxcol};
    print "\n";
}
}
```

The output will be something like:

```
test.xls - 01: [ Sheet1      ]  4 Cols,   4 Rows
A1      B1      -       D1
A2      B2      -       -
A3      -       C3      D3
A4      B4      C4      -
test.xls - 02: [ Second Sheet ]  5 Cols,   3 Rows
x       -       x       -       x
-       x       -       x
x               x               x
```

Note that the example uses the defined-or operator (//) from Perl 6. This is available as a patch for Perl 5.8.x and will be available in Perl 5.10.

Empty cells are often undef values, which is not the same as an empty string "". If you use the above code with strict and warnings, there will be a warning for every empty cell if you do not use the defined-or. Showing empty fields as - is more visibly attractive than using whitespace.

Written in more portable code, this is equivalent to:

```
print join "\t" => map
{
    my $val = $sheet->{cell}[$_][$row];
    defined $val ? $val : "-";
} 1 .. $sheet->{maxcol};
```

How It Works

Spreadsheet::Read does no parsing of the spreadsheets itself, instead using the native parsers to do the hard work. For Microsoft Excel, it uses Spreadsheet::ParseExcel, for OpenOffice.org, Spreadsheet::ReadSXC, and for CSV, Text::CSV_XS.

Using Spreadsheet::Read, you do not have to worry about spreadsheet internal formats, or the way the native parser presents the data to the programmer. The interface is the same and is independent of the spreadsheet you use. If you need to get to the guts for anything this interface does not (yet) support, you can always fall back to the real parser, because without it, Spreadsheet::Read does not work anyway.

Spreadsheet::Read tries to achieve a set of commonly supported features of all of the parsers it can use and aims to extend that in the future to make the use of the native parsers unnecessary (such as color attributes, display formats, font face and sizes, and character encoding). All native parsers support that in a different way, if they support it at all. For example, CSV does not have a defined way of identifying the character encoding of the data.

Hacking the Hack

The more spreadsheet formats this module supports, the more value it gains in portability and eventually for your script's maintainability.

Currently, the module supports a hook for Spreadsheet::Perl, but there is no parser support for it yet. It would probably do this module well to isolate the conversions for the different parsers in separate modules, such as Spreadsheet::Read::Excel, to avoid cluttering the main interface.

The module comes with one conversion script: xlscat, which takes a file in any of the supported spreadsheet formats and converts it to either readable ASCII or CSV. Use xlscat -? to see the supported options. If you have useful scripts, they may be worth bundling with this module.

The module does not die if any of the parsers is not installed, making it useful if you only use OpenOffice.org and do not yet bother with Excel (or vice versa). It is quite easy and valuable to add your own parser support and supply a patch to the author to include it in future releases.

 Factor Out Database Code

H A C K
#22   Separate SQL and Perl to make your life easier.

Small scripts have a way of growing up into essential programs. Unfortunately, they don't always mature design-wise. Far too often a business-critical program starts life as a quick-and-dirty just-get-it-done script and evolves mostly by accretion, not the clear and thoughtful hand of good design.

This is especially true in programs that work with data in various formats or which embed other languages such as HTML or SQL. Fortunately, it only takes a little bit of discipline—if no small amount of work—to clean up this mess and make your code somewhat easier to maintain.

The Hack

The only trick is to remove all SQL from within the code and to isolate it in its own module. You don't have to abstract away or factor out all of the database access code or the various means by which you fetch data or bind to parameters—just untangle the Perl and non-Perl code.

Be strict. Store *every* instance of SQL in the module. For example, if you have a subroutine such as:

```
sub install_nodemethods
{
    my $dbh = shift;

    my $sth = $dbh->prepare(<<'END_SQL');
SELECT
    types.title AS class, methods.title AS method, nodemethod.code AS code
FROM
    nodemethod
LEFT JOIN
    node AS types ON types.node_id = nodemethod.supports_nodetype
END_SQL

    $sth->execute( );

    # ... do something with the data
}
```

store the SQL in the SQL module in its own subroutine:

```
package Lots::Of::SQL;

use base 'Exporter';
use vars '@EXPORT';

@EXPORT = 'select_nodemethod_attributes';

sub select_nodemethod_attributes ()
{
    return <<'END_SQL';
    SELECT
        types.title     AS class,
        methods.title   AS method,
        nodemethod.code AS code
    FROM
        nodemethod
    LEFT JOIN
        node AS types ON types.node_id = nodemethod.supports_nodetype
    END_SQL
}
```

Running the Hack

Now call the query from the refactored original subroutine:

```
use Lots::Of::SQL;

sub install_nodemethods
{
    my $dbh = shift;

    my $sth = $dbh->prepare( select_nodemethod_attributes() );
    $sth->execute();

    # ... do something with the data
}
```

> Putting the empty prototype on the SQL abstraction func-
> tion tells Perl that it can inline the (constant) return value
> whenever other code calls this function. You get the benefit
> of hiding all that SQL behind a readable name without pay-
> ing a runtime price.

Hacking the Hack

Of course, stuffing all of that code into one potentially huge module isn't
exactly the end result of refactoring—but with a bit more polish, it's a good
step. Exporting all of the SQL subroutines is overkill that doesn't really bal-
ance out the niceness of being able to maintain the same SQL just once for
any application that uses the database.

Why not export just what you need?

Consider that every operation on a table is its own exporter group, then create an exporter tag for that operation. For example, if you have the tables
users, stories, and comments, group each *type* of SQL query into a tag:

```
package Lots::Of::SQL;

use base 'Exporter';
use vars qw( @EXPORT_OK %EXPORT_TAGS );

@EXPORT_OK = qw(
    select_user     insert_user     update_user
    select_story    insert_story    update_story
    select_comment insert_comment
    select_stories
    select_user_stories
    select_user_comments
);

%EXPORT_TAGS = (
```

```
user    =>
[ qw(
    select_user insert_user update_user select_user_stories
    select_user_comments
)],
story   =>
[ qw(
    select_story insert_story update_story select_user_stories
    select_stories
)],
comment => [ qw( select_comment insert_comment select_user_comments )],
);
```

Then a hypothetical User module can use Lots::Of::SQL ':user'; and receive only the SQL it needs.

This isn't the end of the story. Suppose you want DBAs or non-Perl types to edit and reuse the SQL. "Build a SQL Library" [Hack #23] has ideas.

Perhaps maintaining those export lists by hand is too much work. Using attributes [Hack #45] could simplify your life.

Maybe static SQL written for a single database isn't your style. Try generating it with a templating system or using an abstract, Perlish representation [Hack #24] instead. You might even switch to a persistence or object-relational mapping module such as Class::DBI. There are plenty of options, once you untangle SQL from Perl.

H A C K Build a SQL Library
#23 Store queries where non-programmers can maintain them.

Most serious programmers know the dangers of mixing their user interface code (HTML, GUI, text) with their business logic. When you have a designer making things pretty, it's too much work for any programmer to integrate change after change to font size, placement, and color.

If you have a DBA, the same goes for your SQL.

Why not keep your queries where they don't clutter up your code and where your DBA can modify and optimize them without worrying about a misplaced brace or semicolon breaking your software? If you use SQL::Library with a plain text file under version control, you can.

The Hack

Install SQL::Library from the CPAN. Extract all of the SQL from your code into one place [Hack #22], and then put it all in a plain text file in INI format:

```
[select_nodemethod_attributes]
SELECT    types.title    AS class,
```

```
            methods.title   AS method,
            nodemethod.code AS code
FROM        nodemethod
LEFT JOIN node            AS types
ON          types.node_id = nodemethod.supports_nodetype
```

The section title (the names in square brackets) is the name of the query and the rest is the SQL. Save the file (for example, *nodemethods.sql*). Then from your code, create a SQL::Library object:

```
use SQL::Library;

my $library = SQL::Library->new({ lib => 'nodemethods.sql' });
```

Running the Hack

Whenever you need a query, retrieve it by name from the library:

```
my $sth = $dbh->prepare( $library->retr( 'select_nodemethod_attributes' ) );
```

From there, treat it as normal.

Hacking the Hack

This isn't very exciting until you get to more complex queries—where the order of joins is important, where the exact nature of queries changes, or where there's lots of manipulation and editing going on. Being able to modify the SQL without touching the code is very handy.

For example, consider a reporting application. Choose a filename to hold the queries. Write a bit of code that processes the queries and feeds them to a library to produce graphs or spreadsheets. (The trick with NAME_lc in "Bind Database Columns" [Hack #25] is very useful here.) Then just loop through all of the queries in the library, preparing and executing them, and processing the results:

```
use SQL::Library;

my $library = SQL::Library->new({ lib => 'daily_reports.sql' });

for my $query ( $library->elements() )
{
    my $sth = $dbh->prepare( $query );
    my %columns;

    $sth->bind_columns( \@columns{ @{ $sth->{NAME_lc} } } );
    $sth->execute( );

    process_report( \%columns );
}
```

Now whenever your users want another query, just write it and store it in the appropriate library file. You never have to touch the reporting program (as long as it can draw its pretty graphs correctly)—and if you can teach your users to write their own queries, you can make your job that much easier.

Query Databases Dynamically Without SQL
Write Perl, not SQL.

SQL is a mini-language with its own tricks and traps. Embedded SQL is the bane of many programs, where readability and findability is a concern. Generated SQL isn't always the answer either, with all of the quoting rules and weird options.

In cases where you don't have a series of fully baked SQL statements you always run—where query parameters and even result field names come from user requests, for example—let SQL::Abstract do it for you.

The Hack

Create a new SQL::Abstract object, pass in some data, and go.

Suppose you have a reporting application with a nice interface that allows people to view any list of columns from a set of tables in any order with almost any constraint. Assuming a well-factored application, the model might have a method resembling:

```perl
use SQL::Abstract;

sub get_select_sth
{
    my ($self, $table, $columns, $where) = @_;

    my $sql           = SQL::Abstract->new( );
    my ($stmt, @bins) = $sql->select( $table, $columns, $where );
    my $sth           = $self->get_dbh( )->prepare( $stmt );

    $sth->execute( );
    return $sth;
}
```

$table is a string containing the name of the table (or view, preferably) to query, $columns is an array reference of names of columns to view, and $where is a hash reference associating columns to values or ranges.

If a user wants to query the users table for login_name, last_accessed_on, and email_address columns for all users whose signup_date is newer than 20050101, the calling code might be equivalent to:

```perl
my $table   = 'users';
my $columns = [qw( login_name last_accessed_on email_address )];
my $where   = { signup_date => { '>=', '20050101' } };
my $sth     = $model->get_select_sth( $table, $columns, $where );
```

The returned $sth is a normal iterable DBI statement handle, suitable for passing to a templating system or other user interface view component. This is very useful for selecting only the interesting parts of a table or view.

Hacking the Hack

There's no reason you have to let users select the kind of information they want to view. Perhaps you have system administrators who should be able to see (and update) any non-key column in the users table, managers who should be able to see and update most personnel-related columns, and normal users who should only see demographic information.

You can use the same underlying model to fetch information from the database—just add a layer over it to exclude requested columns that the particular user of the system shouldn't see. Assuming that you have an object representing the user type with a method that returns the allowed columns for a particular table, call restrict_columns( ) before get_select_sth( ):

```
sub restrict_columns
{
    my ($self, $user, $table, $columns) = @_;
    my $user_columns               = $user->get_columns_for( $table );
    return [ grep { exists $user_columns->{ $_ } } ] @$columns;
}
```

Instead of maintaining separate SQL queries for each type of user accessing the system, you can maintain a list somewhere of appropriate view and update columns for each type of user, reusing the query generator. If you keep the list of types and allowed columns in the database or in a configuration file somewhere, you have data-driven programming and an easy-to-maintain system.

HACK #25   Bind Database Columns

Use placeholders for data retrieved from the database, not just sent to it.

Experienced database programmers know the value of placeholders in queries. (Inexperienced database programmers will soon find out why they're important, when unquoted data breaks their programs.) When you execute a query and pass in values, the database automatically quotes and inserts them into the prepared query, usually making for faster, and always making for safer, code.

Perl's DBI module has a similar feature for retrieving data from the database. Instead of copying column after column into variables, you can *bind* variables to a statement, so that they will contain the appropriate values for each row fetch( )ed.

Of course, this technique appears less flexible than retrieving hashes from the DBI, as it relies on the order of data returned from a query and loads of scalar variables...or does it?

The Hack

Suppose that you have a templating application that needs to retrieve some fields from a table* and wants to contain the results in a hash. You could write a subroutine named bind_hash( ):

```
sub bind_hash
{
    my ($dbh, $hash_ref, $table, @fields) = @_;

    my $sql = 'SELECT ' . join(', ', @fields) . " FROM $table";
    my $sth = $dbh->prepare( $sql );

    $sth->execute( );
    $sth->bind_columns( \@$hash_ref{ @{ $sth->{NAME_lc} } } );

    return sub { $sth->fetch( ) };
}
```

The only really tricky part of the code is using the reference operator (\) on a hash slice. When fed a list, this operator produces a list of references to the values in the list—and a hash slice returns a list of the values, themselves scalars. The NAME_lc property of an active statement handle contains an anonymous array of lowercased field names that the statement will retrieve. This can improve portability.

Running the Hack

Suppose that you have a users table† and you want to retrieve the names, birthdays, and shoe sizes of all of the users, and print them nicely. That's easy:

```
# assume you already have $dbh connected

my %user;

my $user_fetch = bind_hash( $dbh, \%user, qw( users name dob shoe_size ) );

while ($user_fetch->( ))
{
    print "$user{name}, born on $user{dob}, wears a size " .
        "$user{shoe_size} shoe\n";
}
```

* Or, better, a view or stored procedure....
† Or view or stored procedure....

This hack only works well when you're fetching a row at a time. It's also not the right way to build a quick and easy object-relational mapper, because by the time you need a new hash for each row, you've already bound it. That's okay—it's still very fast and flexible and lends itself well to the iterator technique [Hack #26].

HACK #26   Iterate and Generate Expensive Data

Hide lists, streams, and expensive data structures behind a simple interface.

Perl's fundamental aggregate data types—hashes and arrays—are wonderfully flexible and often just what you want. That's often, not always. Sometimes you really need to process data that's expensive to calculate, part of a huge list that won't fit into memory, or just never ends.

When that happens, use a function reference as a data structure. Seriously.

The Hack

Imagine that you've just taken a job as a network administrator, replacing someone who completely failed to do any documentation. You know that you have all sorts of devices on the network with static IP addresses and you have a rough idea of the network blocks, but you don't know which addresses are in use.

Rather than finding every device, checking its settings, and reassigning things, you can write a little program to loop through each address and try to contact the device. It's a good first approximation. How do you check every netblock though? Use Net::Netmask to generate a list of IP addresses.

That could get messy though—do you really want to loop over a list of potentially millions of addresses? This is a good place to use a generator.

```perl
use Net::Netmask;

sub create_generator
{
    my @netmasks;

    for my $block (@_)
    {
        push @netmasks, Net::Netmask->new( $block );
    }

    my $nth = 1;

    return sub
    {
```

```
        return unless @netmasks;
        my $next_ip = $netmasks[0]->nth( $nth++ );

        if ( $next_ip eq $netmasks[0]->last( ) )
        {
            shift @netmasks;
            $nth = 1;
        }

        return $next_ip;
    }
}
```

Running the Hack

Pass create_generator( ) a list of IP network blocks and netmasks and it will return a function reference that, when called, returns either the next address in the series or the undefined value if you've exhausted everything. It does this by closing over two variables, the list of Net::Netmask objects in @netmasks and a counter variable $nth. The latter represents the current position in the list of available addresses for the current Net::Netmask object.

To test an IP address for an active device, just pull a new address from the iterator by executing it:

```
my $next_address   = create_generator( '192.168.1.0/8', '10.0.0.0/16' );

while (my $address = $next_address->( ))
{
    # try to communicate with machine at $address
}
```

If you have a huge group of addresses to check, this is much more memory- and time-friendly than generating a list of hundreds of thousands of addresses all at once.

Hacking the Hack

With a generator as large as this one and the inevitable delay for network communication, you might want a way to suspend and resume from a certain point. If you turned the generator function reference into an object, you could add a serialize( ) or store( ) method that saves the current state. Then you can resume from almost any point. All you need to save is the base( ) and bits( ) information from each active Net::Netmask object (presumably in the proper order) and the current value of $nth.

Of course, in a program that probably has network communication as its most significant bottleneck, you may want to check several addresses in parallel. "Pull Multiple Values from an Iterator" [Hack #27] can help.

Mark Jason Dominus's *Higher Order Perl* (Morgan Kaufmann, 2005) shows how to use functional programming techniques in Perl, including iterators and generators. This book is worth studying in detail.

Pull Multiple Values from an Iterator
#27   Make your iterators and generators highly context-sensitive.

Iterators and generators are fantastically useful for data that takes too long to generate, may never run out, or costs too much memory to keep around. Not every problem works when reading one item at a time though, and finding a nice syntax for pulling only as many items as you need can be tricky.

Perl's notion of context sets it apart from many other programming languages by doing what you mean. When you want a single item, it will give you a single item. When you want nothing, it can give you nothing. When you want a list, it will oblige. That power is yours through the wantarray( ) operator, too.

Wouldn't it be nice if Perl could tell how many items you want from an iterator or generator without you having to be explicit? Good news—it can.

Better Context than wantarray( )

Robin Houston's Want module extends and enhances wantarray( ) to give more details about the calling context of a function. Besides distinguishing between void and scalar context, Want's howmany( ) function can tell *how many* list items the calling context wants, from one to infinity.

The Code

Consider a simple generator that implements a counter. It takes the initial value, the destination value, and an optional step size (which defaults to 1). When it reaches the destination, it returns the undefined value.

```
sub counter
{
    my ($from, $to, $step)  = @_;
    $step                   ||= 1;

    return sub
    {
        return if $from > $to;
        my $value      = $from;
        $from         += $step;
        return $value;
    };

}
```

Creating and using a counter, perhaps one that counts from 1 to 10 by threes, is easy:

```
my $counter = counter( 1, 10, 3 );
my $first   = $counter->( );
```

What if you want the next three steps though? You could call it in a loop, but wouldn't it be nicer to call it with:

```
my ($first, $second, $third) = $iterator->( );
```

That's where multi_iterator( ) comes in. Feed it an iterator or generator and it returns a function that acts as a drop-in replacement for the iterator or generator but respects the calling context:

```
use Want 'howmany';

sub multi_iterator
{
    my ($iterator) = @_;

    return sub
    {
        my $context = wantarray( );

        return                  unless defined $context;
        return $iterator->( ) unless         $context;
        return map { $iterator->( ) } 1 .. howmany( );
    };
}
```

The multi-iterator first must check for void context (so it returns nothing and never kicks the contained iterator), then scalar context (so it can kick the iterator once). Then it kicks the iterator as many times as necessary to produce the number of expected values. Whatever the behavior of the contained iterator or generator when it exhausts its possible values, the multi-iterator will pass along to the caller.

This takes one more step than before, but the results speak for themselves:

```
my $counter       = counter( 1, 10, 3 );
my $iterator      = multi_iterator( $counter );

# multiple variables, list context
my ($first, $second) = $iterator->( );

# void context
$iterator->( );

# single variable, scalar context
my $third         = $iterator->( );

# single variable, list context
my ($fourth)      = $iterator->( );
```

$first contains the value 1 and $second the value 4. So far so good. $third contains 7 and $fourth 10. All subsequent accesses will contain undef.

Hacking the Hack

Being able to iterate over multiple iterators in parallel would be very useful. That's doable here.

This technique works outside of iterators as well; in any place you distinguish between list and scalar context and may need to know more about one-element list context versus *n*-element list context, howmany( ) is useful.

Want has many other interesting context-related features; it's worth exploring further on its own. Fortunately, its documentation is very useful.

Be careful about assigning the results of the iterator call to an array, which effectively has infinite elements. It may not do what you want if you have an infinite generator or iterator (unless you want an infinitely large array consuming infinite amounts of memory and taking infinite time to complete).

## CHAPTER FOUR

Working with Modules
Hacks 28–42

Perhaps the greatest invention of Perl 5 is the idea of modules. They allow people to modify the language and reuse code far beyond what Larry and the Perl 5 porters ever envisioned. (Who could have predicted CPAN or Acme::*, for example?)

If you're doing any serious work with Perl, you'll spend a lot of time working with modules: installing them, upgrading them, loading them, working around weird and unhelpful features, and even distributing them. It makes a lot of sense to understand how Perl and modules interact and how to work with them effectively.

Here are several ideas that show off the varied ways that you can extend your programs. CPAN is only an arm's length away. Be ready.

HACK #28 Shorten Long Class Names

Type only what you need to type. You know what you mean.

Are you tired of using Perl classes with Really::Long::Package::Names::You::Cant::Remember? Use aliased and forget about them. This handy CPAN module creates short, easy-to-remember aliases for long class names.

The Hack

Given the hypothetical example just cited, use aliased to load the class and create an alias all at once:

```
use aliased 'Really::Long::Package::Names::You::Cant::Remember';

my $rem = Remember->new( );
```

When aliased loads a class, it automatically creates a constant subroutine, in the local name space named after the final part of the package name. This subroutine returns the full package name. Because it's a constant, it's actually very efficient; Perl will inline the package name, so that by the time your code has compiled, Perl sees it as if you had actually typed:

```
use aliased 'Really::Long::Package::Names::You::Cant::Remember';

my $rem = Really::Long::Package::Names::You::Cant::Remember->new( );
```

You gain simplicity and lose, well, nothing.

Resolve conflicts. Sometimes you might want to alias two classes that have the same final portion of their package names. In such cases, specify the alias that you want to use to disambiguate the two classes:

```
use aliased 'My::App::Contact';
use aliased 'My::App::Type::Contact' => 'ContactType';

my $contact_type = ContactType->new( );
my $contact      = Contact->new({ type => $contact_type });
```

Importing with aliased. Sometimes, even in object-oriented programming, you need to import symbols from a module. aliased allows you to do so while still creating an alias. The only wrinkle is that you *must* explicitly specify an alias. Why? Because then you pass in a list of import symbols, and if you didn't specify an alias name, the first symbol would be the alias! Here's how it works:

```
use aliased 'My::App::Contact' => 'Contact', qw( EMAIL PHONE );

my $contact = Contact->new({
    kind  => EMAIL,
    value => 'perlhacks@oreilly.com',
});
```

If you hadn't put that 'Contact' there, then the alias would have been EMAIL and that wouldn't do what you meant.

Manage Module Paths
HACK #29
Keep your code where it makes sense to you, not just to Perl.

Perl's a flexible language and it tries to make few assumptions about your environment. Perhaps you're a system administrator with root access and a compiler and can install modules anywhere you want. Perhaps you only have shell access on a shared box and have to submit a change request to have something installed. Perhaps you want to test one set of modules against one program but not another.

Whatever the case, Perl gives you options to manage where it looks for modules. Suppose you have a program in your ~/*work* directory that uses a module named Site::User. By default, Perl will search all of the directories in the special @INC variable for a file named *Site/User.pm*. That may not always include the directory you want (especially if, in this case, you want ~/*work/ lib*). What can you do?

Within Your Program

The simplest and most self-contained way to change Perl's search path is within your program by using the lib pragma. This happens at compile-time [Hack #70], as soon as perl encounters the statement, so put it before any use line for the module you want to load. For example:

```
use lib 'lib';
use Site::User;
```

adds the *lib/* directory—relative to the current directory—to the front of Perl's search path list. Similarly:

```
no lib 'badlib';
use Site::User;
```

removes the *badlib/* directory from Perl's list of search paths. If you have two versions of Site::User installed and want to make sure that Perl doesn't pick up the wrong version from the wrong directory, exclude it.

From the Command Line

Sometimes you don't have the option or the desire to modify a program, though, especially when you're merely testing it. In that case, use the lib pragma from the command line when invoking the program by using perl's -M switch:

```
$ perl -Mlib=lib show_users.pl
```

This is equivalent to use lib 'lib'. To exclude a path, prepend a hyphen to lib:

```
$ perl -M-lib=badlib show_users.pl
```

 The -I flag also lets you include paths, but it does not let you *exclude* them.

With an Environment Variable

Of course, modifying every program or remembering to add a command-line switch to every invocation is a tremendous hassle. Fortunately, there's a third option: set the PERL5LIB environment variable to a colon-separated list of directories to add to the search path. Depending on your shell, this may be:

```
$ export PERL5LIB=/home/user/work/lib:/home/user/work_test/lib:$PERL5LIB
```

```
% setenv PERL5LIB /home/user/work/lib:/home/user/work_test/lib:$PERL5LIB
```

There's no good and easy way to exclude a directory for the search path here; put the correct directory at the front of the path.

If you put the appropriate invocation in the appropriate startup file (such as */etc/profile* or the equivalent), users do not even have to know that this path is there. Of course, if they run programs from cron or another environment without these variables, some paths may not be present.

An easier option may be to write a simple shell script that sets the environment properly and then launches the actual perl binary, passing along the command-line options appropriately.

When Recompiling Perl

Your final recourse is to set the appropriate paths when compiling Perl [Hack #67]. This isn't as bad as it sounds, but it does take a little bit more dedication. Once you have downloaded and unpacked Perl, run the Configure script. Answer all of the questions appropriately until it asks:

```
Enter a colon-separated set of extra paths to include in perl's @INC
search path, or enter 'none' for no extra paths.

Colon-separated list of additional directories for perl to search? [none]
```

Type there the list of directories to add to Perl's built-in @INC. Note that perl will search this directory *after* it searches its core directories, so if you want to load something in place of a core module, you must manipulate the path with one of the other techniques.

HACK #30 Reload Modified Modules

Update modules in a running program without restarting.

Developing a long-running program can be a tedious process, especially when starting and stopping it can take several seconds or longer. This is most painful in cases where you just need to make one or two little tweaks to see your results. The Ruby on Rails web programming toolkit in development mode gets it right, automatically noticing when you change a library and reloading it in the running server without you having to do anything.

Perl can do that too.

The Hack

All it takes is a simple module named `Module::Reloader`:

```
package Module::Reloader;

use strict;
use warnings;

my %module_times;

INIT
{
    while (my ($module, $path) = each %INC)
    {
        $module_times{ $module } = -M $path;
    }
}

sub reload
{
    while (my ($module, $time) = each %module_times)
    {
        my $mod_time    = -M $INC{$module};
        next if $time == $mod_time;

        no warnings 'redefine';
        require ( delete $INC{ $module } );
        $module_times{ $module } = $mod_time;
    }
}

1;
```

At the end of compile time [Hack #70], the module caches the name and modification time of all currently loaded modules. Its reload( ) function checks the current modification time of each module and reloads any that have changed since the last cache check.

Running the Hack

Use the module as usual. Then, when you want to reload any loaded modules, call `Module::Reloader::reload( )`. In a long-running server process, such as a pure-Perl web server running in development mode for a framework, this is easy to do right before processing a new incoming request.

Provided that the modules being modified don't keep around any weird state between requests, the request will see the new behavior.

Hacking the Hack

The module as written *does* attempt to avoid spurious warning messages by suppressing `Subroutine %s redefined at...` error messages, but a compilation error in a module may cause strange behavior and necessitate a server restart. This is for development purposes only; it's very difficult to write code that behaves perfectly in a production environment—too many things could go wrong.

Changing the definition of classes while you have active instances of those classes can do scary things. It may be worthwhile to exclude certain modules, perhaps by specifying filters for modules to include or to exclude.

This module currently does not erase the symbol tables of reloaded modules; that may be useful in certain circumstances. (It may be hazardous in others, where multiple modules affect symbols in a given package.)

HACK #31 Create Personal Module Bundles

Create a personal bundle of your favorite modules.

It never fails. I'm working on a new computer, a friend's computer, or a work computer and I've installed my favorite modules and written some code.

```
use My::Favorite::Module;
My::Favorite::Module->washes_the_dishes();
```

Then I run the program.

```
Can't locate My/Favorite/Module.pm in @INC (@INC contains ...
```

I did it again. I forgot to install the one module I really needed. Hopefully it's the last one. Of course, even if you never forget to install your favorites, it's still a pain to laboriously install a bunch of modules every time you have a new Perl installation.

That's where personal bundles come in.

The Hack

A personal bundle is very easy to make. Just create a normal CPAN distribution. You don't even need to write tests for it: the modules you list will (hopefully) test themselves.

Instead, create an empty package with the modules you want listed in your POD contents section [Hack #32]. For example, suppose that you're a testing fanatic. You want to install your favorite testing modules, so you decide to call your bundle `Bundle::Personal::Mine` (where *Mine* is your PAUSE ID).

```
package Bundle::Personal::Mine;

$VERSION = '0.42';

1;

__END__

=head1 NAME

Bundle::Personal::Mine - My favorite testing modules

=head1 SYNOPSIS

perl -MCPAN -e 'install Bundle::Personal::Mine'

=head1 CONTENTS

Test::Class

Test::Differences

Test::Exception

Test::MockModule

Test::Pod

Test::Pod::Coverage

Test::WWW::Mechanize

=head1 DESCRIPTION

My favorite modules.

... rest of POD, if any ...
```

Then just package up your tarball and stow it in a safe place (or even upload it to the CPAN).

Running the Hack

From then on, to install all of your favorite modules, just type **cpanp i Bundle::Personal::Mine** for CPANPLUS, **perl -MCPAN -e 'install Bundle:: Personal::Mine'** for CPAN, or whatever your favorite module installation incantation is.

Hacking the Hack

When preparing a personal bundle, be selective about what you include. If you include a module that routinely fails tests, the entire bundle installation might fail. If that happens, try to install the errant module manually and return to installing the bundle. It's generally a bad idea to force the installation of a module with failing tests until you understand why they fail. This is especially true when working on a new machine.

Other uses for such bundles include software development kits, corporate bundles, and application support modules. The CPAN already has bundles for Bundle::Test, Bundle::BioPerl, Bundle::MiniVend, and so on. Go to your favorite CPAN mirror and search for bundles. The bundle you want to create may already exist.

Should you really upload your own bundle to the CPAN? It depends. If you maintain a redistributable application that requires several CPAN modules, creating an installation bundle can help users install it and packagers package it. If you're the only person using your bundle, it probably won't do anyone else much good.

 ## HACK #32   Manage Module Installations

Bundle up required modules to make installations easier.

Embracing the Perl way means taking advantage of the CPAN when possible. There are thousands of reusable, easily installable modules that do almost anything you can imagine—including making your coding life much easier and simpler.

Some day you'll have to distribute your software, upgrade Perl, or do something else that means that you can't rely on having all of your existing modules available. Never fear; just create a bundle that the CPAN module can use to install all of the necessary modules for you!

The Hack

The CPAN module doesn't only download and install modules. It can also give you a catalog of what you have installed on your system. The autobundle command takes this list and writes it to a bundle file—a very simple, mostly POD module that CPAN can use later (or elsewhere) to install necessary modules.

If you only support one application, you can use a technique such as in "Trace All Used Modules" [Hack #74] to figure out everything you need to install.

All you have to do is launch the shell, issue the autobundle command, and note where it creates the bundle file:

```
$ cpan

cpan shell -- CPAN exploration and modules installation (v1.7601)
ReadLine support enabled

cpan> autobundle

# time passes...

Wrote bundle file
  /usr/src/.cpan/Bundle/Snapshot_2005_11_13_00.pm
```

Running the Hack

Copy or move the bundle file from its current location. Then when you upgrade or reinstall Perl, or when you move to another box, move the bundle file to the *Bundle/* directory beneath the CPAN module's working directory. Then, from the CPAN shell in the new machine or installation:

```
$ cpan

cpan shell -- CPAN exploration and modules installation (v1.7601)
ReadLine support enabled

cpan> install Bundle::Snapshot_2005_11_13_00

# time really passes...
```

It will go through the bundle list in order, intstalling all modules as necessary. At least, it will try.

Hacking the Hack

If you look at the bundle file, you might notice that it includes lots and lots of modules—maybe more than you need and certainly plenty of core modules. Worse yet, depending on how you've configured your CPAN and how well the modules you want to install mark their dependencies, you may need to babysit the installation to get it to succeed. You may even have to restart it a few times.

If possible, set CPAN to follow all prerequisites without asking when configuring it for the first run. (You can always change it back later.) That will help. The next best thing to do is to prune the module list. When possible, try to arrange dependencies appropriately. (Modules change enough that it's unlikely you'll be able to do this perfectly.)

Finally, you can prune out all of the core modules by running the bundle file through Module::CoreList [Hack #73]. That way, you have a somewhat smaller list of modules to install.

```perl
use Module::CoreList;

my ($bundle, $version) = @ARGV;
$version                ||= $];
@ARGV                   = $bundle;
my $core_list           = $Module::CoreList::version{ $version };
die "Unknown version $version\n" unless $core_list;

# find module list
while (<>)
{
    print;
    last if $_ eq "=head1 CONTENTS\n";
}

print "\n";

# process only module/version lines
while (<>)
{
    if ( $_ eq "=head1 CONFIGURATION\n" )
    {
        print;
        last;
    }

    chomp;
    next unless $_;

    my ($module, $version) = split( /\s+/, $_ );
    $version = 0 if $version eq 'undef';

    next if exists $core_list->{ $module }
            and $core_list->{ $module } >= $version;

    print "$module $version\n\n";
}

# print everything else
print while <>;
```

Run this program, passing the name of the bundle file and, optionally, the version of Perl against which to check. Redirect the output to a new bundle file:

```
$ perl prune_bundle.pl Snapshot_2005_11_03_00.pm > PrunedSnapshot.pm
$
```

Now you have an easier time deciding which modules you really need to install.

Presolve Module Paths

Make programs on complex installations start more quickly.

In certain circumstances, one of Perl's major strengths can be a weakness. Even though you can manipulate where Perl looks for modules (@INC) at runtime according to your needs [Hack #29], and even though you can use thousands of modules from the CPAN, your system has to find and load these modules.

For a short-running, repeated program, this can be expensive, especially if you have many paths in @INC from custom testing paths, sitewide paths, staging servers, business-wide repositories, and the like. Fortunately, there's more than one way to solve this. One approach is to resolve all of the paths just once, and then use your program as normal.

The Hack

"Trace All Used Modules" [Hack #74] shows how putting a code reference into @INC allows you to execute code every time you use or require a module. That works here, too.

```
package Devel::Presolve;

use strict;
use warnings;

my @track;

BEGIN { unshift @INC, \&resolve_path }

sub resolve_path
{
    my ($code, $module) = @_;
    push @track, $module;
    return;
}

INIT
{
    print "BEGIN\n{\n";

    for my $tracked (@track)
    {
        print "\trequire( \$INC{'$tracked'} = '$INC{$tracked}' );\n";
    }

    print "}\n1;\n";
    exit;
}
```

```
1;
```

Devel::Presolve's resolve_path( ) captures every request to load a module, stores the module name, and returns. Thus Perl attempts to load the module as normal. After the entire program has finished compiling, but before it starts to run [Hack #70], it prints to STDOUT a BEGIN block that loads all of the modules by absolute filepath then exits the program.

Running the Hack

Put Devel::Presolve somewhere in your path. Then run your slow-starting program while loading the module. Redirect the output to a file of your choosing:

```
$ perl -MDevel::Preload slow_program.pl > preload.pm
```

preload.pm will contain something similar to:

```
BEGIN
{
    require( $INC{'CGI.pm'}      = '/usr/lib/perl5/5.8.7/CGI.pm' );
    require( $INC{'CGI/Util.pm'} = '/usr/lib/perl5/5.8.7/CGI/Util.pm' );
    require( $INC{'vars.pm'}     = '/usr/lib/perl5/5.8.7/vars.pm' );
    require( $INC{'constant.pm'} = '/usr/lib/perl5/5.8.7/constant.pm' );
    require( $INC{'overload.pm'} = '/usr/lib/perl5/5.8.7/overload.pm' );
}

1;
```

You can either include the contents of this file at the start of *slow_program.pl* or load it as the first module. If you do the latter, put the file in a directory at the *front* of @INC, lest you erase any performance gains.

Note that the trick of assigning to %INC within the require avoids a potentially nasty module-reloading bug, where Perl doesn't see require '/usr/lib/perl5/5.8.7./CGI.pm' as loading the same file as use CGI; does.

Hacking the Hack

Pre-resolving paths likely won't help long-running programs. For short-running programs where startup time can dwarf calculation time, it may, depending on how complex your @INC is. Be especially careful that upgrading Perl or installing new versions of modules may invalidate this cache—it *is* a cache—and cause strange errors. This technique may work better only when you want to deploy a program to a production system, but likely not when you're merely developing or testing.

Create a Standard Module Toolkit

Curb your addiction to explicit use statements.

Most experienced Perl programmers rely on a core set of modules and sub-routines that they use in just about every application they create. For example, if you work with XML documents on a daily basis (and you certainly have our deepest sympathy there), then you probably use either XML::Parser or XML::SAX or XML::We::Built::Our::Own::Damn::Solution all the time.

If those documents contain lists of files that you need to manipulate, then you probably use File::Spec or File::Spec::Functions as well, and perhaps File::Find too. Maybe you need to verify and manipulate dates and times on those files, so you regularly pull in half a dozen of the DateTime modules.

If the application has an interactive component, you might continually need to use the prompt() subroutine from IO::Prompt [Hack #14]. Likewise, you might frequently make use of the efficient slurp() function from File::Slurp. You might also like to have Smart::Comments instantly available [Hack #54] to simplify debugging. Of course, you always specify use strict and use warnings, and probably use Carp as well.

A Mess of Modules

This adds up to a tediously long list of standard modules, most of which you need to load every time you write a new application:

```
#! /usr/bin/perl

use strict;
use warnings;
use Carp;
use Smart::Comments;
use XML::Parser;
use File::Spec;
use IO::Prompt qw( prompt );
use File::Spec::Functions;
use File::Slurp qw( slurp );
use DateTime;
use DateTime::Duration;
use DateTime::TimeZone;
use DateTime::TimeZone::Antarctica::Mawson;
# etc.
# etc.
```

It would be great if you could shove all these usual suspects in a single file:

```
package Std::Modules;

use strict;
use warnings;
```

```
use Carp;
use Smart::Comments;
use XML::Parser;
use File::Spec;
use IO::Prompt qw( prompt );
use File::Spec::Functions;
use File::Slurp qw( slurp );
use DateTime;
use DateTime::Duration;
use DateTime::TimeZone;
use DateTime::TimeZone::Antarctica::Mawson;
# etc.

1;
```

and just use that one module instead:

```
#! /usr/bin/perl

use Std::Modules;
```

Of course, that fails dismally. Using a module that uses other modules isn't the same as using those other modules directly. In most cases, you'd be importing the components you need into the wrong namespace (into Std:: Modules instead of main) or into the wrong lexical scope (for use strict and use warnings).

The Hack

What you really need is a way to create a far more cunning module: one that cuts-and-pastes any use statements inside it into any file that uses the module. The easiest way to accomplish that kind of sneakiness is with the Filter::Macro CPAN module. As its name suggests, this module is a source filter that converts what follows it into a macro. Perl then replaces any subsequent use of that macro-ized module with the contents of the module. For example:

```
package Std::Modules;
use Filter::Macro;     # <-- The magic happens here

use strict;
use warnings;
use Carp;
use Smart::Comments;
use XML::Parser;
use File::Spec;
use IO::Prompt qw( prompt );
use File::Spec::Functions;
use File::Slurp qw( slurp );
use DateTime;
use DateTime::Duration;
```

```
use DateTime::TimeZone;
use DateTime::TimeZone::Antarctica::Mawson;
# etc.
# etc.

1;
```

Now, whenever you write:

```
#! /usr/bin/perl

use Std::Modules;
```

all of those other use statements inside Std::Modules are pasted into your code, in place of the use Std::Modules statement itself.

Hacking the Hack

There's also a more modular and powerful variation on this idea available. The Toolkit module (also on CPAN) allows you to specify a collection of standard module inclusions as separate files in a standard directory structure. Once you have them set up, you can automatically use them all just by writing:

```
#! /usr/bin/perl

use Toolkit;
```

The advantage of this approach is that you can also set up "conditional usages"—files that tell Toolkit to import specific subroutines from specific modules, but only when something actually uses those subroutines. For example, you can tell Toolkit not to always load:

```
use IO::Prompt qw( prompt );
use File::Slurp qw( slurp );
```

but only to load the IO::Prompt module if something actually uses the prompt( ) subroutine, and likewise to defer loading File::Slurp for slurp( ) until actually necessary.

That way, you can safely specify dozens of handy subroutines and modules in your standard toolkit, but only pay the loading costs for those you actually use.

HACK #35 Write Demos from Tutorials

Give tutorial readers example code to run, tweak, and examine.

Reading code is one thing. Running code is another. Example code is wonderfully useful, but nothing beats playing with it—changing values, moving subroutines around, and seeing what happens if you touch just one more thing.

You'll never escape writing documentation. You *can* escape having to explain the basics over and over again if that documentation includes working, runnable code that people can customize for their needs. If you've already realized that including pure-POD modules is a great way to document programs, take the next step and make the tutorials themselves write out their examples.

The Hack

Writing a POD-only tutorial is easy. For example, the basic SDL::Tutorial shows how to create a screen using Perl and the SDL bindings:

```
use SDL::App;

# change these values as necessary
my  $title                 = 'My SDL App';
my ($width, $height, $depth) = ( 640, 480, 16 );

my $app = SDL::App->new(
    -width  => $width,
    -height => $height,
    -depth  => $depth,
    -title  => $title,
);

# your code here; remove the next line
sleep 2;
```

Running the Hack

Better yet, if you run the tutorial from the command line, it writes out this program to a file of your choosing:

```
$ perl -MSDL::Tutorial=sdl_demo.pl -e 1
```

Looking at the tutorial itself [Hack #2], it's only a use statement, a heredoc, and the documentation. How does Pod::ToDemo know to write the file and exit? Further, what if someone accidentally uses SDL::Tutorial as a module within a real program—will it write or overwrite a file and throw an error?

Nope; that's part of the magic.

Inside the Hack

Pod::ToDemo has two tricks. The first is writing code that will execute when you run the demo file from the command line only. caller( ) isn't just for checking the calling subroutine—it walks the entire call stack. The module's import( ) method has this code:

```
my @command = caller( 3 );

return if @command and $command[1] ne '-e';
```

That is, look three levels up the call stack. If the filename of that call frame is *not* -e (the correct command-line invocation to write a demo file), then someone has accidentally used a demo module in a real program, and the import( ) method returns without doing anything.

> Why three levels? The previous level is the implicit BEGIN block surrounding the use call in the demo module [Hack #70]. The next one up is the load of the demo module itself (-M on the command line creates its own block). The top level is the command-line invocation itself.

The rest of the import( ) method itself merely installs another method into the demo module, calling it import( ). By the time the rest of the module finishes compiling, when Perl goes to call that module's import( ), it'll be there—and it can write the file as necessary.

Hacking the Hack

This is the easy way to use Pod::ToDemo. There's also a more difficult way. Consider if you already show the example code within the tutorial, perhaps in one large chunk and perhaps not. Duplicating the code within the string to pass to Pod::ToDemo and the tutorial itself would be a mistake. In that case, generate the code however you like, pulling it out of the POD, and pass a subroutine reference to Pod::ToDemo. The module will call that instead, when appropriate, letting you write the demo file as you like.

This trick would also work to parameterize the demo file based on command-line arguments.

Replace Bad Code from the Outside

Patch buggy modules without touching their source code.

Until computers finally decide to do what we mean, not what we say, programs will have bugs. Some you can work around. Others are severe enough that you have to modify source code.

When the bugs are in code you don't maintain and you don't have a workaround, Perl's dynamic nature can be an advantage. Instead of keeping local copies of externally managed code, sometimes patching that code from the outside is the simplest way to make your code work again.

The Hack

Imagine that you're building a large application that uses a hypothetical Parser module that, for whatever reason, calls exit( ), not die( ), when it fails. The relevant code might look something like:

```perl
package Parser;

sub parse
{
    my ($class, $text) = @_;
    validate_text( $shift );
    bless \$text, $class;
}

sub validate_text
{
    my $text = shift;
    exit 1 unless $text =~ /^</;
}

1;
```

You might normally expect to use this module with code such as:

```perl
use Parser;

my $parser = eval { Parser->parse( 'some example text' ) };
die "Bad input to parser: $@\n" if $@;
```

However because of the exit( ), your program will end. It may be perfectly legitimate that the text to parse in this example is invalid, so Parser can't handle it, but the exit( ) is just wrong—it gives you no opportunity to alert the user or try to fix the problem. If validate_text( ) were a method, you could subclass the module and override it, but you don't have this option.

Fortunately, you *can* override the exit( ) keyword with a function of your own, if you do it at the right time:

```perl
package Parser;
use subs 'exit';
package main;

use Parser;
sub Parser::exit{die shift;}
```

Before Perl can parse the Parser package, you must tell it to consider all occurrences of exit( ) as calls to a user-defined function, not the built-in operator. That's the point of switching packages and using the subs pragma.

Back in the main package, the odd-looking subroutine declaration merely declares the actual implementation of that subroutine. Now instead of exiting, all code that calls exit( ) in Parser will throw an exception instead.

Hacking the Hack

If you don't really care about validation, if you prefer a sledgehammer solution, or if you don't want to replace exit( ) in the entire package, you can replace the entire validate_text( ) function:

```
use Parser;
local *Parser::validate_text;
*Parser::validate_text = sub
{
    my $text = shift;
    die "Invalid text '$text'\n" unless $text =~ /^</;
};
```

Doing this in two steps avoids a warning about using a symbol name only once. Using local replaces the code only in your current dynamic scope, so any code you call *from* this scope will use this function instead of the old version.

To replace the subroutine globally, use Parser as normal, but remove the line that starts with local. Replace it with no warnings 'redefine'; to avoid a different warning.

If you need to switch behavior, make the replacement validate_text( ) into a closure, setting a lexical flag to determine which behavior to support. This variant technique is highly useful in testing code.

Drink to the CPAN

Play London.pm's CPAN Drinking Game—but responsibly.

The CPAN drinking game tests your knowledge of the CPAN. The goal of the game, depending on who you ask, is either to prove that you have an incredibly deep knowledge of the CPAN or to get incredibly drunk. An alternate goal is to learn about modules you never even knew existed. Just try to remember them.

Running the Hack

The first player, Audrey, takes a drink and names a CPAN module: Devel:: Cover. Play passes to Barbie, who's sitting immediately to Audrey's right. Barbie needs to drink and then come up with a released module which starts with C, the first letter of the *last* part of Audrey's module. If he can't, he drinks and play passes to the next player.

If Barbie names a module with three parts, perhaps Crypt::SSLeay::X509, play skips over chromatic, who's sitting to his right. The same applies if he managed to pull out a module name with four, five, or more parts.

Domm picks up with X. He drinks and pulls out XML::XPath. Because the last part starts with the same letter as the first part, the direction of play reverses and it's chromatic's turn.

chromatic drinks and, sadly, can't come up with anything and has to pass. He's now out of the game. Audrey drinks and names XML::Simple. Play continues counterclockwise to Domm, who needs to come up with something starting with S.

The winner is the last remaining player.

Hacking the Hack

Try whiskey!

Seriously, as bar-rific as the game sounds, you don't have to drink alcohol. Try another beverage—hot tea is good, root beer is good, and anything with caffeine can change the rule for losing in interesting ways.

Some variants of the game require Barbie to drink *until* he can name a module. This can take a while.

The author recommends never challenging Audrey to the CPAN drinking game.

Improve Exceptional Conditions
HACK #38   Die with style when something goes wrong.

Perl's exception handling is sufficiently minimal. It's easy to recover when things go wrong without having to declare every possible type of error you might possibly encounter. Yet there are times when you know you can handle certain types of exceptions, if not others. Fortunately, Perl's special exception variable $@ is more special than you might know—it can hold objects.

If you can stick an object in there, you can do just about anything.

The Hack

How would you like more context when you catch an exception? Sure, if someone uses the Carp module you can sometimes get a stack trace. That's not enough if you want to know exactly what went wrong.

For example, consider the canonical example of a system call gone awry. Try to open a file you can't touch. Good style says you should die( ) with an exception there. Robust code should catch that exception—but there's so much useful information that the exception string could hold, why should you have to parse the message to figure out which file it was, for example, or what the error was, or how the user tried to open the file?

Exception::Class lets you throw an exception as normal while making all of the information available through instance methods.

Suppose you've factored out all of your file opening code into a single function:

```
use File::Exception;

sub open_file
{
    my ($name, $mode) = @_;

    open my $fh, $mode, $name or
        File::Exception->throw( file => $name, mode => $mode, error => $! );

    return $fh;
}
```

Instead of calling die( ), the function throw( )s a new File::Exception object, passing the file name, mode, and system error message. File:: Exception subclasses Exception::Class::Base to add two more fields and a friendlier error message:

```
package File::Exception;

use SUPER;
use Exception::Class;

use base 'Exception::Class::Base';

sub Fields
{
    my $self = shift;
    return super(), qw( file mode );
}

sub file { $_[0]->{file} }
sub mode { $_[0]->{mode} }

sub full_message
{
    my $self = shift;
    my $msg  = $self->message();

    my $file = $self->file();
    my $mode = $self->mode();

    return "Exception '$msg' when opening file '$file' with mode '$mode'";
}

1;
```

The only curious piece of the code is the `Fields()` method. `Exception::Class::Base` uses this to initialize the object with the proper attributes.

`full_message()` creates and returns the string used as the exception message. This is what `$@` would contain if this were a normal exception. As it is, `Exception::Class::Base` overrides object stringification [Hack #99] so the objects appear as normal `die()` messages to users who don't realize they're objects.

Running the Hack

Call open_file( ) as usual—within an eval( ) block:

```
my $fh;
$fh = eval { open_file( '/dev/null', '<' ) };
warn $@ if $@;

$fh = eval { open_file( '/dev', '>' ) };
warn $@ if $@;
```

Reading from */dev/null* is okay (at least on Unix-like systems), but writing to */dev* or any other directory is a problem:

```
Exception 'Is a directory' when opening file '/dev' with mode '>'
    at directory_whacker.pl line 10.
```

The real power comes when you treat the object as an object:

```
$fh = eval { open_file( '/dev', '>' ) };

if (my $error = $@)
{
    warn sprintf "Tried to open %s '%s' as user %s at %s: %s\n",
        $error->mode( ), $error->file( ), $error->uid( ),
        scalar( localtime( $error->time( ) ) ),
        $error->error( );
}
```

What are the other methods? They're methods available on all `Exception::Class` objects.

> Make a copy of `$@` as soon as possible, lest another eval( ) block somewhere overwrite your object out from underneath you.

Now instead of having to parse the string for potentially useful information, you can debug and, if possible, recover with better debugging information:

```
Tried to open > '/dev' as user 1000 at Tue Jan 17 21:58:00 2006:
    Is a directory
```

Hacking the Hack

Exception::Class objects are objects—so they can have relationships with each other. You can subclass them and make an entire hierarchy of exceptions, if your application needs them. You can also catch and redispatch them based on their type or any other characteristic you want.

Best of all, if someone doesn't want to care that you're throwing objects, she doesn't have to. They still behave just like normal exceptions.

HACK #39 Search CPAN Modules Locally

Search the CPAN without leaving the command line.

Websites such as *http://search.cpan.org/* are fantastic for finding the Perl module you need from the CPAN, but firing up a web browser, navigating to the page, and waiting for the results can be slow.

Similarly, running the CPAN or CPANPLUS shell and doing i *search term* is also slow. Besides that, you might not even have a network connection.

The Hack

The last time the CPAN or CPANPLUS shell connected to a CPAN mirror it downloaded a file listing every single module—*03modlist.data.gz*. You can see the file at *ftp://cpan.org/modules/03modlist.data.gz*. Because you have that local copy, you can parse it, check the modules that match your search terms, and print the results.

Additionally you can check to see if any of them are installed already and highlight them.

```perl
#!perl -w

# import merrily
use strict;
use IO::Zlib;
use Parse::CPAN::Modlist;

# get the search pattern
my $pattern    = shift || die "You must pass a pattern\n";
my $pattern_re = qr/$pattern/;

# munge our name
my $self       = $0; $self =~ s!^.*[\\/]!!;

# naughty user
die ("usage : $self <query>\n") unless defined $pattern;

# get where the local modulelist is from CPAN(PLUS?)::Config
```

```
my $base;
eval { require CPANPLUS::Config; CPANPLUS::Config->import( ); };
unless ($@)
{
    my $conf = CPANPLUS::Config->new( );
    # different versions have the config in different places
    for (qw(conf _build))
    {
        $base = $conf->{$_}->{base} if exists $conf->{$_};
    }
}

goto SKIP if defined $base;

eval { require CPAN::Config; CPAN::Config->import( ) };

unless ($@)
{
    local $CPAN::Config;
    $base = $CPAN::Config->{'keep_source_where'}."/modules/";
}

goto SKIP if defined $base;

die "Couldn't find where you keep your CPAN Modlist\n";

SKIP:
my $file    = "${base}/03modlist.data.gz";

# open the file and feed it to the mod list parser
my $fh      = IO::Zlib->new($file, "rb")  or die "Cannot open $file\n";
my $ml      = Parse::CPAN::Modlist->new(join "", <$fh>);

# by default we want colour
my $colour  = 1;

# check to see if we have Term::ANSIColor installed
eval { require Term::ANSIColor };

# but if we can't have it then we can't have it
$colour     = 0 if $@;

# now do the actual checking

my $first   = 0;

# check each module
for my $module (map { $ml->module($_) } $ml->modules( ))
{
    my $name = $module->name( );
    my $desc = $module->description( );
```

```
    # check to see if the pattern matches the name or desc
    next unless  $name =~ /$pattern_re/i or $desc =~ /$pattern_re/i;

    # aesthetics
    print "\n-- Results for '$pattern' --\n\n" unless $first++;

    # check to see if it's installed
    eval  "require $name";

    # print out the title - coloured if possible
    if ( $colour && !$@ )
    {
        print Term::ANSIColor::color('red'),
            "$name\n",
            Term::ANSIColor::color('reset');
    }
    elsif (!$@)
    {
        print "!! $name\n";
    }
    else
    {
        print "$name\n";
    }

    # print out the name and description
    print "- $desc\n\n";
}

    exit 0;
```

First, the code tries to find the local module list. This can be in several places. It initially checks for CPANPLUS, assuming that anyone who has that installed will use it over the less featureful CPAN. Different versions of CPANPLUS store the file in different locations, so the code checks both.

If that fails, the program performs the same check for CPAN. If that doesn't work, the program ends.

If the file is present, the code uncompresses it with IO::Zlib and passes it to Parse::CPAN::Modlist to parse it.

The next part checks to see if Term::ANSIColor is available. If so, it can highlight installed modules.

The Parse::CPAN::Modlist::modules() method returns only the names of modules in the list, so the code must load the appropriate Module object to get at the other metadata. Using map { } in the for loop is incredibly convenient.

For efficency, there's an early check if the name or description matches the input pattern. Notice how the results banner (Results for '$pattern') only prints if there is at least one result.

The code attempts to require the module to see if it is available. If so, the program must highlight the name with color, if available, or exclamation marks otherwise. Finally, the program prints the description and tries the next module.

Hacking the Hack

There are plenty of ways to improve this program.

Currently it assumes that the CPANPLUS module list is the most up to date. It should probably check both CPANPLUS and CPAN if possible, look for the appropriate *03modlist.data.gz* in each case, and push it onto a list of potential candidates before using the most recently modified version.

This hack also relies on *03modlist.data.gz* being up to date. If you don't use the CPAN or CPANPLUS shell regularly, this might not be the case.

There are several possible solutions.

First, the program could just die if the module list is too old. This is the simplest (and most defeatist) solution.

Second, you could write a cron job that periodically updates the module list. This has the advantage that even if you have no network currently available, you know it's still reasonably fresh.

Finally, you could check to see whether the module list is older than a certain threshold. If so, you could warn or force the chosen provider to download a newer one. This has the disadvantage of not working if you cannot connect to your CPAN mirror.

Currently, the code checks both the name and the description—which can produce a lot of useless results. It should be possible to build a more complicated query parser that gives users finer-grained control over the results.

Finally, the code doesn't necessarily have to require modules to see if they exist. It could use logic similar to perldoc -l [Hack #2] to find their locations.

Package Standalone Perl Applications

HACK #40   Distribute a full Perl application to users.

The three main ways to distribute an application are via an installer, via a standalone executable, or via source. These choices vary a lot across platforms. Windows users prefer installers, especially *.msi* files. Mac fans are quite happy with *.app* files, which usually come in disk images. Most Linux variants use installers (*.deb* and *.rpm*) but others prefer source.

What if your application is a Perl program?

Perl may seem like an atypical GUI language, but it does have bindings for GUI toolkits including Tk, wxWidgets, Qt, and GTK. Perl can be useful in the GUI realm as a rapid-development foundation or simply to add a couple of dialogs to a mostly background process. One great entry barrier, however, is that most platforms do not bundle these GUI toolkits with Perl—and some platforms do not bundle Perl at all. Though there are packaged distributions of Perl itself, the add-on modules that usually accompany any sophisticated Perl project are typically source code. This poses a problem for most Windows users and many Mac users for whom this is too low-level a task. Only the sysadmin-rich world of Linux and Unix regularly tolerates sudo cpan install Foo commands.

The Hack

The PAR project attempts to to create a solution to bundling the myriad files that usually compose a Perl application into a manageable monolith. PAR files are simply ZIP files with manifests. If you have PAR installed on your computer, you can write Perl code that looks like:

```
#!perl -w

use PAR 'foo.par';
use Foo;
...
```

and if *Foo.pm* is inside the *foo.par* file, perl will load it as if it were a normal installed module. Even more interestingly, you can write:

```
#!perl -w

use PAR 'http://www.example.com/foo.par';
use Foo;
...
```

which will download and cache the *foo.par* archive locally. How's that for a quick update?

You may have noticed the sticky phrase above "If you have PAR installed…" That is a catch-22 of sorts. PAR helps users to skip the software installation steps, but first they have to…install software!

To get around this, PAR takes another page from the ZIP playbook: self-extracting executables. The PAR distibution comes with a program called pp that allows a developer to wrap the core of Perl and any additional project-specific Perl modules into a PAR file with a *main.pl* and an executable header to bootstrap the whole thing. This produces something like /usr/bin/perl with all of its modules embedded inside.

Running the Hack

Consider a basic `helloworld.pl` application:

```perl
#!perl -w

use strict;
use Tk;

my $mw = MainWindow->new( );

$mw->Label(-text => 'Hello, world!')->pack( );
$mw->Button(-text => 'Quit', -command => sub { exit })->pack( );

MainLoop( );
```

To run this, you have to have Perl and Tk installed* and perhaps X11 running (via open `/Applications/Utilities/X11.app`). Run `perl helloworld.pl` to see a window like that in Figure 4-1.

Figure 4-1. "Hello, world" in Perl/Tk

Now suppose that you want to give this cool new application to other Mac users. Telling them to first install Fink, Tk, and X11 just for "Hello, World!" is ludicrous. Instead, build an executable with pp:

```
% pp -o helloworld helloworld.pl
```

That creates a 3 MB executable, *helloworld*, which includes the entirety of both Perl and Tk. Send it to a friend who has a Mac (and X11, because this version of Tk isn't Aqua-friendly) and she can run it. If you were to make a Windows version it would be even easier on end users—on Windows, Tk binds directly to the native GUI, so X11 is not a prerequisite.

Aside from portability, another PAR benefit is version independence. The example executable, though built against Perl 5.8.6 on Mac OS X 10.4, should also work well on 10.3 or 10.2, even though those OSes shipped with older versions of Perl. This is because PAR included every part of 5.8.6 that the example needed in the executable.

---

* On my Mac OS X 10.4 box, I do this via `fink install tk-pm586`

Hacking the Hack

If you download that executable, you can open it with any zip tool:

```
% zipinfo helloworld
Archive:  helloworld   3013468 bytes    689 files
drwxr-xr-x  2.0 unx        0 b- stor 23-Oct-05 14:21 lib/
drwxr-xr-x  2.0 unx        0 b- stor 23-Oct-05 14:21 script/
-rw-r--r--  2.0 unx    20016 b- defN 23-Oct-05 14:21 MANIFEST
-rw-r--r--  2.0 unx      210 b- defN 23-Oct-05 14:21 META.yml
-rw-r--r--  2.0 unx     4971 b- defN 23-Oct-05 14:21 lib/AutoLoader.pm
-rw-r--r--  2.0 unx     4145 b- defN 23-Oct-05 14:21 lib/Carp.pm
... [snipped 679 lines] ...
-rw-r--r--  2.0 unx    12966 b- defN 23-Oct-05 14:21 lib/warnings.pm
-rw-r--r--  2.0 unx      787 b- defN 23-Oct-05 14:21 lib/warnings/register.
pm
-rw-r--r--  2.0 unx      186 t- defN 23-May-05 22:22 script/helloworld.pl
-rw-r--r--  2.0 unx      262 b- defN 23-Oct-05 14:21 script/main.pl
689 files, 2742583 bytes uncompressed, 1078413 bytes compressed:  60.7%
```

You may see that the file sizes don't match. That's because the EXE also contains the whole Perl interpreter outside of the ZIP portion. That adds an extra 200% to file size in this case.

Is it fast? No. Perl must unzip the file prior to use (which happens automatically, of course). Is it compact? No, 3 MB for Hello World is almost silly. Is it convenient? Yes—and that is often the most important quality when shipping software to users.

An interesting consequence of this distribution model is that the executable contains all of the source code. For some companies this may represent a problem (with some possible solutions listed at *http://par.perl.org/*). On the other hand it is also a benefit in that you might satisfy any GPL requirements without having to offer a separate source download.

An important note for Windows is that, thanks to ActiveState, you do not need a C compiler to build Perl yourself. They provide an installable package that includes Tk pre-built. See links on *http://par.perl.org/* for pre-compiled installers for PAR.

HACK #41   Create Your Own Lexical Warnings

Add your own warnings to the `warnings` pragma.

Perl 5.6 added a useful pragma called `warnings` that expanded and enhanced upon the `-w` and `-W` switches. This pragma introduced warnings scoped lexically. Within a lexical scope you can enable and disable warnings as a whole or by particular class.

For example, within a say() function emulating the Perl 6 operator, you could respect the current value of $, (the output field separator) and not throw useless warnings about its definedness with:

```
use warnings;

# ... more code here...

sub say
{
    no warnings 'uninitialized';
    print join( $,, @_ ), "\n";
}
```

See perllexwarn for a list of all of the types of warnings you can enable and disable.

When you write your own module, you can even *create* your own warnings categories for users of your code to enable and disable as they see fit. It's easy.

The Hack

To create a warning, use the warnings::register pragma in your code. That's it. The UNIVERSAL::can module* does this.

Within the module, when it detects code that uses UNIVERSAL::can() as a function, it checks that the calling code has enabled warnings, then uses warnings::warn() to report the error:

```
if (warnings::enabled())
{
    warnings::warn( "Called UNIVERSAL::can() as a function, not a method" );
}
```

Running the Hack

How does this look from code that merely uses the module? If the calling code doesn't use warnings, nothing happens. Otherwise, it warns as normal. To enable or disable the *specific* class of warning, use:

```
# enable
use warnings 'UNIVERSAL::can';

# disable
no warnings 'UNIVERSAL::can';
```

---

* Which detects, reports, and attempts to fix the anti-pattern of people calling UNIVERSAL::can() as a function, not a method.

Hacking the Hack

You can also re-use existing warnings categories. For example, if you want to mark a particular interface as deprecated, write a wrapper for the new function that warns when users use the old one:

```
sub yucky_function
{
    my ($package, $filename, $line) = caller( );

    warnings::warnif( 'deprecated',
        "yucky_function( ) is deprecated at $filename:$line\n" );

    goto &yummy_function;
}
```

> This version of goto replaces the original call in the call stack by calling the new function with the current contents of @_.

Now when users use the warnings pragma with no arguments (or enable deprecated warnings), they'll receive a warning suggesting where and how to update their code.

HACK #42 Find and Report Module Bugs

Fix problems in CPAN modules.

In an ideal world, all software is fully tested and bug free. Of course that's rarely the case.

Using Perl modules offers many advantages, including more thoroughly validated routines, tested and optimized solutions, and the fact that someone has already done part of your job for you. Sometimes, though, you may find that the shiny module that does exactly what you need actually does something different than it should have.

Here's some code that creates a proxy object FooProxy. When you create an instance of this proxy object, it should behave just like an instance of the original Foo object, but FooProxy could modify specific behavior of the Foo object, perhaps to log method calls or check access [Hack #48], without altering the Foo package itself:

```
package FooProxy;

sub new
{
    my $class = shift;
    my $foo   = Foo->new( @_ );
```

```
    bless \$foo, $class;
}

sub can
{
    my $self = shift;
    return $$self->can( @_ );
}

1;
```

Here's some code that instantiates a FooProxy object, and being paranoid, attempts to double-check that the created object looks just like a Foo object:

```
# Create a proxy object
my $proxy = FooProxy->new( );

# Make sure the proxy acts like a Foo
if ($proxy->isa('Foo'))
{
    print "Proxy is a Foo!\n";
}
else
{
    die "Proxy isn't a Foo!";
}
```

When you run this script, you might notice a problem. When you call a Foo method on the $fooproxy object, the method complains that the object isn't Foo. What's going on?

Instead of diving straight into the debugger or throwing print statements throughout the code, step back and take a logical approach [Hack #53]. Here's the Foo definition:

```
package Foo;
use UNIVERSAL::isa;

sub new
{
    my $class = shift;
    bless \my $foo, $class;
}

sub isa
{
    1;
}

1;
```

Foo uses the CPAN module UNIVERSAL::isa to protect itself against people calling the method UNIVERSAL::isa( ) as a function.* When someone calls UNIVERSAL::isa($some_foo, 'Class'), UNIVERSAL::isa should detect the isa( ) method of the Foo object, and call that. In this case, though, isa( ) is executing in the context of FooProxy. This looks like a problem with the UNIVERSAL::isa module; you should file a bug report!

Write a Test

Instead of just reporting the bug generically and leaving the author to diagnose, fix, and verify, give the author an excellent head start by writing a test. Taking it one step further, you can even add this test directly to the module's own collection of tests. After downloading and unpacking *UNIVERSAL-isa-0.05.tar.gz*, look for its *t/* subdirectory. Each *.t* file in this directory represents a unit test with one to many subtests. Add a new test to the package by creating a new *.t* file. UNIVERSAL::isa, however, already includes a *bugs.t* file, so you can just add the new test there.

You could rewrite the example code and add it to *bugs.t*. Just don't forget to increment the test count appropriately, because you're adding tests:

```
# really delegates calls to Foo
{
    package FooProxy;

    sub new
    {
        my $class = shift;
        my $foo   = Foo->new( @_ );
        bless \$foo, $class;
    }

    sub can
    {
        my $self = shift;
        return $$self->can( @_ );
    }
}

my $proxy = FooProxy->new( );
isa_ok( $proxy, 'Foo' );
```

Run the test and make sure it fails. If so, it's a good test; it demonstrates what you consider to be a real bug.

---

* Foo defines its own isa( ), so you *must* call $some_foo->isa( ) instead.

Running the test is usually as simple as:

```
$ prove -lv t/bugs.t
# test output here...
```

Submitting a bug report. Now you've done a lot of the work for the author. Not only have you narrowed the problem down to a particular module, you have produced a test case that he or she can include with the module to ensure that the bug gets fixed and stays fixed in future revisions. Instead of submitting a bug report that merely explains what you think the problem is (or just the symptom), you can provide an implemented test case that demonstrates the problem and will prove that the ultimate fix really works.

It's helpful to have the Perl community review your findings to confirm your analysis. Perl Monks (*http://www.perlmonks.org/*) is a free community for Perl programmers. Many of the best-known names in the Perl community—authors, instructors, and even language designers—frequent Perl Monks and dispense their wisdom freely. It's easy to be sure that you've found a legitimate bug, only to find out that you misunderstood the expected behavior. Further, you might get more useful feedback, such as a pointer that the module you're using is outdated, and there's a much better replacement, or that another module more closely meets your needs.

Once you have confirmation that this is a bug, submit your report to the CPAN Request Tracker at *http://rt.cpan.org/.** This site provides a simple interface to submit bug reports to the appropriate package maintainer, and then check the status of the report. This site supports user accounts (including your existing PAUSE ID) that are useful for tracking your numerous bug reports, but you don't have to create an account. If you choose to continue without an account, you may specify an email address with the bug report, and you'll receive updates when the module maintainer updates your ticket.

On the site, first search for distributions. This will give you a form where you can enter the package distribution name, `UNIVERSAL::isa`, and find a list of active bugs against it. From here, you can report your new bug, assuming someone else hasn't already submitted it!

In the submission form, fill in the requested information. For the subject, please be specific and concise. Instead of `UNIVERSAL::isa is broken`, consider `isa() reports incorrect package type (?)`. Choose an appropriate severity, and indicate the module version or versions in which you observed the defect. There's a box to describe in more detail what you observed and

---

* Of course, the author might prefer another means of reporting. Check the module's documentation to be sure.

how this behavior differs from your expectation. Note the comments on the submission page that suggest other useful information to include.

There is also a place to attach a file. Along with the basic bug report, you can submit a patch to the module to add your test case. To create the patch, extract the package, creating a versioned directory with the pure downloaded form. Next, copy that package directory to another directory without the version number:

```
$ cp -r UNIVERSAL-isa-0.05 UNIVERSAL-isa
```

Make your changes (incorporate the test script) to the files in *UNIVERSAL-isa*, and then make a patch against the official release. First, in each package directory, do make clean to clean up any build-related files. Now, in the directory above both package directories, run diff with the unified and recursive flags, to make the file readable and to pick up all of the changed files:

```
$ diff -ur UNIVERSAL-isa-0.05 UNIVERSAL-isa > isa_misbehaving.patch
```

This command will produce a patch that, when applied to the files in *UNIVERSAL-isa-0.05/*, will reproduce the changes you made to the module's test file. Simply include this patch with your bug report, and you'll give the package maintainer a huge head start on fixing the problem.

Attach the patch you created, and submit the form.

Check your email or the site periodically for the status of your bug. Obviously, if there's a fix, you will want to grab the new version quickly, but you also need to see if the author has rejected your bug. If so, research the issue more to determine whether the issue is truly where you thought it was, or if you need to debug your own code further.

Hacking the Hack

You can do more than merely submitting a bug report. With a well-written test case in hand, it's not as daunting a task to fix the bug yourself. Along with the patch that adds your unit tests, you could even submit a patch against the entire package source. The package tests, including the one you added, will verify that the code change is correct, so the maintainer just has to review the changes and apply them.

 As it turns out, the bug is that the particular version of UNIVERSAL::isa called the method UNIVERSAL::can( ) as a function, not a method. Oops.

Regardless of whether you provide a fix to the package maintainer, submitting a good bug report with effective unit tests adds value to CPAN for all its users.

## CHAPTER FIVE

Object Hacks

Hacks 43–50

Perl has objects, you bet! Beyond the oddity of bless, the repurposing of subroutines, packages, and references, OO Perl has a lot of power and tremendous flexibility. Maybe you've only blessed hash references because you need record objects—but have you considered the benefits of stronger encapsulation, automatic serialization, and enforced access control?

The more you know about Perl, the more options you have for creating and using higher-level abstractions. The next time your coworkers have a nasty problem they just can't solve, look in your bag of OO tricks and smile and say, "Don't worry. We can do anything with Perl."

HACK #43 Turn Your Objects Inside Out

Encapsulate your attributes strongly.

Perl 5's object orientation is minimalistic. It gives you enough to get the job done while not preventing you from doing clever things. Of course, the default approach is usually the simplest one (or the cleverest), not the cleanest or most maintainable.

Most objects are blessed hashes, because they're easy to understand and to use. Unfortunately, they can be difficult to debug and they don't really provide any encapsulation, thus tying you to specific implementation schemes.*

Fortunately, fixing that is easy.

The Hack

An object in Perl needs two things, a place to store its instance data and a class in which to find its methods. A blessed hash (or array, or scalar, or

---

* See "Seven Sins of Perl OO Programming" in *The Perl Review* 2.1, Winter 2005.

subroutine, or typeglob, or…) stores its data *within* the object you pass around. If you dereference the reference, you can read and write that data from anywhere, even outside the class.

An inside out object stores its data elsewhere, often in a lexical variable scoped to the class. From outside the lexical scope, you can't (*usually*—see "Peek Inside Closures" **[Hack #76]**) access that data without using the object's accessors.

> Damian Conway's first book, *Object Oriented Perl* (Manning, 2000) showed various ways to use closure-based encapsulation. His recent *Perl Best Practices* (O'Reilly, 2005) recommended using them as a best practice. The Perl hacker known simply as Abigail has also touted the virtues of inside out objects for several years. See the documentation of Class::Std for a fuller treatment of the issue.

Running the Hack

A simple, naïve inside out object implementation for a record class might be:

```
# create a new scope for the lexicals
{
    package InsideOut::User;

    use Scalar::Util 'refaddr';

    # lexicals used to hold instance data
    my %names;
    my %addresses;

    sub new
    {
        my ($class, $data) = @_;

        # bless a new scalar to get this object's id
        bless \(my $self), $class;

        # store the instance data
        my $id              = refaddr( $self );
        $names{    $id }    = $data->{name};
        $addresses{ $id }   = $data->{address};

        return $self;
    }

    # accessors, as $self->{name} and $self->{address} don't work
    sub get_name
    {
```

```
                    my $self = shift;
                    return $names{ refaddr( $self ) };
            }

        sub get_address
        {
                    my $self = shift;
                    return $addresses{ refaddr( $self ) };
        }

        # many people forget this part
        sub DESTROY
        {
                    my $self = shift;
                    my $id   = refaddr( $self );
                    delete $names{      $id };
                    delete $addresses{ $id };
        }
    }

    1;
```

That's a little more typing, but it's definitely a lot cleaner. Now you can sub-class or reimplement InsideOut::User without having to use a blessed hash—just follow the interface this defines and your code will work.

Of course, the more complex the object, the more typing you have to do. Wouldn't it be nice to automate this?

Hacking the Hack

Class::Std, Class::InsideOut, and Object::InsideOut are three current modules on the CPAN that take some of the work out of inside out objects for you. They all have various tricks and features. Class::Std is nice in that it automatically creates accessors and mutators, calls better constructors and destructors, and uses a declarative attribute-based syntax [Hack #45].

The same class using Class::Std is:

```
    {
        package InsideOut::User;

        use Class::Std;

        my %names     :ATTR( :get<name>    :init_arg<name>    );
        my %addresses :ATTR( :get<address> :init_arg<address> );
    }
```

This code automatically generates the get_name( ) and get_address( ) accessors as well as a constructor that pulls the initial values for the objects out of a hash reference with the appropriate keys. The syntax isn't *quite* as nice as that of Perl 6, but it's much, much shorter than the naïve Perl 5 version—and provides all of the same features.

Serialize Objects (Mostly) for Free

#44 Store object data without mess, confusion, or big blobs of binary data.

Some programs really need persistent data, and sometimes mapping between objects and multiple tables in a fully-relational database is just too much work. This is especially true in cases where being able to edit data quickly and easily is important—there's no interface more comfortable than your favorite text editor **[Hack #12]**.

Instead of hard-coding configuration in a program, wasting your precious youth creating the perfect database schema, or doing XML sit-ups, why not serialize your important object data to YAML?

The Hack

If you use hash-based objects, it's very easy to serialize the data—just make a copy of the hash and serialize it:

```
use YAML 'DumpFile';

sub serialize
{
    my ($object, $file) = @_;
    my %data            = %$object;
    DumpFile( $file, \%data );
}
```

This assumes, of course, that $object is the object you want to serialize and $file is the path and file to which to save the object.

If you use inside out objects **[Hack #43]**, you have a bit more work to do:

```
package Graphics::Drawable;
{
    use Class::Std;

    my %coords_of     :ATTR( :get<coords>   :init_arg<coords>   );
    my %velocities_of :ATTR( :get<velocity>  :init_arg<velocity> );
    my %shapes_of     :ATTR( :get<shape>     :init_arg<shape>    );

    sub get_serializable_data
    {
        my $self  = shift;

        my %data;

        for my $attribute (qw( coords velocity shape ))
        {
```

```
            my $method = 'get_' . $attribute;
            $data{ $attribute } = $self->$method( );
        }

        return \%data;
    }
}
```

Now your `serialize( )` function can avoid breaking encapsulation and call `get_serializable_data( )` instead. An object at the origin (coordinates of (0, 0, 0)) with a velocity of one unit per time unit along the X axis ((1, 0, 0)) and a `Circle` shape serializes to:

```
---
coords:
  - 0
  - 0
  - 0
shape: Circle
velocity:
  - 1
  - 0
  - 0
```

If you want to make more objects, copy the file to a new location and modify it. Just be careful to keep the code valid YAML.[*]

Restoring objects is easy; just use YAML's `LoadFile( )` method:

```
use YAML 'LoadFile';

sub deserialize
{
    my ($class, $file) = @_;
    my $data           = LoadFile( $file );
    return $class->new( $data );
}
```

Assuming your class constructor takes a hash reference keyed on attribute names (as `Class::Std` does), you're all set. Of course, this all presumes some sort of object factory that can manage instances, map files and paths to classes, and store and retrieve objects, let alone handle errors. `Class::StorageFactory` on the CPAN handles this.

If you have all of this—and only need data from an object's public interface (both constructor attributes and data accessible through accessors) to recreate the object—serializing to YAML or another simple plain-text format (JSON?) is fast, easy, flexible, and almost free.

---

[*] A task much easier than writing valid XML by hand...

Add Information with Attributes

#45

Give your variables and subroutines a little extra information.

Subroutines and variables are straighforward. Sure, you can pass around references to them or make them anonymous and do weird things with them, but you have few options to change what Perl does with them.

Your best option is to give them attributes. Attributes are little pieces of data that attach to variables or subroutines. In return, Perl runs any code you like. This has many, many possibilities.

The Hack

Suppose that you have a class and want to document the purpose of each method. Some languages support *docstrings*—comments that you can introspect by calling class methods. Perl's comments are pretty boring, but you can achieve almost the same effect by annotating methods with subroutine attributes.

Consider a Counter class, intended to provide a default constructor that counts the number of objects created. If there's a Doc attribute provided by the Attribute::Docstring module, the class may resemble:

```
package Counter;

use strict;
use warnings;

use Attribute::Docstring;

our $counter :Doc( 'a count of all new Foo objects' );

sub new :Doc( 'the constructor for Foo' )
{
    $counter++;
    bless { }, shift;
}

sub get_count :Doc( 'returns the count for all foo objects' )
{
    return $counter;
}

1;
```

The prototype comes after the name of the subroutine and has a preceding colon. Otherwise, it looks like a function call. The documentation string is the (single) argument to the attribute.

Running the Hack

The easiest way to create and use attributes is with the `Attribute::Handlers`
module. This allows you to write subroutines named after the attributes you
want to declare. The implementation of `Attribute::Docstring` is:

```
package Attribute::Docstring;

use strict;
use warnings;

use Scalar::Util 'blessed';
use Attribute::Handlers;

my %doc;

sub UNIVERSAL::Doc :ATTR
{
    my ($package, $symbol, $referent, $attr, $data, $phase) = @_;
    return if $symbol eq 'LEXICAL';

    my $name               = *{$symbol}{NAME};
    $doc{ $package }{ $name } = $data;
}

sub UNIVERSAL::doc
{
    my ($self, $name) = @_;
    my $package       = blessed( $self ) || $self;

    return unless exists $doc{ $package }{ $name };
    return               $doc{ $package }{ $name };
}

1;
```

To make the `Doc` attribute available everywhere, the module defines a subroutine called `UNIVERSAL::Doc`. This subroutine itself has an attribute, `:ATTR`,
which identifies it as an attribute handler.

For any subroutine or variable that declares a `Doc` attribute, the subroutine
receives several pieces of information. Here, the important ones are the package containing the subroutine, the symbol—from which the typeglob access
can retrieve the name, and the data provided to the attribute. In the `Counter`
class, the attribute handler receives a package name of `Counter` and the typeglob with the name `new` for the symbol when Perl finishes compiling the `new( )`
method. It then stores the attribute data (the docstring itself) in a hash keyed
first on the name of the package and then on the name of the symbol.

Because of the difference between how Perl treats lexical and global variables, the handler can't do much if it receives a lexical symbol (that is, when $symbol is LEXICAL). Then again, these are private to the package so they're not worth documenting in this way anyway.

The similarly named doc( ) method works on any class or object, so that calling Counter->doc('new') or $counter->doc('get_count') both return the docstring for the appropriate method. It simply looks up the docstring in the appropriate package for the given name and returns it.

Hacking the Hack

One potential enhancement is to add the appropriate sigil to the name, so that the docstrings for a variable named $count and a method named count( ) will not overwrite each other. That would require a change to UNIVERSAL::doc( ) so that $name contains the sigil (or, with no sigil, defaults to the method).

Another possibility is to take UNIVERSAL::Doc( ) out of UNIVERSAL, instead importing it into any package that uses this module. That unclutters UNIVERSAL somewhat at the expense of cluttering calling classes. That may or may not be a useful tradeoff.

Attributes may span lines, but you cannot use heredocs, unfortunately.

Make Methods Really Private
Enforce encapsulation with a little more flair.

Perl's object orientation is powerful in many ways, allowing the creation and emulation of almost any kind of object or class system. It's also very permissive, enforcing no access control by default. Any code can poke and prod methods and parents into any class at any time and can call even ostensibly private methods regardless of the intent of the code's original author.

By convention, the Perl community considers methods with a leading underscore as private methods that you shouldn't override or call outside of the class or rely on any specific semantics or workings. That's usually a good policy, but there's little enforcement and it's only a convention. It's still possible to call the wrong method accidentally or even on purpose.

Fortunately, there are better (or at least scarier) ways to hide methods.

The Hack

One easy way to manipulate subroutines and methods at compile time is with subroutine attributes [Hack #45]. The Class::HideMethods module adds an attribute to methods named Hide that makes them unavailable and mostly uncallable from outside the program:

```perl
package Class::HideMethods;

use strict;
use warnings;
use Attribute::Handlers;

my %prefixes;

sub import
{
    my ($self, $ref)      = @_;
    my $package           = caller();
    $prefixes{ $package } = $ref;
}

sub gen_prefix
{
    my $invalid_chars = "\0\r\n\f\b";

    my $prefix;

    for ( 1 .. 5 )
    {
        my $char_pos = int( rand( length( $invalid_chars ) ) );
        $prefix      .= substr( $invalid_chars, $char_pos, 1 );
    }

    return $prefix;
}

package UNIVERSAL;

sub Private :ATTR
{
    my ($package, $symbol, $referent, $attr, $data, $phase) = @_;

    my $name    = *{ $symbol }{NAME};
    my $newname = Class::HideMethods::gen_prefix( $package ) . $name;
    my @refs    = map { *$symbol{ $_ } } qw( HASH SCALAR ARRAY GLOB );
    *$symbol    = do { local *symbol };

    no strict 'refs';
    *{ $package . '::' . $newname } = $referent;
    *{ $package . '::' . $name    } = $_ for @refs;
    $prefixes{ $package }{ $name }  = $newname;
}

1;
```

To hide the method, the code replaces the method's symbol with a new, empty typeglob. This would also delete any variables with the same name, so the code copies them out of the symbol first, and then back into the new, empty symbol. Now you know how to "delete" from a typeglob.

Running the Hack

Using this module is easy; within your class, declare a lexical hash to hold the secret new method names. Pass it to the line that uses Class::HideMethods:

```
package SecretClass;

my %methods;
use Class::HideMethods \%methods;

sub new            { bless {}, shift }
sub hello :Private { return 'hello'  }
sub goodbye        { return 'goodbye' }

sub public_hello
{
    my $self  = shift;
    my $hello = $methods{hello};
    $self->$hello();
}

1;
```

Remember to call all private methods with the $invocant->$method_name syntax, looking up the hidden method name instead.

To prove that it works, try a few tests from outside the code.

```
use Test::More tests => 6;

my $sc = SecretClass->new();
isa_ok( $sc, 'SecretClass' );

ok( ! $sc->can( 'hello' ),        'hello() should be hidden'           );
ok( $sc->can( 'public_hello' ),   'public_hello() should be available' );
is( $sc->public_hello(),
    'hello', '... and should be able to call hello()' );
ok( $sc->can( 'goodbye' ),        'goodbye() should be available'      );
is( $sc->goodbye(), 'goodbye',    '... and should be callable'         );
```

Not even subclasses can call the methods directly. They're fairly private!

Inside the hack. Perl uses symbol tables internally to store everything with a name—variables, subroutines, methods, classes, and packages. This is for the benefit of humans. By one theory, Perl doesn't really care what the name of a method is; it's happy to call it by name, by reference, or by loose description.

That's sort of true and sort of false. Only Perl's *parser* cares about names. Valid identifiers start with an alphabetic character or an underscore and contain zero or more alphanumeric or underscore characters. Once Perl has parsed the program, it looks up whatever symbols it has in a manner similar to looking up values in a hash. If you can force Perl to look up a symbol containing otherwise-invalid characters, it will happily do so.

Fortunately, there's more than one way to call a method. If you have a scalar containing the name of the method (which you can define as a string containing any character, not just a valid identifier) or a reference to the method itself, Perl will invoke the method on the invocant. That's half of the trick.

The other magic is in removing the symbol from the symbol table under its unhidden name. Without this, users could bypass the hidden name and call supposedly hidden methods directly.

Without the real name being visible, the class itself needs some way to find the names of private methods. That's the purpose of the lexical %methods, which is not normally visible outside of the class itself (or at least its containing file).

Hacking the Hack

A very clever version of this code could even do away with the need for %methods in the class with hidden methods, perhaps by abusing the constant pragma to store method names appropriately.

This approach isn't *complete* access control, at least in the sense that the language can enforce it. It's still possible to get around this. For example, you can crawl a package's symbol table, looking for defined code. One way to thwart this is to skip installing methods back in the symbol table with mangled names. Instead, delete the method from the symbol table and store the reference in the lexical cache of methods.

That'll keep out determined people. It won't keep out *really* determined people who know that the PadWalker module from the CPAN lets them poke around in lexical variables outside their normal scope [Hack #76]...but anyone who wants to go to that much trouble could just as easily fake the loading of Class::HideMethods with something that doesn't delete the symbol for hidden methods. Still, it's really difficult to call these methods by accident or on purpose without some head-scratching, which is probably as good as it gets in Perl 5.

HACK
#47 Autodeclare Method Arguments
You know who you are. Stop repeating your $self.

Perl's object orientation is very flexible, in part because of its simplicity and minimalism. At times that's valuable: it allows hackers to build complex object systems from a few small features. The rest of the time it can be painful to do simple things.

Though not everyone always calls the invocant in methods $self, everyone has to declare and manage the invocant and other arguments. That's a bit of a drag—but it's fixable. Sure, you could use a full-blown source filter [Hack #94] to remove the need to shift off $self and process the rest of your argument list, but that's an unnecessarily large hammer to swing at such a small annoyance. There's another way.

The Hack

Solving this problem without source filters requires three ideas. First, there must be some way to mark a subroutine as a method, because not all subroutines *are* methods. Second, this should be compatible with strict, for good programming practices. Third, there should be some way to add the proper operations to populate $self and the other arguments.

The first is easy: how about a subroutine attribute [Hack #45] called Method? The third is also possible with a little bit of B::Deparse [Hack #56] and eval magic. The second is trickier....

A surprisingly short module can do all of this:

```
package Attribute::Method;

use strict;
use warnings;

use B::Deparse;
use Attribute::Handlers;

my $deparse = B::Deparse->new( );

sub import
{
    my ( $class, @vars ) = @_;
    my $package          = caller( );

    my %references       =
    (
        '$' => \undef,
        '@' => [ ],
        '%' => { },
    );

    push @vars, '$self';

    for my $var (@vars)
    {
        my $reftype              = substr( $var, 0, 1, '' );
```

```
        no strict 'refs';
        *{ $package . '::' . $var } = $references{$reftype};
    }
}

sub UNIVERSAL::Method :ATTR(RAWDATA)
{
    my ($package, $symbol, $referent, undef, $arglist) = @_;

    my $code                = $deparse->coderef2text( $referent );
    $code                   =~ s/{/sub {\nmy (\$self, $arglist) = \@_;\n/;

    no warnings 'redefine';
    *$symbol                = eval "package $package; $code";
}

1;
```

All of the variables, including $self, have to be lexical within methods, lest bad things happen when calling one method from another, such as accidentally overwriting a global variable somewhere. The handler for the Method attribute takes the compiled code, deparses it, and inserts the sub keyword and the argument handling line before the rest of the code. All of the arguments to the attribute are the names of the lexical variables within the method.

Compiling that with eval produces a new anonymous subroutine, which the code then inserts into the symbol table after disabling the Subroutine %s redefined warnings.

Running the Hack

From any class in which you tire of declaring and fetching the same arguments over and over again, write instead:

```
package Easy::Class;

use strict;
use warnings;

use Attribute::Method qw( $status );

sub new :Method
{
    bless { @_ }, $self;
}

sub set_status :Method( $status )
{
    $self->{status} = $status;
}
```

```
sub get_status :Method
{
    return $self->{status};
}

1;
```

For every method marked with the :Method attribute, you get the $self invo-
cant declared for free. For every method with that attribute parameterized
with a list of variable names, you get those variables as well.

Notice the strange and deep magic in import( ) as well as the list of arguments passed to it; this is what bypasses the strict checking. If you use
instead only the refs and subs strictures, you don't even have to pass the
variables you want to Attribute::Method.

Hacking the Hack

Is this better than source filters? It's certainly not as syntactically tidy. On
the other hand, attribute-based solutions are often less fragile than source
filtering. In particular, they don't prevent the use of other source filters or
other attributes. It also almost never fails—if your subroutines have errors,
Perl will report them when compiling from the point of view of the original
code before even calling the attribute handler. This technique works best in
classes with several methods that take the same arguments.

Another *possible* way to accomplish this task is to rewrite the optree of the
code reference (with B::Generate and a *lot* of patience) to add the ops to
assign the arguments to the proper variables. Of course, you'll also have to
insert the lexical variables into the pad associated with the CV, but if you
know what this means, you probably know how to do it.

Finding and fixing any lexicals that methods close over isn't as bad in com-
parison. See "Peek Inside Closures" [Hack #76].

> See Ricardo Signes's Sub::MicroSig for an alternate approach
> to the same problem.

Control Access to Remote Objects
HACK #48
Enforce access control to your objects.

Perl's idea of access control and privacy is politeness. Sometimes this is useful—you don't have to spend a lot of time and energy figuring out what to
hide and how. Sometimes you *need* to rifle through someone else's code to
get your job done quickly.

Other times, security is more important than ease of coding—especially when you have to deal with the cold, hostile world at large. Though you may need to make your code accessible to the wilds of the Internet, you don't want to let just anyone do anything.

Modules and frameworks such as SOAP::Lite make it easy to provide web service access to plain old Perl objects. Here's one way to make them somewhat safer.

The Hack

First, decide what kinds of operations you need to support on your object. Take a standard web-enabled inventory system. You need to fetch an item, insert an item, update an item, and delete an item. Then identify the types of access: creating, reading, writing, and deleting.

You *could* maintain a list in code or a configuration file somewhere mapping all the access controls to all the methods of the objects in your system. That would be silly, though; this is Perl! Instead, consider using a subroutine attribute [Hack #45].

```perl
package Proxy::AccessControl;

use strict;
use warnings;

use Attribute::Handlers;

my %perms;

sub UNIVERSAL::perms
{
    my ($package, $symbol, $referent, $attr, $data) = @_;
    my $method                             = *{ $symbol }{NAME};

    for my $permission (split(/\s+/, $data))
    {
        push @{ $perms{ $package }{ $method } }, $permission;
    }
}

sub dispatch
{
    my ($user, $class, $method, @args) = @_;

    return unless $perms{ $class }{ $method } and $class->can( $method );

    for my $perm (@{ $perms{ $class }{ $method } })
    {
        die "Need permission '$perm\n'" unless $user->has_permission( $perm );
    }
}
```

```
        $class->$method( @args );
    }

    1;
```

Declaring permissions is easy:

```
package Inventory;

use Proxy::AccessControl;

sub insert :perms( 'create' )
{
    my ($self, $attributes) = @_;
    # ...
}

sub delete :perms( 'delete' )
{
    my ($self, $id) = @_;
    # ...
}

sub update :perms( 'write' )
{
    my ($self, $id, $attributes) = @_;
    # ...
}

sub fetch :perms( 'read' )
{
    my ($self, $id) = @_;
    # ...
}
```

You can also mix and match permissions:

```
sub clone :perms( 'read create' )
{
    my ($self, $id, $attributes) = @_;
    # ...
}
```

Proxy::AccessControl provides an attribute handler perms that registers a space-separated list of permissions for each marked method. It also provides a dispatch( ) method—the barrier point into the system between the controller routing incoming requests and the actual Perl objects handling the requests.

The only thing left to do (besides actually writing the business logic code) is to make your controller run everything through Proxy::AccessControl::dispatch( ). This function takes three parameters. The first is a $user object that represents the access capabilities of the external user somehow. (Your code needs to allow authentication and creation of this object.) The $class and $method parameters identify the proper class and method to call, if the user has permission to do so.

Hacking the Hack

dispatch() is a coarsely-grained approach to proxying. Perhaps creating dedicated proxies that speak web services or remote object protocols natively would be useful. Behind the scenes, they could take only one extra parameter (the user object) and, for each proxied method, provide their own implementation that performs the access checks before delegating or denying the request as necessary.

There's no reason to limit access control to permissions alone, either. You could control access to objects based on the number of concurrent accesses, the phase of the moon, the remote operating system, the time of day, or whatever mechanism you desire. Anything you can put in an attribute's data is fair game.

HACK Make Your Objects Truly Polymorphic
#49 Build classes based on what they do, not how they inherit.

Many tutorials and books declare confidently that inheritance is a central feature of object-oriented programming.

They're wrong.

Polymorphism is much, much more important. It matters that when you call log() on an object that knows how to log its internal state it does so, not that it inherits from some abstract Logger class somewhere or that it calculates a natural log. Perl 6 encourages this type of design with roles. In Perl 5, you can either build it yourself or use Class::Trait to decompose complex operations into natural, named groups of methods.

That sounds awfully abstract—but if you have a complex problem you *can* decompose appropriately, you can write just a little bit of code and accomplish quite a bit.

The Hack

Imagine that you're building an application with properly abstracted model, view, and controller. You have multiple output types—standard XHTML, cut-down-XHTML for mobile devices, and Ajax or JSON output for RESTful web services and user interface goodness.

Every possible view has a corresponding view class. So far the design makes sense. Yet as your code handles an incoming request and decides what to do with it, how do you decide which view to use? Worse, if you have multiple views, how do you build the appropriate classes without going crazy for all of the combinations?

If you cheat a little bit and declare your views as traits, you can apply them to the model objects and render the data appropriately.

Here's an example model from which the concrete Uncle and Nephew classes both inherit:

```perl
package Model;

sub new
{
    my ($class, %args) = @_;
    bless \%args, $class;
}

sub get_data
{
    my $self = shift;
    my %data = map { $_ => $self->{$_} } qw( name occupation age );
    return \%data;
}

1;
```

The views are pretty simple, too:

```perl
package View;

use Class::Trait 'base';

package TextView;

use base 'View';

sub render
{
    my $self = shift;
    printf( "My name is %s.  I am an %s and I am %d years old.\n",
        @{ $self->get_data() }{qw( name occupation age )} );
}

package YAMLView;

use YAML;
use base 'View';

sub render
{
```

```
    my $self = shift;
    print Dump $self->get_data( );
}

1;
```

The text view displays a nicely formatted English string, while the YAML view spits out a serialized version of the data structure. Now all the controller class has to do is to create the appropriate model object and apply the appropriate view to it before calling render( ):

```
# use model and view classes

# create the appropriate model objects
my $uncle  = Uncle->new(
    name => 'Bob', occupation => 'Uncle', age => 50
);
my $nephew = Nephew->new(
    name => 'Jacob', occupation => 'Agent of Chaos', age => 3
);

# apply the appropriate views
Class::Trait->apply( $uncle,  'TextView' );
Class::Trait->apply( $nephew, 'YAMLView' );

# display the results
$uncle->render( );
$nephew->render( );
```

Running the Hack

The code produces:

```
My name is Bob.  I am an Uncle and I am 50 years old.
---
age: 3
name: Jacob
occupation: Agent of Chaos
```

Hacking the Hack

If that were all that traits and roles are, that would still be useful. There's more though! Class::Trait also provides a does( ) method which you can use to query the capabilities of an object. If you could possibly receive an object that already has a built-in view (a debugging model, for example), call does to see if it does already do a view:

```
Class::Trait->apply( $uncle, $view_type ) unless $uncle->does( 'View' );
```

You also don't have to have your traits inherit from a base trait. If all of the code that uses objects and classes with traits checks does( ) instead of Perl's isa( ) method, you can have traits that do the right thing without having any relationship, code- or inheritance-wise, with any other traits.

This is especially useful for working with proxied, logged, or tested models and views.

HACK #50 Autogenerate Your Accessors

Stop writing accessor methods by hand.

One of the Perl virtues is laziness. This doesn't mean not doing your work, it means doing your work with as little effort as possible. When you find yourself typing the same code over and over again, stop! Make the computer do the work.

Method accessors/mutators (getters/setters) are a case in point. Here's a simple object-oriented module:

```perl
package My::Customer;

use strict;
use warnings;

sub new { bless {}, shift }

sub first_name
{
    my $self         = shift;
    return $self->{first_name} unless @_;
    $self->{first_name} = shift;
    return $self;
}

sub last_name
{
    my $self         = shift;
    return $self->{last_name} unless @_;
    $self->{last_name} = shift;
    return $self;
}

sub full_name
{
    my $self = shift;
    return join ' ', $self->first_name( ), $self->last_name( );
}

1;
```

and a small program to use it:

```perl
my $cust = My::Customer->new( );
$cust->first_name( 'John' );
```

```
$cust->last_name( 'Public' );
print $cust->full_name( );
```

That prints John Public.

Of course, if this is really is a customer object, it needs to do more. You might need to set a customer's credit rating, the identity of a primary sales-person, and so on.

As you can see, the first_name and last_name methods are effectively dupli-cates of one another. New accessors are likely to be the very similar. Can you automate this?

The Hack

There are many modules on the CPAN which handle this, all in slightly dif-ferent flavors. Here are two—one of the most widespread and one of the least constraining.

Class::MethodMaker. One of the oldest such module is Class::MethodMaker, originally released in 1996. It is very feature rich, and although the docu-mentation can seem a bit daunting, the module itself is very easy to use. To convert the My::Customer code, write:

```
package My::Customer;

use strict;
use warnings;

use Class::MethodMaker[
    new    => [qw( new )],
    scalar => [qw( first_name last_name )],],];

sub full_name
{
    my $self = shift;
    return join ' ', $self->first_name( ), $self->last_name( );
}
```

The constructor is very straightforward, but what's up with first_name and last_name? The arguments passed to Class::MethodMaker cause it to create two getter/setters which contain scalar values. However, even though this code appears to behave identically, it's actually much more powerful.

Do you want to check that no one ever set an object's first_name, as opposed to having set it to an undefined value?

```
print $cust->first_name_isset( ) ? 'true' : 'false';
```

Even if you set first_name to undef, first_name_isset( ) will return true. Of course, sometimes you will want to be unset, even after you've set it. That works, too:

```
$cust->first_name( 'Ozymandias' );
print $cust->first_name_isset( ) ? 'true' : 'false'; # true
$cust->first_name_reset( );
print $cust->first_name_isset( ) ? 'true' : 'false'; # false
```

Class::BuildMethods. Class::MethodMaker also has built-in support for arrays, hashes, and many other useful features. However, it requires you use a blessed hash for your objects. In fact, most of the accessor builder modules on the CPAN make assumptions about your object's internals. One exception to this is Class::BuildMethods.

Class::BuildMethods allows you to build accessors for your class regardless of whether it's a blessed hash, arrayref, regular expression, or whatever. It does this by borrowing a trick from inside out objects **[Hack #43]**. Typical code looks like:

```
package My::Customer;

use strict;
use warnings;

use Class::BuildMethods qw(
  first_name
  last_name
);

# Note that you can use an array reference, if you prefer
sub new { bless [ ], shift }

sub full_name
{
    my $self = shift;
    return join ' ', $self->first_name( ), $self->last_name( );
}

1;
```

Use this class just like any other. Internally it indexes the accessor values by the address of the object. It handles object destruction for you by default, but allows you to handle this manually if you need special behavior on DESTROY (such as releasing locks).

Class::BuildMethods is very simple, by design. Like most other accessor generators, it provides some convenience features, but only in the form of default values and data validation:

```
use Class::BuildMethods
  'name',
```

```
gender => { default  => 'male' },
age     => { validate => sub
{
    my ($self, $age) = @_;
    carp 'You can''t enlist if you''re a minor'
        if ( $age < 18 && ! $self->is_emancipated() );
}};
```

With this code, gender() will return male unless you set it to some other value. age() shows how to provide flexible validation. Because the validate() method points to a subroutine reference rather than providing special validation handlers, the author's assumptions of how you should validate your code don't constrain you.

Class::BuildMethods always assumes that a setter takes a single value, so you must pass references for arrays and hashes. It also does not provide class methods (a.k.a. static methods). These limitations may mean this code doesn't fit your needs, but this module was designed to be simple. You can read and understand the docs in one sitting.

Running the Hack

Accessor generation, when it fits your needs, can remove a tremendous amount of grunt work. This is hacking your brain. As a Perl programmer, true laziness means that you waste less time on the fiddly bits so you can spend more time worrying about the hard stuff.

## CHAPTER SIX

Debugging
Hacks 51–59

Not all programs work the first time. Even if you use test-driven development and know exactly what you need to write and how to write it, you will eventually encounter code that you don't understand and which doesn't quite work right. One frequent (and frequently bad) problem-solving technique is voodoo programming, where you change a line or character here and there, hoping to stumble upon the correct incantation.

You can do better! Mastering a few Perl tricks and understanding a few tips can help you wrestle unwieldy code into submission. Amaze your coworkers. Save precious time. Find and fix failures faster! Here's how.

HACK
#51
Find Compilation Errors Fast
Trace problem code as quickly as possible.

As helpful as Perl is, sometimes a missing semicolon, parenthesis, or closing quotation mark send it into a morass of confusion. Error messages clutter your logs or your console window and, try as hard as you might, you can't see what's not there or what's just a little bit wrong.

When trouble strikes, try a simple technique to zoom in on the error as quickly as possible.

The Hack

When your program really goes kablooey, the best thing to do is not to let Perl try to run it, even through your test programs. If things are going that badly wrong, take a tip from the Haskell world and convince yourself that if it at least compiles, it has to be fairly okay.* Just make it compile already!

---

* I kid because I like.

Go to the command line and tell Perl to compile the program with warnings and then stop. If your program is *what_went_wrong.pl*, use:

```
$ perl -wc what_went_wrong.pl
```

If there's no error, Perl will report a happy okay message. Great! Go on to making your tests pass. Otherwise, grab the first error message and figure out how to solve it.

Binary searching for bugs. What if that error message makes no sense? Perl does its best to figure out the offending line, but because of the flexible syntax that allows you to span multiple lines and use postfix conditional expressions, sometimes the best it can say is "something's wrong". In that case, narrow down your search time considerably with a binary search.

Pick a place somewhere in the middle of the file, preferably between subroutines or methods. Add the __END__ token at the start of a line. Effectively this turns the rest of the code into data, so Perl will ignore it. Run perl -wc again. If the error message occurs, the error is in the first half of the file. If the error disappears, the error is in the second half of the file. Move the __END__ token appropriately halfway between whichever end of the file has the error and your current position and try again.

Sometimes you can't move the token without breaking up a block, which definitely causes compilation errors. In that case, use a pair of =cut POD directives to comment out the offending code. Within a handful of iterations, you'll zero in on the problem and you should have an easier time deciding *how* to fix it.

Hacking the Hack

This technique also works decently for figuring out where an error occurs, especially if you don't have logging or tracing statements in the code. Instead of commenting out code selectively, dump appropriate data with YAML or another serialization module at appropriate places to narrow down the error.

This approach often works, but it can fail when you do odd things, such as using a source filter. Beware.

HACK #52   Make Invisible Characters Apparent
See what your variables really contain.

Perl has a handful of good debugging techniques. For example, you can fire up the debugger [Hack #59] or write test cases [Hack #53]. If you're just experimenting, or need a quick-and-dirty answer right now, sometimes the easiest technique is to add a few print( ) statements here and there.

This has its drawbacks, though, especially when the printed output *looks* correct but obviously isn't. Before you flip through the debugger documentation and rejig your debugging statements into test cases, consider a few tricks to make the invisible differences that your computer sees visible to you too. (Then make your test cases, use the debugger, and smarten your comments.)

Bracket Your Variables

A very common mistake is to forget to chomp( ) data read from external sources. Suppose that you're processing a list of files read from another file:

```
while (<$file_list>)
{
    warn "Processing $_";
    next unless -e $_;
    process_file( $_ );
}
```

All of the files *look* correct in the warn( ) output, but the process_file( ) code never occurs.

 warn( ) is better than print( ) because it goes to STDERR by default, which makes it redirectable separately.

Change the debugging line to make the filename more visible:

```
while (<$file_list>)
{
    warn "Processing '$_'";
    next unless -e $_;
    process_file( $_ );
}
```

Adding single quotes (or any other visible character) around the filename will likely reveal that all of the filenames within the loop have newlines at the end (or whatever the current input record separator, $/, contains). The solution is obvious:

```
while (<$file_list>)
{
    chomp;
    next unless -e $_;
    process_file( $_ );
}
```

Bracket Interpolated Lists

The previous technique only works well on scalar variables. Lists and arrays are more tricky. Fortunately, the special punctuation variable $" controls the separator used when interpolating a list into a string.

Suppose that you're writing a ranking system for a table-tennis league. You've come to the end of the program and you want to display the top ten players:

```
my @ranked;

for my $rank ( 1 .. 10 )
{
    $ranked[$rank] = get_player_by_rank( $rank );
}
```

Of course, players may tie—leaving two players at the third rank and no players at the fourth rank. The naïve approach of assuming the array contains exactly ten entries may fail, especially if get_player_by_rank( ) always only returns a single player or potentially returns an array reference of multiple players.

Printing the array may be no help:

```
for my $rank ( 1 .. 10 )
{
    $ranked[$rank] = get_player_by_rank( $rank );
}

warn "Ranks: [@ranked]\n";
```

Everything interpolates into a single string, leaving you to count to see which is missing.

Instead, set $" to a nice, visible string:

```
local $" = '] [';
warn "Ranks: [@ranked]\n";
```

This puts the delimiters between the entries, making it much easier to see which slot is empty.

> If only you could override stringification on that particular array and print the index as well as the element at that index …roll on, Perl 6!

Serialize Your Data

If this is too much for you to handle manually, bring in the big guns of a serialization module to do your debugging for you. Data::Dumper has enjoyed a long reign as a nice debugging aid, but YAML provides even more readability and conciseness. To see a nested data structure (or even a scalar, array, or hash without having to worry about the right delimiters), use the Dump( ) function:

```
my $user = User->load( id => 54272 );
warn Dump( $user );
```

This prints a nice, compact representation of the data in the $user object without the excessive indentation and indirection that Data::Dumper can often provide.

Another good, if complex option, is using Devel::Peek to see exactly what Perl thinks of your variable. When you need it, you really need it. The rest of the time, take a breath, and then spend two minutes writing the test case.

HACK #53 Debug with Test Cases

Make exploratory code reusable.

Many programmers have subdirectories full of little test snippets; it's common to write a few programs to explore a feature of the language or a new library. It's also common to do this with false laziness, eyeballing output and tweaking an idea here or there.

Usually that's okay, but occasionally you *know* you wrote code to explore something you need to know *right now*—if only you could find it and decipher what you were thinking.

If you know how to write test cases with Perl's standard testing tools, you can end this madness and make even your experiments reusable and maintainable.

The Hack

Suppose you've just learned that Perl's default sorting algorithm changed from unstable to stable for Perl 5.8.0. The Internet reveals that, with a stable sorting algorithm, elements that have the same position in the sorting order will retain the positions relative to each other that they had in the input.

Writing test code. What does that really mean in practice? It's time to write some code:

```
my @elements =
(
    [ 2, 2 ], [ 2, 1 ], [ 2, 0 ],
    [ 1, 0 ], [ 1, 1 ], [ 1, 2 ],
);

my @sorted   = sort { $a->[0] <=> $b->[0] } @elements;
```

```
    local $"    = ', ';
    print "[ @$_ ]\n" for @sorted;
```

A stable sorting algorithm should produce the output:

```
    [ 1, 0 ]
    [ 1, 1 ]
    [ 1, 2 ]
    [ 2, 2 ]
    [ 2, 1 ]
    [ 2, 0 ]
```

Because the algorithm sorts only on the first element, all of the ones should come before the twos. Because the algorithm is stable, all of the second values of the ones should increase and all of the second values of the twos should decrease.

From test code to test cases. Of course, six months later that code may be somewhat impenetrable. It has decent variable names, but it's quick and dirty and likely uncommented. What does it prove? Why? Even worse, the first time it ran it has no debugging information—it's easy to misread the output when flipping back and forth between it and the code to recreate the algorithm in your head.

That's the point of test cases: removing tedium and making expectations clear, unambiguous, and automatable. Here's the same file rewritten as executable tests:

```
    use Test::More tests => 4;

    my @elements =
    (
        [ 2, 2 ], [ 2, 1 ], [ 2, 0 ],
        [ 1, 0 ], [ 1, 1 ], [ 1, 2 ],
    );
    my @sorted   = sort { $a->[0] <=> $b->[0] } @elements;

    is( $sorted[0][0], 1, 'numeric sort should put 1 before 2'  );
    is( $sorted[0][1], 0, '... keeping stability of original list' );
    is( $sorted[2][1], 2, '... through all elements'            );
    is( $sorted[3][1], 2, '... not accidentally sorting them'    );
```

With a little more work up front, your expectations are clearer. If there's a failure, you see where it fails without having to trace the algorithm in your head again. You can also see which part of your assumptions (or code) failed in detail as fine-grained as you care to test. Even better, you can add more tests to check further behavior, such as mingling the definition of the ones and twos further.

In case an upgrade changes the behavior of your production code, you can also run the test cases to narrow down the problem.

Hacking the Hack

Ideally, someone's already tested this sort of code—the Perl 5 porters. If you have access to the source code of Perl (in this case) or the library you're testing, you can skim the test suite for examples to borrow and modify or learn from outright. In this case, code in *t/op/sort.t* tests Perl's stable sort. Even just skimming the test descriptions can reveal a lot of information about the ideas behind the implementation.

Debug with Comments

Let your documentation help you remove bugs.

There are two types of people who debug code: those who fire up Perl's built-in debugger and those who sprinkle print statements through their code. If you're in the second group, you probably know that one big problem with debugging by hand is that, once you remove the bugs, you have to go through and remove all the debugging statements as well.

What if you could safely leave them in the code? After all, if you needed them once, you'll probably need them again, when the next bug appears.

The Hack

"Something left in the code, but ignored" is pretty much the definition of a comment, so it's no surprise that you can use comments to turn off debugging statements. There's a much more interesting alternative, however: using comments to turn *on* debugging statements. The Smart::Comments CPAN module does just that: it turns comments *into* debugging statements.

Displaying variables. When you use Smart::Comments, any subsequent comment with three or more leading #s becomes a debugging statement and prints whatever the comment says to STDERR. For example, if you can't work out why your @play_calls variable is getting more elements than you expected:

```
my $call      = "26, 17, 22, hut!";
my @play_calls = split /\s*,?\s*/, $call;
```

insert some smart comments to report what's happening:

```
# make '###' magical...
use Smart::Comments;

my $call      = "26, 17, 22, hut!";

### $call

my @play_calls = split /\s*,?\s*/, $call;

### @play_calls
```

When you run that code, Smart::Comments will find the triple-# comments and print out whatever they contain:

```
$ perl play_book.pl

### $call: '26, 17, 22, hut!'

### @play_calls: [
###                    '2',
###                    '6',
###                    '1',
###                    '7',
###                    '2',
###                    '2',
###                    'h',
###                    'u',
###                    't',
###                    '!'
###                 ]

$
```

Immediately you can see that the split is splitting your text at every single character (because your splitting pattern, /\s*,?\s*/, matches an empty string so split splits everywhere).

The real smartness comes in, however, when you write more structured comments:

```
use Smart::Comments;

my $call      = "26, 17, 22, hut!";

### input: $call

my @play_calls = split /\s*,?\s*/, $call;

### split to: @play_calls
```

which produces the output:

```
$ perl play_book.pl

### input: '26, 17, 22, hut!'

### split to: [
###                    '2',
###                    '6',
###                    '1',
###                    '7',
###                    '2',
###                    '2',
###                    'h',
###                    'u',
###                    't',
```

```
###             '!'
###          ]

$
```

Making Assertions. Even more useful, the module also allows you to write comments that act like assertions:

```
use Smart::Comments;

my $call      = "26, 17, 22, hut!";

my @play_calls = split /\s*,?\s*/, $call;

#### require: @play_calls == 4
```

Assertion comments like this only produce a report (and an exception!) if the assertion fails. In that case, the smartness really shows through, because the smart comments not only report the failure, but they also automatically report all the variables used in the test, so you can see *why* the assertion failed:

```
$ perl play_book_with_assertion.pl

### @play_calls == 4 was not true at play_book_with_assertion.pl line 7.
###     @play_calls was: [
###                        '2',
###                        '6',
###                        '1',
###                        '7',
###                        '2',
###                        '2',
###                        'h',
###                        'u',
###                        't',
###                        '!'
###                      ]

$
```

Best of all, when you finish debugging, you can switch off all the debugging statements simply by removing—or just commenting out—the use Smart:: Comments statement:

```
# use Smart::Comments;

my $call      = "26, 17, 22, hut!";

### input: $call

my @play_calls = split /\s*,?\s*/, $call;

### split to: @play_calls
```

Because the code no longer loads the module, triple-# comments are no longer special. They remain ordinary comments, and Perl consequently ignores them:

```
$ perl play_book.pl

$
```

Configuring smartness levels. By the way, you might have noticed that the require: assertion in the third example used #### instead of ### as its comment introducer. Using differing numbers of #s allows you to be selective about turning smart comments on and off. If you load the module and explicitly tell it which comment introducers are smart, then it will only activate comments with those particular introducers. For example:

```
use Smart::Comments '####';   # Only ####... comments are "smart"
                              # Any ###... comments are ignored

my $call       = "26, 17, 22, hut!";

### $call

my @play_calls = split /\s*,?\s*/, $call;

### @play_calls

#### require: @play_calls == 4
```

This final example turns off the debugging statements, leaving only the assertion active.

If editing your source code to enable and disable Smart::Comments is too onerous, consider making a shell alias [Hack #4] to load the module and execute a named program. The appropriate command line to run a program with Smart::Comments enabled is:

```
$ perl -MSmart::Comments split_test.pl
```

To activate only specific comment introducers, as in the earlier example, write:

```
$ perl -MSmart::Comments="" split_test.pl
```

with the appropriate number of # characters in the quotes.

Show Source Code on Errors
#55 Don't guess which line is the problem—see it!

Debugging errors and warning messages isn't often fun. Instead, it can be tedious. Often even finding the problem takes too long.

Perl can reveal the line number of warnings and errors (with warn and die and the warnings pragma in effect); why can't it show the source code of the affected line?

The Hack

The code to do this is pretty easy, if unsubtle:

```
package SourceCarp;

use strict;
use warnings;

sub import
{
    my ($class, %args) = @_;

    $SIG{__DIE__}  = sub { report( shift, 2 ); exit } if $args{fatal};
    $SIG{__WARN__} = \&report                         if $args{warnings};
}

sub report
{
    my ($message, $level) = @_;
    $level                ||= 1;
    my ($filename, $line) = ( caller( $level - 1 ) )[1, 2];
    warn $message, show_source( $filename, $line );
}

sub show_source
{
    my ($filename, $line) = @_;
    return '' unless open( my $fh, $filename );

    my $start = $line - 2;
    my $end   = $line + 2;

    local $.;
    my @text;
    while (<$fh>)
    {
        next unless $. >= $start;
        last if     $. >  $end;
        my $highlight = $. == $line ? '*' : ' ';
        push @text, sprintf( "%s%04d: %s", $highlight, $., $_ );
    }

    return join( '', @text, "\n" );
}

1;
```

The magic here is in three places. report( ) looks at the call stack leading to its current position, extracting the name of the file and the line number of the calling code. It's possible to call this function directly with a message to display (and an optional level of calls to ignore).

show_source( ) simply reads the named file and returns a string containing two lines before and after the numbered line, if possible. It also highlights the specific line with an asterisk in the left column. Note the localization and use of the $. magic variable to count the current line in the file.

import( ) adds global handlers for warnings and exceptions, if requested from the calling module. The difference between the handlers is that when Perl issues a lexical warning, it doesn't affect the call stack in the same way that it does when it throws an exception.

Running the Hack

This short program shows all three ways of invoking SourceCarp:

```
#!/usr/bin/perl

use strict;
use warnings;

use lib 'lib';
use SourceCarp fatal => 1, warnings => 1;

# throw warning
open my $fh, '<', '/no/file';
print {$fh}...

# report from subroutine
report_with_level();

sub report_with_level
{
    SourceCarp::report( "report caller, not self\n", 2 );
}

# throw error
die "Oops!";
```

Hacking the Hack

There's no reason to limit your error and warning reporting to showing the file context around the calling line. caller( ) offers much more information, including the variables passed to each function in certain circumstances.* It's possible to provide and present this information in a much more useful manner.

Overriding the global __WARN__ and __DIE__ handlers is serious business as it can interfere with large programs. A more robust implementation of this hack might work nicely with Carp, not only because it is more widely compatible, but also because that module offers more features. Another possibility is to integrate this code somehow with Log::Log4perl.

HACK #56 Deparse Anonymous Functions

Inspect the code of anonymous subroutines.

Perl makes it really easy to generate anonymous subroutines on the fly. It's very handy when you need a bunch of oh-so similar behaviors which merely differ on small points. Unfortunately, slinging a bunch of anonymous subroutines around quickly becomes a headache when things go awry.

When an anonymous sub isn't doing what you expect, how do you know what it is? It's anonymous, fer cryin' out loud. Yet Perl knows what it is—and you can ask it.

The Hack

Suppose that you've written a simple filter subroutine which returns all of the lines from a file handle that match your filter criteria.

```perl
sub filter
{
    my ($filter) = @_;

    if ('Regexp' eq ref $filter)
    {
        return sub
        {
            my $fh = shift;
            return grep { /$filter/ } <$fh>;
        };
    }
    else
    {
        return sub
        {
            my $fh = shift;
            return grep { 0 <= index $_, $filter } <$fh>;
        };
    }
}
```

* See perldoc -f caller.

Using the subroutine is simple. Pass it a precompiled regex and it will return lines which match the regular expression. Pass it a string and it will return lines which contain that string as a substring.

Unfortunately, later on you wonder why the following code returns every line from the file handle instead of just the lines which contain a digit:

```
my $filter = filter(/\d/);
my @lines  = $filter->($file_handle);
```

Data::Dumper is of no use here:

```
use Data::Dumper;
print Dumper( $filter );
```

This results in:

```
$VAR1 = sub { "DUMMY" };
```

Running the Hack

Using the Data::Dump::Streamer serialization module allows you to see inside that subroutine:

```
use Data::Dump::Streamer;
Dump( $filter );
```

Now you can see the body of the subroutine more or less as Perl sees it.

```
my ($filter);
$filter = undef;
$CODE1 = sub {
          my $fh = shift @_;
          return grep({0 <= index($_, $filter);} <$fh>);
        };
```

From there, it's pretty apparent that Perl didn't recognize that you were trying to pass in a regular expression and the bug is trivial to fix:

```
my $filter = filter(qr/\d/);
my @lines  = $filter->($file_handle);
```

Hacking the Hack

Behind the scenes, Data::Dump::Streamer uses the core module B::Deparse. In essence it does the following:

```
use B::Deparse;
my $deparse = B::Deparse->new();
print $deparse->coderef2text($filter);
```

which outputs:

```
{
    my $fh = shift @_;
    return grep({0 <= index($_, $filter);} <$fh>);
}
```

The primary difference is that Data::Dump::Streamer also shows the values of any variables that the subroutine has closed over. See "Peek Inside Closures" [Hack #76] for more details. This technique is also good for displaying diagnostics when you eval code into existence or receive a subroutine reference as an argument and something goes wrong when you try to execute it.

The B::Deparse documentation gives more information about the arguments that you can pass to its constructor for even better control over the output.

HACK #57 Name Your Anonymous Subroutines

Trade a little anonymity for expressivity.

Despite the apparently oxymoronic name, "named anonymous subroutines" are an undocumented feature of Perl. Originally described by "ysth" on Perl Monks, these are a wonderful feature.

Suppose your program merrily runs along with a carefree attitude—but then dies an ugly death:

```
Denominator must not be zero! at anon_subs.pl line 11
    main::__ANON__(0) called at anon_subs.pl line 17
```

What the heck is main::__ANON__(0)? The answer may be somewhere in code such as:

```
use Carp;

sub divide_by
{
    my $numerator = shift;
    return sub
    {
        my $denominator = shift;
        croak "Denominator must not be zero!" unless $denominator;
        return $numerator / $denominator;
    };
}

my $seven_divided_by = divide_by(7);
my $answer           = $seven_divided_by->(0);
```

In this toy example, it's easy to see the problem. However, what if you're generating a ton of those divide_by subroutines and sending them all throughout your code? What if you have a bunch of subroutines all generating subroutines (for example, if you've breathed too deeply the heady fumes of Mark Jason Dominus' *Higher Order Perl* book)? Having a bunch of subroutines named __ANON__ is very difficult to debug.

> $seven_divided_by is effectively a *curried* version of divide_
> by( ). That is, it's a function that already has one of multiple
> arguments bound to it. There's a piece of random functional
> programming jargon to use to impress people.

The Hack

Creating an anonymous subroutine creates a glob named *__ANON__ in the
current package. When caller( ) and the rest of Perl's guts look for names
for anonymous subroutines, they look there. Using carp and croak will
quickly reveal this.

The solution is therefore to override this name temporarily. The easy way is
to have the parent subroutine name the anonymous one:

```
sub divide_by
{
    my $numerator = shift;
    my $name      = (caller(0))[3];
    return sub
    {
        local *__ANON__ = "__ANON__$name";
        my $denominator = shift;
        croak "Denominator must not be zero!" unless $denominator;
        return $numerator / $denominator;
    };
}
```

Running the program now produces the output:

```
Denominator must not be zero! at anon_subs.pl line 12
        __ANON__main::divide_by(0) called at anon_subs.pl line 18
```

Hacking the Hack

While that's better and it may fit your needs, it's not the most flexible solution. If you create several anonymous subroutines, they will all have the
same name. It's more powerful to name the anonymous subroutines by
passing the creator subroutine a name—or taking it from an argument, as
appropriate.

```
use Carp;

sub divide_by
{
    my ($name, $numerator) = @_;
    return sub
    {
        local *__ANON__ = "__ANON__$name";
        my $denominator = shift;
```

```
        croak "Denominator must not be zero!" unless $denominator;
        return $numerator / $denominator;
    };
}

my $three_divided_by = divide_by( 'divide_by_three', 3 );
my $answer           = $three_divided_by->(0);
```

The output looks like you expect:

```
Denominator must not be zero! at anon_subs.pl line 12
    __ANON__main::divide_by_three(0) called at anon_subs.pl line 18
```

Note that this code as written does *not* work under the debugger. The solution is to disable a debugger flag *before* Perl compiles the anonymous subroutines:

```
        my $old_p;
        BEGIN { $old_p = $^P; $^P &= ~0x200; }

        sub divide_by
        {
            # ...
        }

        BEGIN { $^P = $old_p; }
```

See perldoc perlvar for an explanation of $^P.

HACK #58 Find a Subroutine's Source

Find out where subroutines come from.

There are few things more annoying than finding a misbehaving subroutine and not being able to figure out where it came from. Some modules export subroutines automatically. Sometimes someone will have imported absolutely everything by using the :all tag in the use line.

Whatever the cause, the first step in fixing an errant subroutine is locating it.

The Hack

You *could* muck around in your symbol table [Hack #72] and use introspection to find the CV and check its STASH information [Hack #78], but Rafael Garcia-Suarez's Sub::Identify does this for you (using the invaluable B backend module internally).

The B module is uncommon, but very handy when necessary. It effectively allows you to explore Perl's inner workings. In this example, svref_2object() takes a code reference and returns an object blessed into the B::CV class. You won't actually find this class declared anywhere, but it's part of the B module internally.

Running the Hack

Just use the stash_name() function:

```
package My::Package;

use Sub::Identify ':all';
use HTML::Entities 'encode_entities';
print stash_name( \&encode_entities );
```

Run this code; it will print HTML::Entities. Even if another module has re-exported &encode_entities into your namespace, Sub::Identify will still report HTML::Entities as the source of the subroutine.

For descriptions of the class hierarchy of these objects and the methods that you can call on them, see OVERVIEW OF CLASSES and SV-RELATED CLASSES in perldoc B. Unfortunately, much of the documentation is rather sparse and reading the source code of this module and the header files of the various Perl data structures, as well as pestering P5P with questions, is often the best way to figure out what you're doing. See also Chapter 8.

HACK #59 Customize the Debugger
Write your own debugger commands.

Adding a command to the debugger (or modifying an existing one) by editing the debugger is a difficult job; to do this, you have to patch the debugger source in *perl5db.pl* and replace it. Sometimes you don't have the necessary privileges to do this, and given the complexity of the debugger, it's a difficult job—especially because you can't debug the debugger.

Yet modifying your tools the way you want them is important. Fortunately, Devel::Command module makes this much simpler. With Devel::Command, you write simple modules to define your commands, and the debugger finds them and loads them for you automatically.

The Hack

Writing a command is simple. There are only a few things to remember:

Input and output

The debugger reads input from DB::IN and writes to DB::OUT. If you want your command to work just like a native debugger command, you need to use these filehandles for input and output. Generally, you'll only need to print to DB::OUT.

Debugger context versus program context

To evaluate an expression in the context of the program that's being debugged (for example, you want to pass the value of a variable in the program to your command), call the *subroutine* &eval on it. To evaluate something in the *debugger's* context, use plain old eval.

A "hello, world" command looks like:

```
package Devel::Command::HelloWorld;
use base 'Devel::Command';

sub command
{
    print DB::OUT "Hello world!\n";
    1;
}

1;
```

Devel::Command defaults to using the command( ) as the actual command code. Run this by putting it somewhere in your @INC and then start the debugger:

```
flatbox ~ $ perl -deO
Default die handler restored.
Patching with Devel::Command::DBSub::DB_5_8

Loading DB routines from perl5db.pl version 1.07
Editor support available.

Enter h or `h h' for help, or `man perldebug' for more help.

main::(-e:1):    0
  DB<1> cmds
cmds
helloworld
  DB<2> helloworld
Hello world!
  DB<3> q
flatbox ~ $
```

The message that begins Patching with... lets you know that Devel:: Command has successfully activated. cmds lists the commands and typing helloworld runs your command.

Overriding a debugger command. Overriding a command is simple: just return true if your command routine wants to handle the command or false if you don't.

```
package Devel::Command::X;

use base 'Devel::Command';

sub command
{
    my ($cmd) = @_;

    if ($cmd =~ /x marks/)
    {
        print DB::OUT "Arrrrr....\n";
        return 1;
    }
    else
    {
        return 0;
    }
}

1;
```

Now the x command knows to be piratical when it sees a command beginning with x marks.

```
flatbox ~ $ perl -de0
Default die handler restored.
Patching with Devel::Command::DBSub::DB_5_8

Loading DB routines from perl5db.pl version 1.07
Editor support available.

Enter h or `h h' for help, or `man perldebug' for more help.

main::(-e:1):    0
  DB<1> $x = [1,2,3]

  DB<2> x $x
0  ARRAY(0x804e2f4)
    0  1
    1  2
    2  3
  DB<3> x marks the spot
Arrrrr....
  DB<4> q
flatbox ~ $
```

Running the Hack

Create a module in the `Devel::Command::` namespace. Install `Devel::Command` from CPAN, and then tell the debugger to load it by adding one line to your debugger initialization file, *.perldb* (or *perldb.ini*, for non-Unix systems):

```
use Devel::Command;
```

That's it. This makes the debugger automatically search `@INC` for modules in the `Devel::Command::` namespace, load them, and install them as commands. By default, it picks a name for the command by downcasing the last namespace qualifier (so, for example, `Devel::Command::My::DoStuff` ends up as the `dostuff` command).

`Devel::Command` also installs its own `cmds` command, which lists all commands that it found and loaded, and dynamically patches the debugger's command processing subroutine with a modified version which knows how to find the commands installed by `Devel::Command`.

Hacking the Hack

To develop tests while using the debugger, try the `Devel::Command::Tdump` module on CPAN. This module loads `Test::More` for you and lets you actually write tests and save them from the debugger.

If you want to see drawings of your data structure in the debugger, `Devel::Command::Viz` and the `graphviz` package will let you do it. Install those, then use the `viz` command on a variable:

```
flatbox ~ $ perl5.8.5 -de0
Patching with Devel::Command::DBSub::DB_5_8_5

Loading DB routines from perl5db.pl version 1.27
Editor support available.

Enter h or `h h' for help, or `man perldebug' for more help.

main::(-e:1):    0
  DB<1> use WWW::Mechanize

  DB<2> $m = WWW::Mechanize->new( )

  DB<3> viz $m
```

You'll see a graphical depiction of the `WWW::Mechanize` object in a pop-up window.

## CHAPTER SEVEN

Developer Tricks
Hacks 60–69

Surviving software development and enjoying it are two very different things. Do you know what your code is doing? Can you look at any piece and know where it belongs and what it means? Do you trust your code? Do you trust your coworkers? What can you do to take back control of your projects, code-wise?

Obviously reducing the friction of writing code will make your life easier, but what about the friction of *designing* and *maintaining* code? Comprehensive testing and collective code standards help. Here are a few ideas to bring up in your next developer meeting that will make you a hero.

HACK
#60
Rebuild Your Distributions

Rebuild your distributions with ease.

If you work with Perl modules built in the standard CPAN format (and you should, as the many available tools make your life easier this way), you generally will have a *Makefile.PL* or *Build.PL* file, *lib/* and *t/* directories, manifests, and so on. If the module uses ExtUtils::MakeMaker, you change your tests, update the module and rebuild the distribution again with a command such as:

```
$ make realclean && perl Makefile.PL && make && make test
```

Modules that use Module::Build require instead:

```
$ ./Build realclean && perl Build.PL && perl ./Build && perl ./Build test
```

It gets annoying typing this over and over again. Worse, if you do this for patches you send to others, you might forget and assume you have a *Makefile* when using Module::Build or a *Build* file when using ExtUtils::MakeMaker. This is tiresome.

The Hack

Instead, put this *rebuild* script in your path and set the appropriate permissions:

```
#!/bin/bash

if [ -f Build.PL ]; then
    makeprog=Build
    makecommand="perl ./Build"
elif [ -f Makefile.PL ]; then
    makeprog=Makefile
    makecommand=make
else
    echo Nothing to reload!
    exit 1
fi

if [ -f $makeprog ]; then
    $makecommand realclean
fi
perl $makeprog.PL && $makecommand && $makecommand test
```

Running the Hack

Whenever you want to rebuild your project, type `rebuild` at the command line in the parent directory of the project and don't worry about whether you're using `Module::Build` or `ExtUtils::MakeMaker`.

Hacking the Hack

If you really want to get carried away, bash scripts put their command line arguments in variables named $1, $2, and so on. It's trivial to add extra commands to build your distribution, your manifest, or whatever else you like:

```
if [ "$1" = dist ]; then
    $makecommand dist
fi
```

HACK #61 Test with Specifications

Let the computer write your tests.

Writing tests is a great way to gain confidence in your code. Each test you write makes a tiny claim about what your code ought to do. When it passes, you have clear evidence to support the claim. If you write enough tests to make a cohesive suite, the tiny claims within the suite combine to imply a general claim that your code works properly.

There are times, however, when writing a suite of tests is the hard way to make a general claim. Sometimes, the claim you want to make seems so simple, yet the tests you have to write seem so voluminous. For these times, it would be nice to be able to turn the process around. Instead of writing tests to make a claim, why not make the claim outright and let the computer write the tests for you? That's the idea behind specification-based testing. The Test::LectroTest family of modules brings this idea to Perl.

The Hack

To make claims about your code, you define *properties* that say that your code must behave in particular ways for a general spectrum of conditions. Then LectroTest automatically gathers evidence to support or refute your claims by executing large, random test suites that it generates on the fly. When it finishes, it prints the results in standard TAP format, just as the other Perl testing tools do.

Suppose you need to test Perl's sqrt function, which you expect to compute the square root of its argument. The first step is to figure out what sqrt ought to do. From your school days, you recall that the square root of a number x is the number that when multiplied by itself (that is, *squared*) gives you back x. For example, the square root of 9 is 3 because 3 times 3 is 9.

The square root function undoes the effect of squaring. You could consider this the defining property of the function. Putting it more formally, you might say: "For all numbers x, the square root of $x \times x$ should equal x." To test this claim, all you need to do is restate it as a LectroTest property:

```
# loads and activates LectroTest
use Test::LectroTest;

Property
{
    ##[ x <- Float ]##              # first  part
    sqrt( $x * $x ) == $x;         # second part
}, name => "sqrt is inverse of square"; # third  part
```

This is a complete Perl program that you can run. It tests a single property, specified in three parts. The first part (in the funny brackets) specifies the domain over which the property's claim should hold. Read it as saying, "For all floating-point numbers x..."

LectroTest actually offers a tiny language for declaring more complex domains, but it's not necessary here.

The second part is a snippet of Perl code that checks the property's claim for a given value of x. If the claim holds, the code must return a true value; otherwise, it must return a false value. In this property, read the code as saying,

"...the square root of $x \times x$ should equal x." For convenience, LectroTest makes the variables mentioned in the first part of the property available in the second part as lexical variables—$x, here.

Because of the imperfections of floating-point arithmetic, a more robust way of testing this claim would be to check whether the difference between $x and sqrt($x * $x) is within an acceptably small range. For simplicity, however, I've used a straight equality test, which could result in a false negative test result.

The third part gives the property a name. It's optional but adds a lot of documentation value, so give your properties meaningful names.

Running the Hack

To test whether your claims hold, just execute the program that contains your properties. In this case, you have only one property, so the program's output might look like:

```
1..1
not ok 1 - 'sqrt is inverse of square' falsified in 3 attempts
# Counterexample:
# $x = "-1.61625080606365";
```

Here, LectroTest says that, for some value of x, it was able to prove your property's claim false. It provides the troublesome value of x as a counterexample that you can use to figure out what went wrong.

Refining your claims. In this case, what went wrong is that the property made an overly broad claim. The square root function only applies to non-negative numbers (ignore imaginary numbers for this hack), and yet the property made its claim about *all* floating-point numbers, which includes those less than zero.

This illustrates an important benefit of the specification-based approach to testing: because it forces you to make your claims explicit, it can reveal hidden assumptions and holes in your thinking. Now you must consider what sqrt *should* do when given a negative number. For Perl, it probably ought to result in an error, so you might revise your property:

```
# helper:  returns true if calling the given function
# results in an error; returns false otherwise

sub gives_error(&)
{
    ! eval { shift->() } and $@ ne "";
}
```

```
Property
{
    ##[ x <- Float ]##
    $x < 0 ? gives_error { sqrt( $x ) }
            : sqrt( $x * $x ) == $x
}, name => "sqrt is inverse of square and dies on negatives";
```

You also could make sqrt's split personality more obvious by writing two properties that together define its behavior:

```
Property
{
    ##[ x <- Float ]##
    $tcon->retry() if $x < 0;        # only test non-negatives
    sqrt( $x * $x ) == $x;
}, name => "sqrt is inverse of square";

Property
{
    ##[ x <- Float ]##
    $tcon->retry() unless $x < 0;  # only test negatives
    gives_error { sqrt( $x ) };
}, name => "sqrt of negative numbers gives error";
```

Calling $tcon->retry( ) tells LectroTest to retry a test case you don't like, starting over with a brand new, random case. Use this call in your properties to subject only sensible cases to your tests. In the first property, for instance, the conditional call to $tcon->retry( ) ensures that LectroTest subjects only non-negative values of x to the sqrt-is-the-inverse-of-squaring test.

The LectroTest-provided $tcon object lets you talk to the underlying test controller to do all sorts of interesting things. See the LectroTest documentation to learn more.

You now have two properties. The first claims, "For all non-negative floating-point numbers x, the square root of $x \times x$ should equal x." The second claims, "For all negative floating-point numbers x, attempting to take the square root of x should result in an error." With practice, it becomes easy to convert LectroTest property specifications into written claims and vice versa. These two claims seem to cover all of the bases, and so it's time to put them to the test.

Interpreting test output. When you run the two-property suite, you get the results:

```
1..2
ok 1 - 'sqrt is inverse of square' (1000 attempts)
ok 2 - 'sqrt of negative numbers gives error' (1000 attempts)
```

Good news! LectroTest subjected each claim to 1,000 random test cases and was unable to find any problems. Still, this happy outcome doesn't *prove* that sqrt works as expected. It merely gives you evidence to support that conclusion. Certainly, the evidence is persuasive—you would think that 2,000 tests ought to be enough to flush out any obvious problems—but it's important not to lose sight of the limitations of testing.

In light of the evidence, though, there is probably no need to test further. The existing results argue persuasively in favor of sqrt, and there's no reason to think there are special circumstances that might make the current degree of testing inadequate. The only corner case in sight is the negative-number case, and you have that covered. At this point, you can probably rest satisfied that sqrt does the right thing.

Taking advantage of specification-based testing. With the specification-based approach, a little testing code goes a long way. It only took about fifteen lines of code to test sqrt fairly rigorously.

Another strength of the approach is that the claims embodied in your testing code are easy to see—just read the properties. These claims are useful beyond their testing value, serving as formal documentation of what you expect your software to do.

Because of these strengths, specification-based tests make a great complement to hand-written tests. When one approach to testing seems difficult, the other is often easy, and combining the approaches makes many complicated testing problems easier. For this reason, you ought to have both approaches in your toolbox.

Specification-based testing is a deep and interesting topic, and this hack only scratches its surface. To learn more, including how to use it with more-traditional Perl testing tools, the documentation for Test::LectroTest is a good starting point.

HACK #62 Segregate Developer and User Tests

Run only the tests you need when you need them.

In general, the more tests you have for a system the better. In specific, the more tests you have, the more time it takes to test your code. In very specific, some tests are more valuable than others. You may reach 95% confidence by running a few test files (*user tests*) and that may be good enough for day-to-day operations. You may also have a few deeper tests (*developer tests*) that use external resources or take a long time to explore all of the potential possibilities for failure—and you don't necessarily want to make everyone run them all at once.

If your project uses Perl's standard module-building tools (at least, Module::
Build, which comes very highly recommended), you can segregate developer and user tests *very* easily, running the time-consuming tests only when
you need to, perhaps right before a release.

The Hack

To customize Module::Build's behavior, almost all you have to know is to
define your own subclass and override the appropriate ACTION_* method.
How about running only the user tests with the normal perl ./Build test
invocation and all tests with perl ./Build disttest?

It's helpful to skim the source of Module::Build::Base [Hack #2] when overriding an action. That's where you can learn that the next method to override is
find_test_files(). The ACTION_test() method calls this to figure out which
tests to run. Override the test finder method to filter out developer tests.
Easy!

Don't celebrate just yet, though: ACTION_disttest() launches another Perl
process to run *Build.PL* and, eventually, perl ./Build test. Because this is
another process, there's no easy way to set a flag or a Perl variable to tell the
second invocation of ACTION_test() to run all tests. Fortunately, you *can* set
an environment variable, perhaps PERL_RUN_ALL_TESTS, that both the parent
and child can see.

All that's left is to decide where the developer tests are; how about in *t/
developer/*.t*? That's enough to write a Module::Build subclass:

```
package Module::Build::FilterTests;

use base 'Module::Build';

use SUPER;
use File::Spec::Functions;

sub ACTION_disttest
{
    local $ENV{PERL_RUN_ALL_TESTS} = 1;
    super();
}

sub find_test_files
{
    my $self  = shift;
    my $tests = super();

    return $tests unless $ENV{PERL_RUN_ALL_TESTS};
```

```
    my $test_pattern = catfile(qw( t developer *.t ) );
    push @$tests, <$test_pattern>;
    return $tests;
}

1;
```

The SUPER module makes calling the parent implementations of overridden methods a little cleaner syntactically. The only other notable feature of the test is the use of the glob operator to find all tests in the *t/developer/* directory.

Running the Hack

In your own *Build.PL* file, load and instantiate a Module::Build::FilterTests object instead of a Module::Build object. Everything else should proceed as normal.

 The easiest way to distribute a custom Module::Build subclass is to distribute it by storing it in *build_lib/* or another directory and to use it from *Build.PL* with a use lib line.

```
$ perl Build.PL
Checking whether your kit is complete...
Looks good
Deleting Build
Removed previous script 'Build'
Creating new 'Build' script for 'SomeModule' version '1.28'
$ perl ./Build
$ perl ./Build test
... user tests run ...
```

To run the developer tests, either set the PERL_RUN_ALL_TESTS environment variable before running perl ./Build test or run the distribution tests with perl ./Build disttests.

Hacking the Hack

Could you do the same by checking for the presence of the environment variable in each test file? Absolutely—but consider that adding a new developer test is as easy as putting it in the *t/developer/* directory without adding any extra magic to the test file. Also you get the test and disttest targets to behave correctly almost for free.

You can further customize the tests, running specific subsets for different test targets. perl ./Build networktests could try to connect to a server, for example. See the Module::Build documentation for more information.

The author particularly recommends that CPAN authors who want to raise their Kwalitee scores skip the POD tests for non-developers.

In theory, you can achieve the same effect with ExtUtils::
MakeMaker. Yet every time the author spelunks into the module's documentation, or worse—code, he wakes up fully
clothed and shivering in the shower several hours later.

HACK #63 Run Tests Automatically

See what's broken right after you break it!

The idea behind test-driven development is that rapid feedback based on
comprehensive test coverage helps you write sane, clean code that never
regresses. Once you know *how* to write tests, the next step is getting sufficient feedback as soon as possible.

What if you could run your tests immediately after you write a file? That's
fast feedback that can help you see if you've broken anything. Best of all,
you don't have to switch from your most beloved editor!

The Hack

The heart of this hack is the onchange program:

```perl
#!/usr/bin/perl

# onchange file1 file2 ... fileN command

use strict;
use warnings;

use File::Find;
use Digest::MD5;

my $Command      = pop @ARGV;
my $Files        = [@ARGV];
my $Last_digest = '';

sub has_changed
{
    my $files = shift;
    my $ctx   = Digest::MD5->new( );

    find( sub { $ctx->add( $File::Find::name, ( stat($_) )[9] ) },
        grep { -e $_ } @$files );

    my $digest      = $ctx->digest( );
    my $has_changed = $digest ne $Last_digest;
    $Last_digest    = $digest;

    return $has_changed;
}
```

```
while (1)
{
    system( $Command ) if has_changed( $Files );
    sleep 1;
}
```

This takes a list of files or directories to monitor and a command to run when they change. Of course, using File::Find means that this processes directories recursively.

Running the Hack

For a Perl application that uses the standard CPAN module structure (modules in *lib/*, tests in *t/*, and either a *Makefile.PL* or *Build.PL* to control everything), running is easy. Open a new terminal, change to your build directory, and run the command:

```
$ onchange Build.PL lib t 'clear; ./Build test'
```

Then every time either a test or a module file changes such that its MD5 signature changes, onchange will rebuild the project and run its tests again.

Hacking the Hack

MD5 signatures aren't the best way to tell if a file has changed. Even changing whitespace can make files look different (though sometimes it can be significant). You could use PPI::Signature, at least on pure-Perl code, to examine files and see if there are any syntactically significant changes.

You don't have to run *all* of the tests every time a module changes; it might be sufficient to run the user tests and the module-specific unit tests—but onchange needs to change to make this happen. If you had some way of correlating module files to their tests, you could even do this automatically.

 HACK **See Test Failure Diagnostics—in Color!**
#64 Highlight the unexpected.

If you follow good development practices and write comprehensive unit tests for your programs, you'll be able to develop faster and more reliably. You'll also eventually run into the problem of too many successes hiding the failures—that is, if you keep your tests always succeeding, you only need to know about the tests that fail.

Why not make them stand out?

Perl's standard testing harness, Test::Harness is actually a nice wrapper around Test::Harness::Straps, which is a parser for the TAP format that standard tests follow. If and when the report that Test::Harness writes isn't sufficient, use Test::Harness::Straps to write your own.

The Hack

There are two barriers to this approach. First, the default behavior of Perl's standard testing tools is to write diagnostic output to STDERR. Test:: Harness doesn't capture this. Second, Test::Harness goes to a bit of trouble to set up the appropriate command line paths to run tests appropriately.

The first problem is tractable, at least if you can use a module such as IPC:: Open3 to capture STDERR and STDOUT. The second problem is a little trickier. The current version of Test::Harness::Straps, which ships with Test::Harness 2.48, doesn't *quite* provide everything publicly that you need to run tests well. Hopefully a future version will correct this, but for now, the hack is to use a private method, _command_line( ), to generate the appropriate command for running the test.

Adding color is very easy, at least on platforms where Term::ANSIColor works. The code can be as simple as:

```perl
#!/usr/bin/perl

use strict;
use warnings;

use IPC::Open3;
use Term::ANSIColor;
use Test::Harness::Straps;

my $strap = Test::Harness::Straps->new( );

for my $file (@ARGV)
{
    next unless -f $file;

    my $output;

    my $command = $strap->_command_line( $file );
    my $pid     = open3( undef, $output, $output, $command );
    my %results = $strap->analyze( $file, $output );

    print $_->{output} for @{ process_results( $file, \%results ) };
}

sub process_results
{
    my ( $file, $results ) = @_;
    my $count              = 0;
```

```
    my @results;
    for my $test ( @{ $results->{details} } )
    {
        $count++;
        next if $test->{ok};

        push @results =>
        {
            test   => $test,
            output => create_test_result(
                $test->{ok}, $count, @{$test}{qw( name reason diagnostics )}
            )
        };
    }

    return \@results;
}

sub create_test_result
{
    my ( $ok, $number, $name, $reason, $diag ) = @_;

    $ok       = $ok ? 'ok' : 'not ok';
    $reason ||= '';
    $reason   = " ($reason)" if $reason;
    $diag   ||= '';

    return color( 'bold red' ) .
           sprintf "%6s %4d %s%s\n%s\n", $ok, $number, $name, $reason,
           color( 'clear yellow' ) . $diag . color( 'reset' );
}
```

The code loops through every test file given on the command line, running it through IPC::Open3::open3( ) to collect the output from both STDERR and STDOUT into $output. It uses Test::Harness::Straps's analyze( ) method to turn the TAP output into a data structure representing the tests, and then processes each result.

Passing tests are uninteresting; only failures with diagnostics are useful, so the process_results( ) function filters out everything else. Test numbers and names print out in bold red and test diagnostics print in clear yellow.

Hacking the Hack

Test::Harness::Straps actually provides much more information, such as the number of total tests expected and actually run, as well as special information about TODO and SKIP tests. It's easy to provide a Test::Harness-style summary of each test file run as well as the total tests.

It's also possible to write a harness that collects output over a network or from other sources. *Perl Testing: A Developer's Notebook* (O'Reilly, 2005) has other examples and suggestions.

Test Live Code
HACK #65

Verify your code against actual use...with little penalty.

Perl culture widely acknowledges automated testing as one step in verifying quality. Most CPAN modules and many large applications, not to mention Perl distributions themselves, have comprehensive test suites that run before installation to show what works and, occasionally, what doesn't work.

In theory, that's enough. In practice, it can be difficult to predict exactly how your code will react to production systems, live customers, and their actual data. Testing against this scenario would be incredibly valuable, but it's much more complex—not to mention probably much slower. If your automated tests are effective, they'll match the behavior of most customer requests.

Fortunately, it's possible to embed tests in production code that test against live data, non-destructively, but that don't generate too much data nor slow down your system.

The Hack

Imagine you have a web application that allows employees to manage their user data stored in a backend LDAP database. Abstraction is the key to a good system. You've created a User object and you've tested that the system vets and verifies all sorts of names and addresses that you could think of. You don't know how the system will react to the messy real world, though.

Instead of hard-coding the creation of the User object, create a factory object that returns a User object or equivalent.

```perl
package UserFactory;

use User;
use UserProxy;

my $count    = 0;

sub create
{
    my $self  = shift;
    my $class = $count++ % 100 ? 'User' : 'UserProxy';
    return $class->new( id => $count, @_ );
}

1;
```

Every hundred requests, the factory will create a `UserProxy` object instead of a `User` object. As long as `UserProxy` implements the same interface as `User` (and actually behaves similarly), the rest of the code should see no difference. `UserProxy` is a bit more complex:

```perl
package UserProxy;

use strict;
use warnings;

use User;
use Test::Builder;

sub new
{
    my ($class, %args) = @_;
    my $proxied         = User->new( %args );
    my $Test            = Test::Builder->create();
    $Test->output( time() . '_' . $proxied->id() . '.tap' );
    $Test->plan( 'no_plan' );
    bless { proxied => $proxied, test => $Test }, $class;
}

sub proxied
{
    my $self = shift;
    return $self->{proxied};
}

sub test
{
    my $self = shift;
    return $self->{test};
}

sub can
{
    my ($self, $method) = @_;
    my $proxied         = $self->proxied();
    return $proxied->can( $method );
}

sub verify_name
{
    my ($self, $name)   = @_;
    my $proxied         = $self->proxied():
    my $test            = $self->test();
    $test->ok( $proxied->verify_name( $name ), "verify_name() for '$name'" )
        || $test->diag( $proxied->verification_error() );
}

# ...

1;
```

When UserFactory creates a UserProxy, the proxy class creates an actual User object with the same arguments. It also wraps some calls to normal User methods with its own methods to run tests. The example verify_name( ) method wraps the call to User->verify_name( ) in a test case, expecting it to pass but logging it with a test diagnostic containing the error if it does not.

Apart from the factory/proxy design, the other part that makes this hack work is the use of Test::Builder in UserProxy->new( ). Each UserProxy object contains its own Test::Builder object and sends its output to a unique file with a name based on the current time and the number of the request. From there, use a cron job to run prove or some other Test::Harness-related program to analyze the tests and notify the proper people if things fail.

Be sure to use Test::Builder 0.60 or newer to have access to create( ).

Hacking the Hack

The more data you can keep about failing requests, the better—you can use this data in your automated tests as you add test cases and fix the bugs.

Test::Builder provides only a few methods. You may want to write your own test library atop Test::Builder based on your needs. An alternate approach is to use Test::Class within your proxy. Though you need to find some way to manage the test output and counter on a per-object basis, the module will handle much of the setup code for you. It will also be very valuable if you want to test multiple types of objects that inherit from common ancestors.

Sampling one out of every hundred requests may be the wrong frequency. There's a whole field of statistical analysis devoted to sample and defect rates. This is a decent place to start, and it's likely an improvement over only automated testing, but it's not perfect for every need.

It may be worth serializing the proxied object and storing it somewhere useful in case of failure. Whether you use Storable or YAML or just save the relevant data somewhere else, having the exact information available to recreate the appropriate customer request will aid debugging.

HACK
#66   Cheat on Benchmarks
Add optimizations where they really matter.

A well-known fact among programmers is that the true sign of superiority of a language is its performance executing various meaningless and artificial benchmarks. One such impractical benchmark is the Ackermann function, which really exercises an implementation's speed of recursion. It's easy to write the function but it's difficult for the computer to calculate and optimize.

> Of course, benchmarks are rarely useful. Yet sometimes they can teach you about good optimization techniques.

If you love Perl, cheat. It's easy.

A fairly fast but maintainable Perl 5 implementation of this function is:

```perl
use strict;
use warnings;

no warnings 'recursion';

sub ackermann
{
    my ($m, $n) = @_;
    return         $n + 1       if $m == 0;
    return ackermann( $m - 1, 1 ) if $n == 0;
    return ackermann( $m - 1, ackermann( $m, $n - 1 ) );
}

print ackermann( 3, 10 ), "\n";
```

Analyzing the function reveals that it takes a long, long time to calculate the value for any interesting positive integers. That's why the code disables the warning for deep recursion.

So, cheat. Add two lines of code to the program before calling ackermann( ) with the seed values to speed it up substantially:

```perl
use Memoize;
memoize( 'ackermann' );
```

> Don't run this with arguments greater than (4, 2) if you plan to use your computer before it finishes computing.

Calculating for (3, 10) with the memoized version took just under 1.4 seconds on the author's computer. The author interrupted the unmemoized version after a minute, then felt bad and restarted. It ran to completion in just over five minutes. These are not scientific results, but the difference in timing is dramatic.

Is this really cheating? A hypothetically complex Perl compiler could notice that ackermann( ) has no side effects and mathematically must return the same output for any two given inputs, so it could perform this optimization itself. You're just helping it along with a core module.

See the Memoize documentation for information on how this works and legit-imate uses of memoization. See the *http://en.wikipedia.org/wiki/Ackermann_function* Wikipedia entry for more about the Ackermann function.

Build Your Own Perl

HACK
#67   Compile Perl just the way you like it.

Perl has so many features that no single binary can do everything everyone wants. If you're debugging XS code, you might want to enable debugging. If you like to experiment, you might want to enable threads. If you need to run Perl on an odd platform where memory or disk space are low, you might want to disable certain features and core modules. You might even want an experimental patch that adds type information (autobox on the CPAN) or the defined-or operator (dor on the CPAN). You might also want to patch Perl yourself or help test out a development release.

Whatever the case, building your own Perl is reasonably easy.

The Hack

Before you start, you need a working C development environment with a compiler, system headers, and a Make utility.

First, download Perl. The latest version is always available from the CPAN at *http://www.cpan.org/src/*. Stable versions have even minor version num-bers (Perl 5.6.x, Perl 5.8.x, Perl 5.10.x) while development versions have odd minor numbers (Perl 5.7.x, Perl 5.9.x). Unless you are ready to report and possibly debug bugs, choose a stable version.

After you have downloaded and unpacked the distribution, change to the new directory. To configure the default build, simply run the *Configure* file:

```
$ sh Configure -de
```

You don't *have* to use the -de flag, but the configuration will prompt you for multitudinous options that few people care about and fewer still all under-stand. However, some options *are* useful.

To install Perl to a different root directory, use the -Dprefix option. For example, if you want to test Perl 5.9.3 and install it to */usr/local/bleadperl-5.9.3*, use the flag -Dprefix=/usr/local/bleadperl-5.9.3.

If you already have a system Perl installed, some of the OS utilities might rely on it. In this case, build and install a parallel Perl rather than overwrite an installed version.

To build a development release, pass the -Dusedevel flag.

To enable threads, use the -Dusethreads flag.

To enable debugging of the perl binary itself, pass the -Doptimize='g' flag.

To see the other configuration options, run:

```
$ sh Configure -h
```

Running the Hack

Now you have Perl configured and can build it. Building is as simple as running your Make utility, usually make but sometimes gmake:

```
$ make
```

If everything goes well, you will have a perl binary in a few minutes, along with compiled versions of the necessary core libraries in *lib/*. Then, run the core tests:

```
$ make test
```

Everything *should* pass. If not, check the appropriate *README.** file for your platform to see if there are any expected failures.

If there are failures, or if you're building a development release, consider using the perlbug utility built with this Perl to report the failures:

```
$ ./perlbug -nok
```

Use the -ok flag instead to report success of a development release.

If you can't send mail from this system, send the output to a file with the -f switch:

```
$ ./perlbug -nok -f build.failure
```

Then mail the file to perlbug@perl.org.

If everything is to your expectation, install your new Perl with:

```
$ make install
```

Switch to the root user or use sudo as necessary, depending on your installation prefix.

Hacking the Hack

The *INSTALL* file in the source distribution contains the most information about building and installing Perl, as well as reporting any bugs to the Perl 5 Porters. If you run into trouble, read that file for answers. The numerous *README.** files contain platform-specific information that affects how Perl builds and runs (read them with perldoc or your favorite pager).

To hack on Perl itself, start by reading *pod/perlhack.pod* in the source directory. This also gives the rsync command used to access the very latest sources, as well as instructions on sending patches.

H A C K **Run Test Suites Persistently**
#68   Speed up your tests.

Large Perl applications with many interconnected modules can take a long time to start up. Perl needs to load, compile, and initialize all of the modules before it can start running your application.

Tests for a large system can be particularly slow. A test suite typically contains lots of small short-lived scripts, each of which pulls in lots of module code at start up. A few seconds of delay per script can add up to a lot of time spent waiting for your test suite to finish.

The cure for long startup times within web-based applications is to run under a persistent environment such as mod_perl or PersistentPerl. PersistentPerl works for command-line programs as well. It's usually as simple as changing the shebang line from #!/usr/bin/perl to #!/usr/bin/perperl.

Running your test suite persistently is slightly more complicated, and doesn't work for every test, but the benefit is a huge speed increase for most of your tests. Running your test suite persistently can speed up your tests by a factor of five on a slow machine.

The Hack

The first step of the hack is to make Test::Builder-based scripts compatible with PersistentPerl. There are several parts to this:

- The script has to reset the Test::Builder counter on startup.
- The script needs to prevent Test::Builder from duplicating STDOUT and STDERR, as this seems to be incompatible with PersistentPerl.
- Scripts with no_plan have to register a PersistentPerl cleanup handler to display the final 1..X line.

Test::PerPerlHelper does all of this for you:

```perl
package Test::PerPerlHelper;

use strict;
use warnings;

use base 'Test::Builder';

require Test::More;

sub import
{
    my $class = shift;

    if (eval {require PersistentPerl} && PersistentPerl->i_am_perperl())
    {
        # rebless the Test::Builder singleton into our class
        # so that we can override the plan and _dup_stdhandles methods
        my $Test = Test::Builder->new();
        bless $Test, __PACKAGE__;
    }

    $class->plan(@_);
}

sub plan
{
    my $class = shift;
    return unless @_;

    my $Test  = Test::Builder->new();

    if (eval {require PersistentPerl} && PersistentPerl->i_am_perperl())
    {
        $Test->reset();

        Test::Builder::_autoflush(*STDOUT);
        Test::Builder::_autoflush(*STDERR);

        $Test->output(*STDOUT);
        $Test->failure_output(*STDERR);
        $Test->todo_output(*STDOUT);

        $Test->no_ending(1);
        my $pp    = PersistentPerl->new();
        $pp->register_cleanup(sub { $Test->_ending });
    }
    $Test->SUPER::plan(@_);
}

# Duplicating STDERR and STDOUT doesn't work under perperl
# so override it with a no-op
sub _dup_stdhandles {  }

1;
```

Under the hood, Test::Builder uses a singleton $Test object to maintain state. No matter how many times you call Test::Builder->new( ), it always returns a reference to the same $Test object. It does this so that all the various CPAN test modules can all share the same test state (especially the test counter).

Test::PerPerlHelper makes itself a subclass of Test::Builder, and then sneakily reblesses the Test::Builder singleton so that it is a Test::PerPerlHelper instead of a Test::Builder. In this way Test::PerPerlHelper can make itself compatible with all of the CPAN Test::* modules by customizing the singleton $Test object.

Test::PerPerlHelper only does this and other PersistentPerl-related compatibility tricks if the test script is running under PersistentPerl, so you can safely run the same test script normally as well.

The only change that you should have to make to your test scripts is make them end in a true value:

```
use Test::More 'no_plan';

ok(1);
ok(2);
ok(3);

1;  # persistent tests need to end in a true value!
```

Creating a wrapper around prove. Next you need to make all of your test scripts run in the same shared PersistentPerl interpreter.

Normally when you run a program under PersistentPerl, the Perl interpreter stays running in the background after your program terminates. The next time you run the program, PersistentPerl will reuse the same backend interpreter. Typically, each program gets its own private interpreter.

However, for test suites, this policy of one interpreter per program causes a problem. When you use Test::Harness's prove program to run your tests, you don't want to make prove itself persistent; you want to make all of your test scripts persistent—and you want them all to share a single interpreter.

The first step is to create a wrapper script called perperl-runscript which you will use to run every test script:

```
#!/usr/bin/perperl -- -M1

use strict;
use Test::PerPerlHelper;
```

```
my $script;
while (my $arg = shift)
{
    # if the arg is a -I switch, add the directory to @INC
    # unless it already exists
    if ($arg =~ /^-I(.*)/ and -d $1)
    {
        unshift @INC, $1 unless grep { $_ eq $1 } @INC;
    }
    else
    {
        $script = $arg;
    }
}

do $script or die $@;
```

Place perperl-runscript somewhere in your $PATH.

Running the Hack

Set the HARNESS_PERL environment variable to perperl-runscript to cause Test::Harness to run every test through this script instead of through Perl. Because the name of this script never changes, PersistentPerl will always use the same backend interpreter to run every test. The -M1 switch on the shebang line tells perperl to only spawn one backend interpreter.

You can set HARNESS_PERL on the same line as prove:

```
$ HARNESS_PERL=perperl-runscript prove -Ilib t/
```

Better still, create a wrapper script around prove called perperl-prove:

```
#!/bin/sh

export HARNESS_PERL=perperl-runscript

prove $*
```

Now you have the choice of running your test suite persistently or non-persistently:

```
$ perperl-prove -Ilib t/
$ prove -Ilib t/
```

To "restart" PersistentPerl, you must kill its backend processes:

```
$ killall perperl_backend
```

You have to restart PersistentPerl if any code outside of the test script itself has changed. However you *don't* have to restart PersistentPerl if only the test script has changed.

Hacking the Hack

There are some limitations with running tests persistently. In particular:

- Scripts that muck about with STDIN, STDOUT, or STDERR will have problems.
- The usual persistent environment caveats apply: be careful with redefined subs, global variables, and so on; required code only gets loaded on the first request, and so forth.
- Test scripts have to end in a true value.

Expect some scripts to cause problems. When you find a script that does not play nicely with PersistentPerl, you can configure the script to skip all its tests when run persistently:

```
use Test::More;
use Test::PerPerlHelper;
if (eval { require PersistentPerl } and PersistentPerl->i_am_perperl() )
{
    Test::PerPerlHelper->plan(
        'skip_all',
        'Redirecting STDIN doesn't work under perperl' );
}
else
{
    plan "no_plan";
}
```

You can also use the "Reload Modified Modules" **[Hack #30]** hack to reload modules without restarting PersistentPerl.

Add the following lines to your test script:

```
use Module::Reloader;
Module::Reloader::reload() if $ENV{'RELOAD_MODULES'};
```

Now you can reload modules by setting the RELOAD_MODULES environment variable to a true value:

```
$ RELOAD_MODULES=1 perperl-prove t/
```

If you don't set the environment variable, then the modules will not be reloaded:

```
$ perperl-prove t/
```

Note that for some reason Module::Reloader doesn't work on the first run of a script; it only starts working on the second run. The first run fails with an error, Too late to run INIT block.

Simulate Hostile Environments in Your Tests

Test devastating failures with aplomb.

When you publish a CPAN module that depends on other modules, you list the prerequisite modules in your *Makefile.PL* or *Build.PL* script.

Using *Build.PL*:

```
my $builder = Module::Build->new(
  # ... other Build.PL options ...
  requires =>
  {
      'Test::More'    => 0,
      'CGI'           => 2.0,
  }
);
```

Using *Makefile.PL*:

```
WriteMakefile(
    # ... other Makefile.PL options ...
    'PREREQ_PM' =>
    {
        'Test::More'    => 0,
        'CGI'           => 2.0,
    }
);
```

However, there are a few ways that this standard prerequisite checking can be insufficient. First, you may have optional prerequisites. For instance, your module will use Foo::Bar if it happens to be installed, but should fail gracefully when Foo::Bar is absent.

Second, if the behavior of a module changed between two versions, you may still want to support both versions. For example, CGI changed how it handles PATH_INFO in version 3.11. Your CGI::Super_Path_Info module probably wants to be compatible with both CGI version 3.11 and also with earlier (and later) versions.

Finally, occasionally a user will install your module by hand to bypass the prerequisite check, hoping to use an older version of Foo::Bar than the one you require. Sometimes your module works fine (maybe with some feature limitations), but your test suite breaks because your tests assumed the presence of a new feature.

For each of these cases. you can make your module and tests more robust. For example, you can skip tests that are incompatible with an older version of a module:

```
use Test::More;
use CGI;
```

```
if ($CGI->VERSION >= 3.11)
{
    plan skip_all => 'skipping compatibility tests for old CGI.pm';
}
else
{
    plan 'tests' => 17;
}
```

You can also skip tests that require the presence of a particular optional module:

```
eval 'require URI;';
if ($@)
{
    plan skip_all => 'optional module URI not installed';
}
else
{
    plan 'tests' => 10;
}
```

Now your tests are (hopefully) more robust, but how do you make sure that they will actually work on a system that is missing some modules and has older versions of others?

Ideally, you want to run your test suite against a few different sets of installed modules. Each set will be different from what you have installed in the main Perl site_lib of your development machine. It's way too much work to uninstall and reinstall ten different modules every time you make a new CPAN release.

The Hack

There are three possibilities: the user has an old version of the module installed, the user does not have the module installed, and the user has some combination of both for multiple modules.

Simulating old versions of modules. Create custom Perl library directories and include these directories when you use prove to run your tests. For instance, to run the tests against an old version of CGI:

```
$ mkdir t/prereq_lib
$ mkdir t/prereq_lib/CGI
$ cp CGI-3.10.pm t/prereq_lib/CGI.pm
$ prove -Ilib -It/prereq_lib t/
```

Including *t/prereq_lib* on the command line to prove puts at the start of @INC, so Perl will load any modules you put in this directory before modules installed in your system's Perl *lib* directories.

Simulating missing modules. That works for older versions of modules, but how do you install the *absence* of a module in a custom library directory so that it takes precedence over a copy already installed on your system?

The solution is to create a zero-length file with the same name as the module. This works because in order for a module to load successfully (via require or use) it has to end in a true value, such as (from actual CPAN modules):[*]

```
1;
666;
"false";
"Steve Peters, Master Of True Value Finding, was here.";
```

A zero-length file doesn't end in a true value, and consequently require fails. It doesn't fail with the same error message as a missing module fails with, but it still fails.

For example, to run the tests in an environment missing URI:

```
$ mkdir -p t/skip_lib
$ touch t/skip_lib/URI.pm
$ prove -Ilib -It/skip_lib t/
```

Running multiple scenarios. You can create multiple different library directories, each containing a different combination of missing and/or old modules:

```
$ mkdir -p t/prereq_scenarios/missing_uri
$ touch t/prereq_scenarios/missing_uri/URI.pm
$ mkdir -p t/prereq_scenarios/old_cgi
$ cp CGI-3.10.pm t/prereq_scenarios/old_cgi/CGI.pm
$ mkdir -p t/prereq_scenarios/new_cgi
$ cp CGI-3.15.pm t/prereq_scenarios/new_cgi/CGI.pm
```

Then run all of these scenarios at once:

```
$ for lib in t/prereq_scenarios/*; do prove -Ilib -I$lib t/; done
```

However this one-liner stops at the first error and doesn't provide any summary information. Here's a more complete version:

```perl
#!/usr/bin/perl

use strict;
use File::Find;

if (@ARGV < 2)
{
    die "Usage: $0 [prereq_scenarios_dir] [args to prove]\n";
}
```

---

[*] The more boring the line of code, the better the opportunity for creativity.

```perl
my $scenarios_dir = shift;

my %scenario_modules;
my $errors;

my @scenarios      = grep { -d } <$scenarios_dir/*>;

for my $lib_dir (@scenarios)
{
    unless (-d $lib_dir)
    {
        $errors   = 1;
        warn "lib dir does not exist: $lib_dir\n";
        next;
    }
    my @modules;

    find(sub
    {
        return unless -f;

        my $dir =  "$File::Find::dir/$_";
        $dir    =~ s/^\Q$lib_dir\E//;
        $dir    =~ s/\.pm$//;
        $dir    =~ s{^/}{};
        $dir    =~ s{/}{::}g;

        push @modules, $dir;
    }, $lib_dir);

    $scenario_modules{$lib_dir} = \@modules;
}

die "Terminating." if $errors;

for my $lib_dir (@scenarios)
{
    my $modules   = join ', ', sort @{ $scenario_modules{$lib_dir} };
    $modules    ||= 'none';
    print "\n" . '#' x 62 . "\n";
    print "Running tests.  Old (or absent) modules in this scenario:\n";
    print "$modules\n";

    my @prove_command = ('prove', "-I$lib_dir", @ARGV);

    system( @prove_command ) && do
    {
        die <<EOF;
##############################################################
One or more tests failed in scenario $lib_dir.
The old or absent modules were:
    $modules
```

```
The command was:
    @prove_command

Terminating.
#############################################################
EOF
    };
}
```

Save this as *prove-prereqs* and run it as:

```
$ prove-prereqs t/prereq_scenarios -Ilib t/
```

Hacking the Hack

PITA, the Perl Image Testing Architecture (*http://search.cpan.org/dist/PITA*) project, goes much further than this hack does. PITA will be able to test your Perl modules under different versions of Perl and even on different operating systems (possibly running within virtual machines on a single computer). It will allow you to automate the testing process and collect the results generated from several testing environments.

## CHAPTER EIGHT

Know Thy Code
Hacks 70–83

Introspection isn't just a self-help exercise. It's a way of asking Perl what it thinks about your program.

Why does that matter? There are plenty of advanced techniques that, properly applied, will save you much time, effort, and trouble. That word "properly" is the sticky one though—unless you know what's proper and what's not, you'll have difficulty mastering advanced Perl.

Despite all the rich nooks and crannies and hidden corners of the core, there are only a few techniques you absolutely must understand. Study well the hacks here and you'll absorb higher lore and unlock secrets that will help you customize Perl, the language, for your specific needs.

HACK #70 Understand What Happens When
Tell compile time from runtime.

Dynamic languages are flexible, neither requiring you to know all of the code you're ever going to run in a program at compile time nor necessarily failing if it's not there at runtime. Perl can live with some ambiguity about seeing functions you haven't defined yet (if ever) and referring to variables that don't necessarily have any values yet.

That doesn't always make life easier for programmers. While Perl's pretty good about knowing what happens when, reading the source code doesn't always make it clear. While it may seem obvious to you that program execution happens top to bottom that's not always how it works.

The Hack

Here's what actually happens.

Compilation. When you first run your program, Perl reads the file and starts compiling from top to bottom. At this point, it looks for symbols (variables and subroutines), registers them appropriately, and converts the text of the program into an internal representation that it can execute. If it encounters syntax errors, it aborts and reports an error message.

Of course, some constructs aren't syntax errors in normal use:

```
#!/usr/bin/perl

my $age = 10;
print $aeg;
```

Perl will only complain about an undeclared variable $aeg when running under the strict pragma. However, the question of how this works is less obvious when you consider that Perl reports this error *before* running the code. Consider:

```
#!/usr/bin/perl
use strict;

my $age = 10;
print $aeg;
```

The secret is that use internally becomes:

```
BEGIN
{
    require 'strict';
    strict->import( ) if strict->can( 'import' );
}
```

Perl then loads the strict module, if it can, and starts compiling that, returning to the main program when it finishes.

Whenever Perl encounters a BEGIN block, it executes its contents immediately, just as it encounters them. Of course, it doesn't execute code outside of the block that a programmer might think is important to the block:

```
my $name = 'Spot';

BEGIN { print "Hello, $name!\n" }
```

Though the BEGIN block executes as soon as Perl encounters it, and though Perl has already associated $name with the appropriate storage spot inside and outside of the block, the assignment will not happen until runtime; the BEGIN block executes *before* the assignment happens, even if it comes later in the file.

Even though it may seem correct that this would work if it were part of a module loaded from the main program (at least with use), the internal BEGIN will still execute before the rest of the code in the file.

Initialization. As soon as Perl finishes compiling, it runs any CHECK blocks found—but in reverse order of their declaration. For example:

```
#!/usr/bin/perl

BEGIN { print "First!\n"  }
CHECK { print "Third!\n"  }
CHECK { print "Second!\n" }
```

prints:

```
First!
Second!
Third!
```

INIT blocks run *after* all CHECK blocks in order of their appearance:

```
#!/usr/bin/perl

BEGIN { print "First!\n"  }
INIT  { print "Fourth!\n" }
CHECK { print "Third!\n"  }
CHECK { print "Second!\n" }
INIT  { print "Fifth!\n"  }
```

prints:

```
First!
Second!
Third!
Fourth!
Fifth!
```

Runtime. When running, execution order happens as you might expect. There aren't any surprises unless you do something tricky (as per most of the rest of the book). One change is that running code by evaling a string—after runtime starts—will only execute any BEGIN blocks found as a result of that operation, not CHECK or INIT blocks.* This program:

```
#!/usr/bin/perl

BEGIN { print "First!\n"  }
INIT  { print "Fourth!\n" }
CHECK { print "Third!\n"  }
CHECK { print "Second!\n" }
INIT  { print "Fifth!\n"  }

eval <<END_EVAL;
BEGIN { print "BEGIN in eval\n!" }
```

---

* This is why Attribute::Handlers and persistent interpreters such as mod_perl do not get along by default.

```
        CHECK { print "CHECK in eval\n!" }
        INIT  { print "INIT in eval\n!"  }
        END_EVAL
```

prints:

```
    First!
    Second!
    Third!
    Fourth!
    Fifth!
    BEGIN in eval!
```

Cleanup. Finally, when it comes time for the program to exit (but not with a compilation error), Perl runs all END blocks in reverse order of their appearance:

```
    #!/usr/bin/perl

        BEGIN { print "First!\n"  }
        INIT  { print "Fourth!\n" }
        CHECK { print "Third!\n"  }
        CHECK { print "Second!\n" }
        INIT  { print "Fifth!\n"  }

        eval <<END_EVAL;
        BEGIN { print "BEGIN in eval\n!" }
        CHECK { print "CHECK in eval\n!" }
        INIT  { print "INIT in eval\n!"  }
        END   { print "Sixth!\n"         }
        END_EVAL

        END   { print "Seventh!\n"       }
        END   { print "Eighth!\n"        }
```

prints:

```
    First!
    Second!
    Third!
    Fourth!
    Fifth!
    BEGIN in eval!
    Sixth!
    Seventh!
    Eighth!
```

Why did the END block in the eval execute first? Although it's an END block and Perl encountered the string first, it executes that block at runtime, so it's the final END block compiled and, thus, the first to execute.

See perlmod for more details.

HACK
#71

Inspect Your Data Structures

Peek into a reference and see how far down it goes.

How do you know the structure of a Perl reference? Is the reference to a hash, an array, an object, a scalar, or something else? Many people suggest the use of Data::Dumper. This module has a method that dumps the data structure as a text string. It works very well, but its main purpose is to serialize a data structure into a string you can eval to recreate the reference and its data.

Most of the time I don't want to save state or eval anything. I just want to see a text representation of the reference. I really like the representation of a data structure that using the x command within the Perl debugger provides.

Dumping References Outside the Debugger

Is it possible to produce this from a Perl program without using the debugger? Yes!

```
use strict;
use Dumpvalue;

my $d    = Dumpvalue->new( );
my $hash =
{
    first_name => 'Tim',
    last_name  => 'Allwine',
    friends    => [ 'Jon','Nat','Joe' ],
};
$d->dumpValue(\$hash);
```

This produces the output:

```
-> HASH(0x80a190)
    'first_name' => 'Tim'
    'friends' => ARRAY(0x800368)
       0  'Jon'
       1  'Nat'
       2  'Joe'
    'last_name' => 'Allwine'
```

This is the same output that the debugger produces. The HASH line says that $hash is a hash reference. The next level of indentation shows the keys of the hash and their corresponding values. first_name for example points to the string Tim but friends points to an array reference. The contents of that array appear, one at a time, indented one step further with their indices within the array and their values.

This technique is handy when you have to maintain code written by other people. Suppose that you're editing a web program with over 2,000 lines of code. Deep in the code, you find a reference named $someref and you want to see its contents. At the top of the file, add the lines:

```
use Dumpvalue;
my $d = Dumpvalue->new( );
```

Then while $d and $someref are in scope, add the line:

```
$d->dumpValue(\$someref);
```

When you run it, the code will dump $someref.

Printing to a File

One complaint with this technique is where dumpValue( ) prints. It usually prints to STDOUT, by default, but actually it prints to the currently selected output filehandle. That's a hint. Add a couple of lines to change the filehandle:

```
open my $fh, '>dump.out';
my $old_fh = select($fh);
$d->dumpValue(\$ref);
close $fh;
select($old_fh);
```

Now when you run the program, the dump string will end up in a file called *dump.out*.

Output in CGI or mod_perl Programs

Dumping the output in CGI or mod_perl programs is more complex. Often you don't want to print to a filehandle at all, as it may change the rendering of the output drastically. Instead, use IO::Scalar to create a filehandle to a string and select that filehandle. Then, undirected print or dumpValue( ) calls will go to this new filehandle. Select the old filehandle and carry on with your program, printing $dump_str when you want.

```
use IO::Scalar;

my $dump_str;
my $io  = IO::Scalar->new(\$dump_str);
my $oio = select($io);

print '<pre>',"\n";        # goes to $dump_str
$d->dumpValue(\$someref);  # as does this
print '</pre>';            # and this too

select($oio);              # old filehandle
print $dump_str;           # stdout again when you want it to
```

Find Functions Safely

#72   Look for code to execute without risking explosions.

The ultimate goal of designing reusable code is genericity—being able to write useful pieces of code that allow future expansion without (much) difficulty or modification. Complete genericity is difficult, as your code has to make *some* assumptions *somewhere*.

Perl's very flexible about how you interact with other code. You can fold, spindle, mutilate, and mangle symbols in any package you want at almost any time. Although this flexibility makes it possible to find code in other packages, sometimes it makes it difficult to know if the function you want is really there, at least safely and without digging through symbol tables.

You can do it, though.

The Hack

If you can avoid the problem, avoid it.

One of the most common ways to interact with other code is to provide an interface you expect it to fulfill. This may be through suggesting that all plug-ins inherit from a base class that provides default methods to overload or through documenting that your code will always call plug-in methods and pass specified arguments.

Subclassing can be fragile, though, especially in Perl where your implementation choices affect everyone else who writes code. (See the implementation of HTTP::Daemon and how it stores instance data, for example.)

If you only need to know that plug-ins or extensions conform to an interface, consider using a Perl 6-ish module such as Class::Roles or Class::Trait. Though there's a little bit of theory to learn before you understand the code, you can make your code more flexible and generic without enforcing more on the extensions than you really need to enforce.

Get cozy with can( ). If you *can't* entirely force a separate interface, as in the case where you want to make some methods publicly callable from user requests on a web site and other methods private to the world, consider namespacing them. For example, imagine a web program that performs mathematical operations based on the contents of the action parameter:

```
sub dispatch_request
{
    my ($self, $q) = @_;
    my $action     = $q->param( 'action' );
    $self->$action( );
}
```

This technique isn't *quite* as bad as invoking $action directly as a symbolic reference, but it provides little safety. An attacker could provide an invalid action, at best crashing the program as Perl tries to invoke an unknown method, or provide the name of a private method somewhere that he really shouldn't call, revealing sensitive data or causing unexpected havoc.

To verify that the method exists somewhere, use the can( ) method (provided by the UNIVERSAL ancestor of all classes):

```
sub dispatch_request
{
    my ($self, $q) = @_;
    my $action    = $q->param( 'action' );
    return unless $self->can( $action );
    $self->$action();
}
```

That prevents attackers from calling undefined methods, but it's little advantage over wrapping the whole dispatch in an eval block. If you change the names of all valid methods to start (or end) with a known token, you can prevent calling private methods:

```
sub dispatch_request
{
    my ($self, $q) = @_;
    my $action    = 'action_' . $q->param( 'action' );
    return unless $self->can( $action );
    $self->$action();
}
```

Now when the user selects the login action, the request dispatches to the method action_login. For even further protection, see "Control Access to Remote Objects" [Hack #48].

Find functions, not methods! That works for methods, but what about functions? Perl 5 at least makes very few internal distinctions between methods and subroutines. can( ) works just as well on package names to find subroutines as it does class names to find methods. If you know you've loaded a plug-in called Logger and want to know if it can register( ), try:

```
my $register_subref = Logger->can( 'register ' );
$register_subref->( ) if $register_subref;
```

can( ) returns a reference to the found function if it exists and undef otherwise.

This also works if you have the package name in a variable:

```
my $register_subref = $plugin->can( 'register ' );
$register_subref->( ) if $register_subref;
```

If you don't know for sure that $plugin contains a valid package name, wrap the can( ) method call in an eval block:*

```
my $register_subref = eval { $plugin->can( 'register ') };
$register_subref->( ) if $register_subref;
```

If the eval fails, $register_subref will be false.

Know What's Core and When

HACK #73   Keep track of the core modules you're using and not using.

Not every Perl installation is fortunate enough to be able to install the latest released version of the core as soon as it is available or to install the freshest modules off of the CPAN as soon as they hit the index. Some developers on legacy systems have to be very careful to avoid the wrath of their system administrators for whom stability is a way of life, not just a goal.

Though Perl 5's standard library has always provided a lot of features, it has grown over time. What's standard and usable everywhere as of Perl 5.8.7 isn't the same as what existed as of Perl 5.004. How can you know, though, without either digging through release notes or watching your carefully constructed code break when put on the testing machine?

Use Module::CoreList.

The Hack

Suppose you've read perldoc perlport and have resolved never to write unportable, hardcoded file paths anymore. You've browsed the documentation of File::Spec and realize that a few careful calls can make your code more likely to work on platforms as exotic as Windows (or even VMS, but that's scary).

Unfortunately for your good intentions, your development platform is a box that shipped with Perl 5.004 from way back when the network really was the computer. Before replacing all of your join('/', @path, $filename) code with calls to shiny catfile( ), your sense of duty and due diligence causes you to ask "Wait, when did File::Spec enter the core?"

Install Module::CoreList from the CPAN, and then bring up a command line:

```
$ perl -MModule::CoreList -e 'print Module::CoreList->first_release(
    "File::Spec" ), "\n"'
5.005
```

---

* Some people recommend calling UNIVERSAL::can( ) as a function, not a method. That's silly; what if the package overrides can( )? You'll get the wrong answer!

Good thing you checked. Now you have three choices: submit the paper-work to upgrade Perl on that machine to something released this millen-nium,* bribe the sysadmin to install File::Spec on that machine, or sadly give up on the idea that this code will work unmodified on Mac OS classic.

Checking by version. Maybe knowing the first occurrence of the module isn't good enough. Consider the case of poor Test::Simple. Though the first ver-sions were useful and good, it wasn't until release 0.30 and the introduction of Test::Builder that the golden age of Perl testing began. If you haven't upgraded Perl in a couple of years and rely on the universal Perl testing backend, what's the minimum version of Perl you can use without having to install a newer Test::Simple?

Pass an optional second value to first_release( ), the version number of the package:

```
$ perl -MModule::CoreList -e 'print Module::CoreList->first_release(
    "Test::Simple", '0.30' ), "\n"'
5.007003
```

Anything released after Perl 5.7.3 contains Test::Builder. Of course, note that this doesn't mean that releases of Perl with *lower* numbers don't contain Test::Builder—Perl 5.6.2, released *after* Perl 5.7.3, contains Test::Simple 0.47.

If you're really curious, and especially if you end up with information about development releases of Perl, browse through the data structures at the end of Module::CoreList by hand [Hack #2] for more detailed information.

When did Module::CoreList make it in the core? Perl 5.9.2.

Trace All Used Modules

HACK
#74

See what modules your program uses—and what modules those modules use!

Perhaps the most useful feature of Perl 5 is module support, allowing the use of existing, pre-written code. With thousands of modules on the CPAN available for free, it's likely that any code you write will use at least a few other pieces of code.

Of course, all of the modules you use optionally use a few modules of their own, and so on. You could find yourself loading dozens of pieces of code for what looks like a simple program. Alternately, you may just be curious to see the relationships within your code.

Wouldn't it be nice to see which modules your code loaded from where? Now you can.

---

* Perl 5.004_05 released in April 1999.

The Hack

The easiest way to gather the information on what Perl modules any piece of code loads is a little-known feature of @INC, the magic variable that governs where Perl looks to load modules. If @INC contains a code reference, it will execute that reference when attempting to load a module. This is a great place to store code to manage library paths, as PAR and The::Net (*http://www.perlmonks.org/?node_id=92473*, not on the CPAN) do. It also works well to collect interesting statistics:

```perl
package Devel::TraceUse;

use Time::HiRes qw( gettimeofday tv_interval );

BEGIN
{
    unshift @INC, \&trace_use unless grep { "$_" eq \&trace_use . '' } @INC;
}

sub trace_use
{
    my ($code, $module) = @_;
    (my $mod_name      = $module) =~ s{/}{::}g;
    $mod_name                     =~ s/\.pm$//;
    my ($package, $filename, $line) = caller();
    my $elapsed        = 0;

    {
        local *INC     = [ @INC[1..$#INC] ];
        my $start_time = [ gettimeofday() ];
        eval "package $package; require '$mod_name';";
        $elapsed       = tv_interval( $start_time );
    }
    $package           = $filename if $package eq 'main';
    push @used,
    {
        'file'   => $package,
        'line'   => $line,
        'time'   => $elapsed,
        'module' => $mod_name,
    };

    return;
}

END
{
    my $first = $used[0];
    my %seen  = ( $first->{file} => 1 );
    my $pos   = 1;

    warn "Modules used from $first->{file}:\n";
```

```
    for my $mod (@used)
    {
        my $message = '';

        if (exists $seen{$mod->{file}})
        {
            $pos = $seen{$mod->{file}};
        }
        else
        {
            $seen{$mod->{file}} = ++$pos;
        }

        my $indent = '  ' x $pos;
        $message  .= "$indent$mod->{module}, line $mod->{line}";
        $message  .= " ($mod->{time})" if $mod->{time};
        warn "$message\n";
    }
}

1;
```

The code begins by storing a reference to trace_use( ) at the head of @ISA. Whenever Perl encounters a use or require statement for a module it hasn't previously loaded, it will loop through each entry in @ISA, trying to load the module from there. As the first entry is a subroutine reference, Perl will call the subroutine with the name of the module to load (at least, translated into a Unix-style file path).

Devel::TraceUse translates the path name back into a module name, looks up the call stack to find the name of the package and file containing the use or require statement as well as the line number of the statement, and then redispatches the lookup, taking itself temporarily out of @INC. This redispatch allows the module to collect information on how long it took to load the module.

 This time isn't absolute; the string eval statement as well as the calls to Time::HiRes take up a near-constant amount of time. However, it's likely consistent, so comparing times to each other is sensible.

The code uses the filename of the caller if there's no explicit package given, stores all of the available information, and pushes that structure into an array of modules used.

At the end of the program, the module prints a report of the modules loaded in the order in which Perl encountered them.

Running the Hack

Perhaps the prove utility from Test::Harness has captured your attention and you want to know what modules it loads. With Devel::TraceUse in your path somewhere, run the command:

```
$ perl -MDevel::TraceUse /usr/bin/prove
Modules used from /usr/bin/prove:
  Test::Harness, line 8 (0.000544)
    Test::Harness::Straps, line 6 (0.000442)
      Test::Harness::Assert, line 9 (0.000464)
      Test::Harness::Iterator, line 10 (0.000581)
      Test::Harness::Point, line 11 (0.000437)
      POSIX, line 313 (0.000483)
        XSLoader, line 9 (0.000425)
    Benchmark, line 9 (0.000497)
      Exporter::Heavy, line 17 (0.000502)
  Getopt::Long, line 9 (0.000495)
    constant, line 221 (0.000475)
  Pod::Usage, line 10 (0.000486)
    File::Spec, line 405 (0.000464)
      File::Spec::Unix, line 21 (0.000432)
    Pod::Text, line 411 (0.000471)
      Pod::ParseLink, line 30 (0.000475)
      Pod::Select, line 31 (0.000447)
        Pod::Parser, line 242 (0.000461)
          Pod::InputObjects, line 205 (0.000444)
          Symbol, line 210 (0.000469)
  File::Glob, line 82 (0.000521)
```

Thus prove uses Test::Harness, Getopt::Long, Pod::Usage, and File::Glob directly, each of which uses several other modules. If you were adding features to prove and wanted to know if using POSIX would add significantly to the resource footprint, you would now know that you already pay the price for it, so you might as well use it.

Hacking the Hack

What could make this module more useful? Right now, it doesn't report the use of Time::HiRes, because it uses that internally. Making timing information optional would be nice. Furthermore, the report always goes to STDERR, which may mingle badly with other program output.

Perhaps you want to filter out certain packages selectively, or trace *all* of the uses of require and use. In lieu of reloading every module every time some piece of code wants to use it, Perl tracks loaded modules by caching their filenames in %INC. To have Devel::TraceUse track every attempt to load a module, whether Perl has loaded it, keep the delegation, but clear out %INC. (Be sure to keep your own cache, though, to prevent subroutine redefinitions and initialization code from running over and over again.)

Find All Symbols in a Package

#75 Explore symbol tables without soft references.

One of the earliest temptations for novice programmers is to use the contents of one variable as part of the name of another variable. After making one too many costly mistakes or showing such code to a more experienced programmer, novices start to use the `strict` pragma to warn them about dubious constructs.

However, several advanced features of Perl, such as the implementation of the `Exporter` module, are only possible by reading from and writing to the symbol table at run time. Normally `strict` forbids this—but it's possible to access global symbols at run time with `strict` enabled.

This is an easy way to find out if a symbol—such as a scalar, array, hash, subroutine, or filehandle—exists.

The Hack

Suppose you want to check whether a specific type of variable is present in a given namespace. You need to know the name of the package, the name of the variable, and the type of the variable.

Defining the following subroutine in the `UNIVERSAL` package makes the class method `contains_symbol` available to any package:[*]

```perl
my %types =
(
    '$' => 'SCALAR',
    '@' => 'ARRAY',
    '%' => 'HASH',
    '*' => 'IO',
    '&' => 'CODE',
);

sub UNIVERSAL::contains_symbol
{
    my ($namespace, $symbol) = @_;
    my @keys                 = split( /::/, $namespace );
    my $type                 = $types{ substr( $symbol, 0, 1, '' ) }
                               || 'SCALAR';

    my $table = \%main::;

    for my $key (@keys)
    {
        $key .= '::';
```

---

[*] Er…class.

```
            return 0 unless exists $table->{$key};
            $table = $table->{$key};
    }

    return 0 unless exists $table->{$symbol};
    return *{ $table->{$symbol} }{ $type } ? 1 : 0;
}
```

To see if a symbol exists, for example to test that `contains_symbol` exists in the `UNIVERSAL` package, call the method like:

```
print "Found it!\n" if UNIVERSAL->contains_symbol( '&contains_symbol' );
```

How does it work? Perl uses the same data structure for hashes as it does for symbol tables. The same operations—storing and retrieving values by key; iterating over keys, values, or both; and checking the existence of a key— work on both. The secret is knowing how to access the symbol table.

The main symbol table is always available as the hash named `%main::`. Every other symbol table has an entry starting there. For example, `strict`'s symbols are available in `$main::{'strict::'}`, while `CGI::Application`'s symbols are in `$main::{'CGI::'}{'Application::'}`. Each level is a new hash reference.

> The quotes are important to identify the name with the colons appropriately.

Within a symbol table, all leaf entries (values that aren't themselves symbol tables) contain typeglobs. A typeglob is similar to a hash, but it cannot contain arbitrary keys—it has a fixed set of keys, as shown in the `%types` array.[*]

Because a typeglob *isn't* a hash, you can't access its members as you would a hash. Instead, you must dereference it with the leading * glob identifier, then subscript it with the name of the slot to check.

Running the Hack

Once you have the glob, you can assign references to it to fill in its slots. For example, to create a new subroutine `growl()` in `Games::ScaryHouse::Monster`, find the symbol table for `Games::ScaryHouse::Monster` and the glob named `growl`. Then assign a reference to a subroutine to the glob and you will be able to call it as `Games::ScaryHouse::Monster::growl()`. Similar techniques work for anything else to which you can take a reference.

---

[*] There are other keys, but they're less common and rarely worth mentioning.

This trick offers *some* benefits over other ways of querying for a symbol, such as using soft references, calling can( ) on subroutines (which may run afoul of inheritance), and wrapping potentially harmful accesses in eval blocks. However do note that an optimization* automatically created a scalar entry in every new glob. Thus if you have a package global hash named %compatriots, contains_symbol( ) will claim that $compatriots also exists.

> This technique does *not* work on lexical variables; they don't live in symbol tables!

Peek Inside Closures
Violate closure-based encapsulation when you really need to.

Very few rules in Perl are inviolate—not even the rule that lexicals are inaccessible outside their scopes. For closures to work (and even lexicals in general), Perl has to be able to access them *somehow*. If you could use the same mechanism, you could read from and write to these variables.

This is very useful for debugging closures and closure-based objects [Hack #43]. It's scary and wrong, but sometimes it's just what you need.

The Hack

Robin Houston's PadWalker module helpfully encapsulates the necessary dark magic in a single place that, most importantly, you don't have to understand to use. Suppose you have a misbehaving counter closure:†

```
sub make_counter
{
    my ($start, $end, $step) = @_;

    return sub
    {
        return if $start == $end;
        $start += $step;
    };
}
```

One way to debug this is to throw test case after test case at it [Hack #53] until it fails and you can deduce and reproduce why. An easier approach is to show all of the enclosed values when you have a misbehaving counter.

---

* Removed as of Perl 5.9.3.

† The erroneous operator is ==. There are actually *two* bugs, though.

Once you have a counter, use PadWalker's closed_over() function to retrieve a hash of all closed-over variables, keyed on the name of the variable:

```
use Data::Dumper;
use PadWalker 'closed_over';

my $hundred_by_nines = make_counter( 0, 100, 9 );

while ( my $item = $hundred_by_nines->() )
{
    my $vars = closed_over( $hundred_by_nines );
    warn Dumper( $vars );
}
```

Running the Hack

Running this reveals that $start, the current value of the counter, quickly exceeds 100.

```
$VAR1 = {
           '$start' => \9,
           '$step' => \9,
           '$end' => \100
         };
$VAR1 = {
           '$start' => \18,
           '$step' => \9,
           '$end' => \100
         };

# ...

$VAR1 = {
           '$start' => \6966,
           '$step' => \9,
           '$end' => \100
         };

# ...
```

$step and $end are okay, but because $start never actually *equals* $end, the closure never returns its end marker.

Changing the misbehaving operator to >= fixes this.*

---

* Consider if the $step is negative, however.

Hacking the Hack

One good turn of scary encapsulation-violation deserves another. The hash that closed_over( ) returns actually contains *references* to the closed-over variables as its values. If you dereference them, you can assign to them. Here's one way to debug the idea that the comparision operator is incorrect:

```perl
while ( my $item = $hundred_by_nines->( ) )
{
    my $vars  = closed_over( $hundred_by_nines );
    my $start = $vars->{'$start'};
    my $end   = $vars->{'$start'};
    my $step  = $vars->{'$step'};

    if ( $$start > $$step )
    {
        $$start = $$end - $$step;
    }
}
```

PadWalker is good for accessing all sorts of lexicals. If you have a subroutine reference of any kind, you can see the names of the lexicals within that subroutine—not just any lexicals it closes over. You can't always get the values, though. They're only active if you're in something that that subroutine actually called somewhere.

Be careful, though; just because you can look in someone's closet doesn't mean that you should.

The CPAN module Data::Dump::Streamer can do similar magic, except that it also deparses the closure. This is useful in other circumstances. The code:

```perl
use Data::Dump::Streamer;
my $hundred_by_nines = make_counter( 0, 100, 9 );
1 while 100 > $hundred_by_nines->( );
Dump( $hundred_by_nines );
```

produces the result:

```perl
my ($end,$start,$step);
$end = 100;
$start = 108;
$step = 9;
$CODE1 = sub {
        return if $start == $end;
        $start += $step;
    };
```

HACK
#77
Find All Global Variables
Track down global variables so you can replace them.

Perl 5's roots in Perl 1 show through sometimes. This is especially evident in the fact that variables are global by default and lexical only by declaration. The strict pragma helps, but adding that to a large program that's only grown over time (in the sense that kudzu grows) can make programs difficult to manage.

One problem of refactoring such a program is that it's difficult to tell by reading whether a particular variable is global or lexical, especially when any declaration may have come hundreds or thousands of lines earlier. Your friends and co-workers may claim that you can't run a program to analyze your program and find these global variables, but *you can*!

The Hack

Perl 5 has several core modules in the B::* namespace referred to as the backend compiler collection. These modules let you work with the internal form of a program as Perl has compiled and is running it. To see a representation of a program as Perl sees it, use the B::Concise module. Here's a short program that uses both lexical and global variables:

```
use vars qw( $frog $toad );

sub wear_bunny_costume
{
    my $bunny = shift;
    $frog     = $bunny;
    print "\$bunny is $bunny\n\$frog is $frog\n\$toad is $toad";
}
```

$frog and $toad are global variables.* $bunny is a lexical variable. Unless you notice the my or use vars lines, it's not obvious to the reader which is which. Perl knows, though:

```
$ perl -MO=Concise,wear_bunny_costume friendly_animals.pl
examples/friendly_animals.pl syntax OK
main::wear_bunny_costume:
n   <1> leavesub[1 ref] K/REFC,1 ->(end)
-       <@> lineseq KP ->n
1           <;> nextstate(main 35 friendly_animals.pl:5) v ->2
6           <2> sassign vKS/2 ->7
4               <1> shift sK/1 ->5
3                   <1> rv2av[t2] sKRM/1 ->4
2                       <$> gv(*_) s ->3
```

---
* They're also friends.

```
5            <0> padsv[$bunny:35,36] sRM*/LVINTRO -6
7            <;> nextstate(main 36 friendly_animals.pl:6) v ->8
a            <2> sassign vKS/2 ->b
8               <0> padsv[$bunny:35,36] s ->9
-               <1> ex-rv2sv sKRM*/1 ->a
9                  <$> gvsv(*frog) s -a
b            <;> nextstate(main 36 friendly_animals.pl:7) v ->c
m            <@> print sK ->n
c               <0> pushmark s ->d
-               <1> ex-stringify sK/1 ->m
-                  <0> ex-pushmark s ->d
l                  <2> concat[t6] sKS/2 ->m
j                     <2> concat[t5] sKS/2 ->k
h                        <2> concat[t4] sKS/2 ->i
f                           <2> concat[t3] sK/2 ->g
d                              <$> const(PV "$bunny is ") s ->e
e                              <0> padsv[$bunny:35,36] s -f
g                              <$> const(PV "\n$frog is ") s ->h
-                           <1> ex-rv2sv sK/1 ->j
i                              <$> gvsv(*frog) s -j
k                        <$> const(PV "\n") s ->l
```

That's a lot of potentially confusing output, but it's reasonably straightforward. This is a textual representation of the optree representing the wear_bunny_costume( ) subroutine. The emboldened lines represent variable accesses. As you can see, there are two different opcodes used to fetch values from a variable. padsv fetches the value of a named lexical from a lexical pad, while gvsv fetches the value of a scalar from a typeglob.

Running the Hack

Knowing this, you can search for all gvsv ops within a compiled program and find the global variables! B::XPath is a backend module that allows you to search a given tree with XPath expressions. To look for a gvsv node in the optree, use the XPath expression //gvsv:

```
use B::XPath;

my $node = B::XPath->fetch_root( \&wear_bunny_costume );

for my $global ( $node->match( '//gvsv' ) )
{
    my $location = $global->find_nextstate();
    printf( "Global %s found at %s:%d\n",
    $global->NAME(), $location->file(), $location->line() );
}
```

fetch_root( ) gets the root opcode for a given subroutine. To search the entire program, use B::XPath::fetch_main_root( ). match( ) applies an XPath expression to the optree starting at the given $node, returning a list of matching nodes.

As each node returned should be a gvsv op (blessed into B::XPath::SVOP), the NAME( ) method retrieves the name of the glob. The find_nextstate( ) method finds the nearest parent control op (or COP) which contains the name of the file and the line number on which the variable appeared.* The results are:

```
$ perl friendly_animals.pl
Global frog found at friendly_animals.pl:8
Global frog found at friendly_animals.pl:9
```

Hacking the Hack

If you want to find only globals named $toad, change the XPath expression and parameterize it by a node attribute:

```
$node->match( '//gvsv[@NAME="toad"]' ))
```

There's no limit to the types of opcodes you can search for in a program beyond what B::XPath supports and the XPath expressions you can write. As long as you can dump a snippet of code into an optree list, you can eventually turn that into an XPath expression. From there, just grab the node information you need and you're on your way.

See also the built-in B::Xref module. It produces a cross reference of variables and subroutines in your code.

HACK
#78

Introspect Your Subroutines

Trace any subroutine to its source.

You can name anonymous subroutines [Hack #57] and deparse them [Hack #56]. You can even peek at their closed-over lexical variables [Hack #76]. There are still more wonders in the world.

Someday you'll have to debug a running program and figure out exactly where package *A* picked up subroutine *B*. One option is to trace all import( ) calls, but that's even less fun than it sounds. Another option is to pull out the scariest and most powerful toolkit in the Perl hacker's toolbox: the B::* modules.

The Hack

Finding a misbehaving function means you need to know two of three things:

---

* It uses a heuristic, so it may not always be *exact*.

- The original package of the function
- The name of the file containing the function
- The line number in the file corresponding to the function

From there, your debugging should be somewhat easier. Perl stores all of this information for every CV* it compiles. You just need a way to get to it.

The usual entry point is through the B module and its svref_2object( ) function, which takes a normal Perl data structure, grabs the underlying C representation, and wraps it in hairy-scary objects that allow you to peek (though not usually poke) at its guts.

It's surprisingly easy to report a subroutine's vital information:

```
use B;

sub introspect_sub
{
    my $sub      = shift;
    my $cv       = B::svref_2object( $sub );

    return join( ':',
        $cv->STASH->NAME( ), $cv->FILE( ), $cv->GV->LINE( ) . "\n"
    );
}
```

introspect_sub( ) takes one argument, a reference to a subroutine. After passing it to svref_2object( ), it receives back a B::CV object. The STASH( ) method returns the typeglob representing the package's namespace—calling NAME( ) on this returns the package name. The FILE( ) method returns the name of the file containing this subroutine. The GV( ) method returns the particular symbol table entry for this subroutine, in which the LINE( ) method returns the line of the file corresponding to the start of this subroutine.

> Okay, using Devel::Peek::CvGV on a subroutine reference is easier.
>
> ```
> use Devel::Peek 'CvGV';
> sub Foo::bar { }
> print CvGV( \&Foo::bar );
> ```
>
> Of course, that prints the *name* of the glob containing the subroutine…but it's a quick way to find even that much information. Now you know *two* ways to do it!

---

* The internal representation of all subroutines and methods.

Running the Hack

Pass in any subroutine reference and print the result somehow to see all of this wonderful data:

```perl
use Data::Dumper;

package Foo;

sub foo { }

package Bar;

sub bar { }
*foo = \&Foo::foo;

package main;

warn introspect_sub( \&Foo::foo );
warn introspect_sub( \&Bar::bar );
warn introspect_sub( \&Bar::foo );
warn introspect_sub( \&Dumper );

# introspect_sub( ) as before...
```

Run the file as normal:

```
$ perl introspect.pl
Foo:examples/introspect.pl:14
Bar:examples/introspect.pl:18
Foo:examples/introspect.pl:14
Data::Dumper:/usr/lib/perl5/site_perl/5.8.7/powerpc-linux/Data/Dumper.pm:495
```

As you can see, aliasing `Bar::foo( )` to `Foo::foo( )` didn't fool the introspector, nor did importing `Dumper( )` from `Data::Dumper`.

Hacking the Hack

That's not all though. You can also see any lexical variables declared within a subroutine. Every CV holds a special array* called a padlist. This padlist itself contains two arrays, one holding the name of lexical variables and the other containing an array of arrays holding the values for subsequent recursive invocations of the subroutine.†

Grabbing a list of all lexical variables declared in that scope is as simple as walking the appropriate array in the padlist:

```perl
sub introspect_sub
{
```

---

* In an AV data structure that represents arrays.

† At least, it's something like that; it gets complex quickly.

```
    my $sub      = shift;
    my $cv       = B::svref_2object( $sub );
    my ($names)  = $cv->PADLIST->ARRAY();

    my $report  = join( ':',
        $cv->STASH->NAME( ), $cv->FILE( ), $cv->GV->LINE( ) . "\n"
    );

    my @lexicals = map { $_->can( 'PV' ) ? $_->PV() : () } $names->ARRAY();

    return $report unless @lexicals;

    $report .= "\t(" . join( ', ', @lexicals ) . ")\n";
    return $report;
}
```

There's one trick and that's that the array containing the names of the lexicals doesn't *only* contain their names. However, knowing that the B::OP-derived objects holding the names will always have a PV( ) method that returns a string representing the appropriate value of the scalar, the code filters out everything else. It works nicely, too:

```
use Data::Dumper;

package Foo;

sub foo
{
    my ($foo, $bar, $baz) = @_;
}

package Bar;

sub bar { }
*foo = \&Foo::foo;

package main;

warn introspect_sub( \&Foo::foo );
warn introspect_sub( \&Bar::bar );
warn introspect_sub( \&Bar::foo );
warn introspect_sub( \&Dumper );

# introspect_sub( ) as modified...
```

This outputs:

```
$ perl introspect_lexicals.pl
Foo:examples/introspect.pl:14
    ($foo, $bar, $baz)
Bar:examples/introspect.pl:18
Foo:examples/introspect.pl:14
    ($foo, $bar, $baz)
Data::Dumper:/usr/lib/perl5/site_perl/5.8.7/powerpc-linux/Data/Dumper.pm:495
```

Easy…at least once you've trawled through `perldoc B` and perhaps the Perl source code (*cv.h* and *pad.c*, if you really need details).

Find Imported Functions
#79   Keep an eye on your namespace.

Importing functions is a mixed blessing. Having functions available from another namespace without having to type their full names is convenient. However, the chance for name collisions and confusion increases with the number of imported symbols.

There are multiple ways to tell the original package of a function, but many of them involve lots of deep magic and, in cases of generated functions, may not tell the whole story. If you really want to know what you've imported and when, the shortest and simplest approach is to use the `Devel::Symdump` module.

The Hack

To get a list of functions from a package, create a new `Devel::Symdump` object and use the `functions()` method on it:

```
use Devel::Symdump;
my $symbols   = Devel::Symdump->new( 'main' );
my @functions = $symbols->functions();
```

That gives you a list of fully-qualified function names as of the time of the call. Load and import from the other modules you need, and then create and query a *new* `Devel::Symdump` object to get a longer list of functions.

Running the Hack

Suppose you want to know what `File::Spec::Functions` imports.* If you can wedge the code to create and query the first `Devel::Symdump` object before the use line executes **[Hack #70]**, all you have to do is perform an array intersection to remove duplicate elements.

```
use Devel::Symdump;

my %existing;

BEGIN
{
```

---

* Sure, you could read the documentation, but your system administrator compressed the documentation and broke it.

```
    my $symbols = Devel::Symdump->new( 'main' );
    @existing{ $symbols->functions() } = ();
}

use File::Spec::Functions;

BEGIN
{
    my $symbols    = Devel::Symdump->new( 'main' );
    my @new_funcs =
        map { s/main:://; $_ }
        grep { not exists $existing{ $_ } } $symbols->functions();
    local $" = "\n    ";
    warn qq|Imported:$"@new_funcs\n|;
}
```

As of Perl 5.8.7, this prints:

```
$ perl show_fsf_symbols.pl
Imported:
  catfile
  curdir
  updir
  path
  file_name_is_absolute
  no_upwards
  canonpath
  catdir
  rootdir
$
```

Are you worried that this won't account for user-defined functions? Don't—by the time the BEGIN blocks run, Perl hasn't seen any yet. You're safe.

Hacking the Hack

Devel::Symdump works on more than just functions. You can find all exported scalars, arrays, hashes, and file and directory handles, as well as all other symbol tables beneath the named one. Beware, though, that all new symbols have a scalar created by default (at least in Perl prior to 5.9.3), so searching for those isn't as useful as you might think.

It would be easy to register a list of all exported functions with the using package, to allow more introspection and runtime. You could even write a module that does this and re-exports them to your package.

Profile Your Program Size

Find out how much memory your program takes, and then trim it!

The difference between a Perl program and a natively compiled binary is far more than just program convenience. Although the Perl program can do far more with less *source* code, in memory, Perl's data structures and bookkeeping can take up more space than you might think. Size matters sometimes—even if you have plenty of memory (if you're not trying to optimize for shared memory in a child-forking application, for example), a program with good algorithms and not tied to IO or incoming requests can still run faster if it has fewer operations to perform.

One of the best optimizations of Perl programs is trimming the number of operations it has to perform. The less work it has to do, the better.

This isn't an argument for obfuscated or golfed code—just good profiling to find and trim the few fat spots left in a program.

The Hack

When Perl compiles a program, it builds an internal representation called the optree. This represents every single discrete operation in a program. Thus knowing how many opcodes there are in a program (or module) and the size of each opcode is necessary to know where to start optimizing.

The B::TerseSize module is useful in this case.* It adds a size( ) method to all ops. More importantly, it gives you detailed information about the size of all symbols in a package if you call package_size( ).

To find the largest subroutine in a package and report on its opcodes, use code something like:

```
use B::TerseSize;

sub report_largest_sub
{
    my $package                 = shift;
    my ($symbols, $count, $size) = B::TerseSize::package_size( $package );
    my ($largest)               =
        sort { $symbols->{$b}{size} <=> $symbols->{$a}{size} }
        grep { exists $symbols->{$_}{count} }
        keys %$symbols;
```

---

* It's *more* useful when used with mod_perl and Apache::Status; see *http://modperlbook.org/html/ch09_04.html*.

```
    print "Total size for $package is $size in $count ops.\n";
    print "Reporting $largest.\n";
    B::TerseSize::CV_walk( 'root', $package . '::' . $largest );
}
```

package_size( ) returns three items: a reference to a hash where the key is the name of a symbol and the value is a hash reference with the count of opcodes for that symbol and the total size of the symbol, the total count of opcodes for the package, and the total size of the package.

report_largest_sub( ) takes the name of a loaded package, finds the largest subroutine in that package (where the heuristic is that only subroutines have a count key in the second-level hash of the symbol information), prints some summary information about the package, and then calls CV_walk( ) which prints a lot of information about the selected subroutine.

Running the Hack

The real meat of the hack is in interpreting the output. B::TerseSize displays statistics for every significant line of code in a subroutine. Thus, calling report_largest_sub( ) on Text::WikiFormat will print pages of output for find_list( ):

```
Total size for Text::WikiFormat is 92078 in 1970 ops.
Reporting find_list.
UNOP   leavesub     0x10291e88 {28 bytes} [targ 1 - $line]
    LISTOP lineseq    0x10290050 {32 bytes}


-------------------------------------------------------------
        COP    nextstate    0x10290010 {24 bytes}
        BINOP  aassign      0x1028ffe8 {32 bytes} [targ 6 - undef]
            UNOP  null       0x1028fd38 {28 bytes} [list]
                OP    pushmark   0x1028ffc8 {24 bytes}
                UNOP  rv2av      0x1028ffa8 {28 bytes} [targ 5 - undef]
                    SVOP  gv         0x1028ff88 {96 bytes}  GV *_
            UNOP  null       0x1028d660 {28 bytes} [list]
                OP    pushmark   0x1028fec0 {24 bytes}
                OP    padsv      0x1028fe68 {24 bytes} [targ 1 - $line]
                OP    padsv      0x1028fea0 {24 bytes} [targ 2 -
                                                              $list_types]
                OP    padsv      0x1028fee0 {24 bytes} [targ 3 - $tags]
                OP    padsv      0x1028ff10 {24 bytes} [targ 4 - $opts]

[line 317 size: 380 bytes]


-------------------------------------------------------------

(snip 234 more lines)
```

The final line gives the key to interpreting the output; it represents line 317 of the file defining this package:

```
315: sub find_list
316: {
317:     my ( $line, $list_types, $tags, $opts ) = @_;
318:
319:     for my $list (@$list_types)
```

This single line costs twelve opcodes and around 380 bytes* of memory. If this were worth optimizing, perhaps removing an unused variable would help.

The previous lines list each op on this line in tree order. That is, the root of the branch is the nextstate control op. It has a sibling, the leaveloop binary op. You can ignore the memory address, but the size of the op in curly braces can be useful. Finally, some ops have additional information in square brackets—especially those referring to lexical variables.

The real use of this information is when you can compare two different implementations of an algorithm to each other to optimize for memory usage or number of ops. Sometimes the code with the fewest number of lines really isn't slimmer.

Hacking the Hack

Do you absolutely hate the output from CV_walk( )? Write your callback and use B::walkoptree_slow( ) or B::walkoptree_exec( ) to call it. Don't forget to use B::TerseSize to make the size( ) method available on ops. You can get package and line number information from nextstate ops.

Unfortunately, doing this effectively probably means stealing the code from B::TerseSize. At least it's reasonably small and self-contained. Look for the methods declared in the B:: namespace.

HACK #81   Reuse Perl Processes
Spend CPU time running programs, not recompiling them.

As nice as it is to be able to type and run a Perl program, compiled programs sometimes have a few advantages. Quickly running processes might spend most of their time launching, not running.

If you have a program you might want to run all the time, but it takes significant time to load the appropriate modules and get ready to run and you just can't spare that time on something that should execute immediately and get

---

* Give or take; B::TerseSize can only guess sometimes.

out of the way or that might have to run dozens of times per second under high load, trade a little memory for speed with PPerl.

The Hack

Matt Sergeant's PPerl module provides a mod_perl-like environment for normal Perl programs. A well-written program can run under PPerl with no modifications.

Suppose you use Chia-liang Kao's amazingly useful SVK distributed revision control system, written in Perl.* You're continually making lots of little checkins, and you've started to notice a bit of a lag as launching the program continually recompiles a handful of complex modules.

Make a copy of the svk program in your path where your shell will find it before the system version. Edit the file and change the first line from:

```
#!/usr/bin/perl -w
```

... to:

```
#!/usr/bin/pperl -w
```

That's it!

Running the Hack

The first time you launch svk, it will take just about as long as normal. Subsequent launches will run much more quickly, as PPerl reuses the launched process—avoiding the repeated hit of compilation.

This works well for other processes too—mail filters written with Mail::Audit or Mail::Filter, SpamAssassin, and any Perl program that can run multiple times idempotently but usually takes little time to run.

Hacking the Hack

As an administrator, to make a persistent svk to share between every developer on the box, create an alias (or equivalent shell script) to launch svk with the --anyuser flag:

```
alias svk='/usr/bin/pperl -- --anyuser /usr/bin/svk'
```

Other useful flags include --prefork to tune the number of persistent processes to launch and --maxclients to set the maximum number of requests

---

* If you don't use it already, try it.

any child will serve before exiting. (This helps keep down memory usage, as multiple requests unshare more and more pages.)

> One feature PPerl currently lacks is to shut down the persistent process after it goes unused for a period of time.

HACK #82 Trace Your Ops

Watch Perl execute individual instructions.

Unlike so-called natively compiled programs, Perl programs are instructions for the Perl virtual machine. When Perl compiles a program, it reduces it to a tree of opcodes, such as "fetch this lexical variable" and "add the attached constant." If you want to see what your program is doing, the best* way is to examine each individual opcode.

The B::* modules—the compiler backend to Perl—give you some flexibility in examining compiled code from Perl. They don't give you many opportunities to play with ops as Perl runs them, however. Fortunately, Runops::Trace does.

The Hack

Runops::Trace replaces Perl's standard runloop with an alternate runloop that calls back to Perl code, passing the B::* object representing the next op that will run. This allows you to request and log any data from that op.

> Perl's standard runloop executes the current op, fetches the next op after that, dispatches any signals that have arrived, and repeats.

For example, to count the number of accesses to global symbols within a program, write a callback logger:

```
package TraceGlobals;

use strict;
use warnings;

use Runops::Trace \&trace_globals;

my %globals;
```

* Though not necessarily the *easiest*.

```
sub trace_globals
{
    return unless $_[0]->isa( 'B::SVOP' ) && $_[0]->name() eq 'gv';
    my $gv   = shift->gv();
    my $data = $globals{ $gv->SAFENAME() } ||= {};
    my $key  = $gv->FILE() . ':' . $gv->LINE();
    $data->{$key}++;
}

END
{
    Runops::Trace->unimport();

    for my $gv ( sort keys %globals )
    {
        my $gv_data = $globals{ $gv };
        my @counts  = keys %$gv_data;

        for my $line ( sort { $gv_data->{$b} <=> $gv_data->{$a} } @counts)
        {
            printf "%04d %s %-> s\n", $gv_data->{$line}, $gv, $line;
        }
    }
}

1;
```

The important work is in trace_globals( ). The subroutine first examines its only argument, throwing out all non-SV opcodes and all non-GV opcodes. (These are opcodes that access typeglobs, or GVs, as the Perl internals call them.) Then it fetches the GV object attached to the op, logging the name of the GV (SAFENAME( )) and the file (FILE( )) and line (LINE( )) where the symbol occurs.

The END block formats and reports this data nicely. The call to Runops::Trace->unimport( ) at the start prevents the tracing module from accidentally trying to trace itself at the end of the program.

Running the Hack

Because of the way Runops::Trace installs its tracing runloop, you must load a tracing module *before* the code you want to trace. The easiest way to do this is from the command line, perhaps on the program from "Find All Symbols in a Package" [Hack #75]:

```
$ perl -MTraceGlobals find_package_symbols.pl
Foo:find_package_symbols.pl:14
        ($foo, $bar, $baz)
Bar:find_package_symbols.pl:18
```

```
Foo:find_package_symbols.pl:14
        ($foo, $bar, $baz)
Data::Dumper:/usr/lib/perl5/site_perl/5.8.7/powerpc-linux/Data/Dumper.pm:484
0001 AddrRef -> /usr/lib/perl5/5.8.7/overload.pm:94
0054 Bits -> /usr/lib/perl5/5.8.7/warnings.pm:189
0003 Cache -> /usr/lib/perl5/5.8.7/Exporter.pm:13
0002 DeadBits -> /usr/lib/perl5/5.8.7/warnings.pm:239
0001 Dumper -> /usr/lib/perl5/5.8.7/Exporter.pm:65
0001 EXPORT -> /usr/lib/perl5/site_perl/5.8.7/powerpc-linux/Data/Dumper.pm:
24
0001 EXPORT_OK -> /usr/lib/perl5/site_perl/5.8.7/powerpc-linux/
        Data/Dumper.pm:25
0001 ISA -> /usr/lib/perl5/site_perl/5.8.7/powerpc-linux/Data/Dumper.pm:23
0002 Offsets -> /usr/lib/perl5/5.8.7/warnings.pm:136
0003 SIG -> /usr/lib/perl5/5.8.7/Exporter.pm:62
0001 StrVal -> /usr/lib/perl5/site_perl/5.8.7/powerpc-linux/
        Data/Dumper.pm:104
0037 _ -> :0
<...>
```

The first part of the output is the normal program output, as the program runs as normal. The second half of the output shows the number of accesses, the name of the symbol, and the file and line of the definition of the symbol. The final line is interesting—it shows the requests made for the glob named _, usually accessed as @_ and not defined in a package or a file.

Hacking the Hack

Finding all of the global symbols is interesting, especially if you want to explore a certain code path where static analysis isn't helpful [Hack #77]. You can do much, much more with a tracing runloop. Consider that the callback function is basically the entry point into an event-driven state machine. Find the type of ops you want to query and perform your behavior based on that.

For example, to measure the amount of time you spend in one package over another, look for the B::COP objects that represent the nextstate op and keep timing information. To see when a variable changes, look for B::SVOP objects accessing that particular variable.

A future enhancement to Runops::Trace may allow you to *change* the next op, declining to handle dangerous or indelicate operations, or even redirecting to different ops. To learn more, read the documentation for B and become familiar with optrees with B::Concise and B::Terse.

Write Your Own Warnings

HACK #83

Improve static code checking.

You have strict under control. You know why you use warnings. Maybe you even use B::Lint to find problems. Are they truly enough for you? If you've ever wished that you could make strict stricter or make warnings preachier, you're in luck.

> Perl::Critic is a similarly excellent tool that audits your code based on Damian Conway's *Perl Best Practices* (O'Reilly).

The Hack

It's impossible to override some built-in functions* **[Hack #91]** like print( ) and printf( ). Usually print( ) succeeds because it writes to an internal buffer—but occasionally Perl has to flush the buffer. print( ) might fail if you write to a file on a full file system, to a closed handle, or for any of several other reasons. If you don't check print( ) and close( ) for success, you might lose data without knowing about it.

The best you can do for unoverridable functions is to create new warnings for unsafe code.

Here's *bad_style.pl*, a short program that opens a file and writes something to it. It has three misfeatures: ignoring the results of print( ) and close( ) and a terribly non-descriptive variable name:

```
open my $fh, '>>', 'bad_style.txt'
    or die "Can't open bad_style.txt for appending: $!\n";
print {$fh} 'Hello!';
close $fh;
```

You *could* review every line of code in your system to find these errors. Better yet, teach B::Lint how to find them for you:

```
package B::Lint::VoidSyscalls;

use strict;
use warnings;

use B 'OPf_WANT_VOID';
use B::Lint;
```

---

* Run perl -MB::Keywords -le 'eval{ prototype $_ } or print for @B::Keywords::Functions' after installing B::Keywords to see a complete list.

```perl
# Make B::Lint accept plugins if it doesn't already.
use if ! B::Lint->can('register_plugin'),
    'B::Lint::Pluggable';

# Register this plugin.
B::Lint->register_plugin( __PACKAGE__, [ 'void_syscall' ] );

# Check these opcodes
my $SYSCALL = qr/ ^ (?: open | print | close ) $ /msx;

# Also look for things that are right at the end of a subroutine
# sub foo { return print() }
my $TERM = qr/ ^ (?: leavesub ) $/msx;

sub match
{
    my ( $op, $checks ) = @_;

    if (    $checks->{void_syscall}
        and $op->name() =~ m/$SYSCALL/msx )
    {
        if ( $op->flags() & OPf_WANT_VOID )
        {
            warn "Unchecked " . $op->name() . " system call "
                . "at " . B::Lint->file() . " on line "
                . B::Lint->line() . "\n";
        }
        elsif ( $op->next->name() =~ m/$TERM/msx )
        {
            warn "Potentially unchecked " . $op->name() . " system call "
                . "at " . B::Lint->file() . " on line "
                . B::Lint->line() . "\n";
        }
    }
}
```

As of Perl 5.9.3, B::Lint supports plugins. Earlier versions
don't, so this code checks the version and loads a fallback if
necessary.

This module also checks for system calls made in potentially void context at
the end of functions—that is, where the next opcode is leavesub.

Running the Hack

Checking *bad_style.pl* with B::Lint::VoidSyscalls is easy:

```
$ perl -MB::Lint::VoidSyscalls -MO=Lint bad_style.pl
Unchecked print system call at bad_style.pl on line 3
Unchecked close system call at bad_style.pl on line 4
bad_style.pl syntax OK
```

Hacking the Hack

The idea is pretty general: find bad stuff in the optree ("Find All Global Variables" [Hack #77] shows how to mine the optree) and tell the user about it. There are plenty of possibilities to add more strictness to your OO code—checking that a class actually exists for class method calls, that the methods being called on those classes exist, and even that the methods being called are appropriate methods for certain classes. Here's an alternate match( ) subroutine that does just that:

```perl
sub match
{
    my $op = shift;

    if ( $op->name() eq 'entersub' )
    {
        my $class  = eval { $op->first->sibling          ->sv->PV };
        my $method = eval { $op->first->sibling->sibling->sv->PV };

        if ( defined $class )
        {
            no strict 'refs';

            # check strict classes
            if ( not %{ $class . '::' } )
            {
                B::Lint::warning "Class $class doesn't exist";
            }
            # check strict class methods
            elsif ( defined $method and not $class->can($method) )
            {
                B::Lint::warning "Class $class can't do method $method";
            }
        }
        elsif (      defined $method
                and not grep { $_->can($method) } classes( B::Lint->file() )
        )
        {
            B::Lint::warning "Object can't do method $method";
        }
    }
}
```

```perl
use File::Slurp 'read_file';

my %classes;
sub classes
{
    my $file = shift;
    $classes{$file} ||= scalar {
        map { $_ => 1 }
        grep { defined %{ $_ . '::' } }
        read_file($file) =~ m/( \w+ (?: (?:::|')\w+ )* )/msxg
    };
    return keys %{ $classes{$file} };
}
```

CHAPTER NINE

Expand Your Perl Foo
Hacks 84–101

What exactly is a Perl guru? Is it someone who's programmed Perl for years and years? Is it someone with a dozen modules on the CPAN? Is it someone with patches in the core or her name in the Preface.*

Perhaps instead a guru is someone who knows something that most people never knew existed. A real guru can apply that knowledge productively and appropriately to solve a difficult problem with apparent ease.

Want to be a Perl guru? Here's some of the magic you may never have suspected. Absorb these secrets. Recognize the situations where you can apply them. Then you too will be a guru.

Double Your Data with Dualvars
#84 Store twice the information in a single scalar.

Some languages are really picky about the contents of a variable. If the variable is a string, it's always a string. If the variable is a number, it's always a number—especially of a certain type and size.

Perl's not that picky; it happily converts back and forth depending on what you do with the variable. Consequently, one variable may hold several different pices of data. You can even peek inside Perl's storage and do different things depending on how you treat your variable—returning entirely different values whether you treat it as a number or a string.

The Hack

Consider a program that has a lot of constants—say, a graphical program [Hack #16] with screen size, color depth, difficulty level, and so on. If you're

---

* Actually, that *might* be a good sign!

215

debugging such a problem, it can be difficult to track variables when you're passing around magic variables. It gets worse when you have to deal with flags that you AND and OR together. How do you know when a number is really an important number or just the coincidental result of a calculation that merely *looks* like an important number?

Instead of having to look up the symbolic names (easy for programmers to remember) for values (easy for a computer to handle) every time you debug something, consider using dualvars:

```
use Scalar::Util 'dualvar';

my $width   = dualvar( 800, 'Screen width'       );
my $height  = dualvar( 600, 'Screen height'      );
my $colors  = dualvar(  16, 'Screen color depth' );

# some code
sub debug_variable
{
    my $constant = shift;
    printf STDERR "%s is %d\n", $constant, $constant;
}
```

Now whenever you encounter a variable you want to inspect for debugging, pass it to debug_variable( ), which will helpfully print something like:

```
Screen width is 800
Screen height is 600
Screen color depth is 16
```

Running the Hack

Every Perl scalar has several slots for several different types of data. The dualvar( ) function from the ever-useful Scalar::Util package takes two: a numeric and a string value. It stores the numeric value in the numeric (NV) slot of the scalar and sets a flag that it's okay to look in that slot in numeric contexts. It does the same for the string value (PV slot, string contexts).

Whenever you access a scalar in a certain type of context, Perl first checks the appropriate flag for that context. If it's okay to use the value in the appropriate slot, Perl does so. Otherwise, it converts an existing value from another slot to the appropriate type, puts the calculated value in the appropriate slot, and sets the flag it checked.

The dualvar nature affects the value stored in the variable, not the variable itself, so it's safe to pass back and forth in and out of functions.

Hacking the Hack

You can also use this trick with the constant pragma if you prefer that for your constants:

```
use constant AUTHOR => dualvar( 006, 'chromatic the superspy author' );
```

If that's not paranoid enough for you, the Readonly module also works with this technique:

```
use Readonly;
Readonly::Scalar my $colors => dualvar(  16, 'Screen color depth' );
```

Replace Soft References with Real Ones

Combine the benefits of name-based references, lexicals, and typo-checking.

One of the first milestones in becoming an effective programmer is the sudden flash of Zen when you first ask the question "How can I use a variable as a variable name?"* The second half of that zap of enlightenment is when you realize why you usually don't need to do that.

Sometimes it's the easiest solution to a problem, though—especially when you're refactoring a large, complex piece of code written by someone who just didn't *get it* yet.

Don't despair; you can have all of the benefits with almost none of the drawbacks.

Suppose you have a sales reporting application such as one the author had to maintain many lives ago. There are multiple types of items for sale, each with its own separate total in the report. You have a parser that reads external data, giving you a key-value pair with the name of the sale category and the value of the item.

Unfortunately, the program uses several lexical-but-file-global variables and you don't have time to change the whole thing to use an obvious %totals hash.

> If that's not scary enough, imagine that the actual system really *did* use symbolic references here (yes, that implies globals, not lexicals!) without error checking and that the sales totals came from the Internet through unencrypted means. Suddenly being a writer seems appealing.

* See *perlfaq7* if you've really *never* asked this.

The code, minus the section you need to change and with a fake data-reading section for the purpose of the example, might look something like:

```perl
use strict;
use warnings;

my ($books_total, $movies_total, $candy_total, $certificates_total, $total);

create_report();
print_report();
exit();

sub print_report
{
    print <<END_REPORT;
SALES
    Books:              $books_total
    Movies:             $movies_total
    Candy;              $candy_total
    Gift Certificates:  $certificates_total

TOTAL:                  $total
END_REPORT
}

sub create_report
{
    # your code here
}

sub get_row
{
    return unless defined( my $line = <DATA> );
    chomp( $line );
    return split( ':', $line );
}

__DATA__
books:10.00
movies:15.00
candy:7.50
certificates:8.00
```

The Hack

Use a hash, as the FAQ suggests, stuffed full of references to the variables you need to update. You can build this very concisely, with only a little bit of duplication, with a sadly underused piece of Perl syntax—the list reference constructor. When given a list of scalars, the reference constructor (\) returns a list of references to those scalars. That's perfect for the list of values to a hash slice!

```
sub create_report
{
    my %totals;
    @totals{ qw( books movies candy certificates total )} =
    \( $books_total, $movies_total, $candy_total,
      $certificates_total, $total
    );

    while (my ($category, $value)  = get_row())
    {
        ${ $totals{ $category } } += $value;
        ${ $totals{total}        } += $value;
    }
}
```

That's better. When your data feed changes next week and gives you a list of product names, not categories, change the list slice assignment to %totals to store multiple references to the same category total scalars under different keys. You still have an ugly mapping of strings to lexical variables, but until you can refactor out the yuck of the rest of the application, you've at least localized the problem in only one spot you need to touch.

Besides, as far as the author knows, the original application is likely still running.

Hacking the Hack

Validation is still a problem here; how do you prevent a typo in the data from an external source from causing a run-time error? With the hash, you *can* check for a valid key with exists (though storing total in the hash as well is a potential bug waiting to happen). This may be an appropriate place to use a locked hash [Hack #87].

Optimize Away the Annoying Stuff
#86 File off the rough edges of your code.

Sit down and look at the code you actually write every day. Is there something tedious that you do all the time, something that is a tiny (but constant) irritation? Maybe it's as simple as adding that final "\n" to the end of just about every print command:

```
print "Showing first ", @results / 2, " of ", scalar @results, "\n";

for (@results[ 0 .. @results / 2 - 1 ])
{
    if (m/($IDENT): \s* (.*?) \s* $/x)
    {
        print "$1 -> ", normalize($2), "\n";
    }
```

```
    else
    {
        print "Strange result: ", substr( $2, 0, 10 ), "\n";
    }
}
```

The Hack

If you find that you have to tack a newline onto the end of most (or even just many) of your print statements, factor out that tiny annoyance:

```
sub say { print @_, "\n" }

# and ever after...

say "Showing first ", @results / 2, " of ", scalar @results;

for (@results[ 0 .. @results / 2 - 1 ])
{
    if (m/($IDENT): \s* (.*?) \s* $/x)
    {
        say "$1 -> ", normalize($2);
    }
    else
    {
        say "Strange result: ", substr( $2, 0, 10 );
    }
}
```

Likewise, if you're forever opening a file and reading in the contents:

```
open my $fh, '<', $filename or die "Couldn't open 'filename'";
my $contents = do { local $/; <$fh> };
```

you could automate that:

```
sub slurp
{
    my ($file) = @_;
    open my $fh, '<', $file or croak "Couldn't open '$file'";
    local $/;
    return <$fh>;
}

# and thereafter:

my $contents = slurp $filename;
```

Hacking the Hack

The key here is to find the repetitive, low-level, mechanical things you do and hoist them out of your code into shorter, cleaner, higher-level abbreviations. Factoring out these common "micropatterns" makes the resulting code more readable and less prone to typos and other mishaps. It also frees you to concentrate on solving your actual problem.

There are already good implementations on CPAN for many of these micro-patterns. For example, see `Perl6::Say`, `File::Slurp`, `List::UtilTerm::ReadKey`, or `Sort::Maker`. Subroutines like `say( )` and `slurp( )` are also prime candidates for adding to your standard toolkit [Hack #34].

HACK #87 Lock Down Your Hashes

Protect against typos in your hashes.

As much as the scalar is the fundamental data type in Perl, the hash is perhaps the most useful—except for one small flaw. Though `use strict` protects against embarrassing typos in variable names, it does nothing to protect against mistyping hash *keys*.

If you're fortunate enough to use Perl 5.8.0 or newer, you can protect yourself with locked hashes.

The Hack

Suppose you're working on code that needs to sling around several hashes and your coworkers keep mistyping key names.[*] Though things all look correct, it's difficult to catch and debug and it causes you plenty of problems.

Rather than searching the entire program's source code (and vetting the contents of all possible variables and configuration files and every place you could get a new hash key), lock the hash's keys:

```perl
use Test::More tests => 2;
use Hash::Util 'lock_keys';

my %locked   = ( foo => 1, bar => 2 );
my %unlocked = ( foo => 1, bar => 2 );
lock_keys( %locked );

eval {   $locked{fool} = 1 };
eval { $unlocked{fool} = 1 };

is( keys %locked,   2, 'hash with locked keys should disallow unknown key' );
is( keys %unlocked, 3, '... but unlocked hash should not' );
```

---

[*] As if anyone would *ever* misspell "referrer."

Running the Hack

Anyone can add any keys and values to %unlocked, but trying to read from or write to a key not in the hash (in this case, fool) when you call lock_keys( ) will fail with the error:

```
Attempt to access disallowed key 'fool' in a restricted hash...
```

Run your test suite and check the line number of the error message to find the culprit. Fix. Repeat.

Note that you can still call exists without triggering the exception. Also, if your co-workers are particularly evil or at least actively malicious, they can call unlock_keys( ) before doing bad things. If this is the case, you have bigger problems than misspellings—such as not having a comprehensive test suite.

> Though this may *seem* like it solves some of the problems of using blessed hashes as the basis of objects, it has several limitations, especially that it still doesn't enforce any encapsulation. See instead "Turn Your Objects Inside Out" [Hack #43].

Clean Up at the End of a Scope

HACK
#88

Execute your cleanup code, no matter how you exit a scope.

Successful programs are robust. Even if errors happen, the programs can adapt, continuing if possible, but always exiting cleanly and sensibly.

Robust programs often need to guarantee that some sort of cleanup happens sometimes, whether that's closing spawned programs properly, flushing buffers, removing temporary files, or giving up an exclusive resource. Some programming languages and platforms provide ways to ensure that your cleanup code always runs. Perl doesn't—but it does provide the hooks to make it possible.

The Hack

Imagine that you have to write a program that processes and analyzes records from a database. The processing isn't idempotent, so you need to keep track of the most recent record processed. You can assume that the record ids increase monotonically. However, admins can interrupt the program as necessary, as the task has a low priority. You want to make sure that, no matter what happens, you always record the id of the most-recently processed item.

Use Scope::Guard and a closure to schedule an end-of-scope operation:

```perl
use Scope::Guard;

sub process_records
{
    my $records  = fetch_records( );
    my $last_rec = 0;
    my $cleanup  = sub { cleanup( $last_rec ) if $last_rec };
    my $guard    = Scope::Guard->new( $cleanup );

    for my $record ( @$records )
    {
        process_record( $record );
        $last_rec = $record;
    }
}

sub cleanup
{
    my $record = shift;

    # mark record as last record successfully completed
}
```

process_records( ) declares a lexical variable, $last_rec, to hold the last record successfully processed. It then builds a closure in $cleanup which calls the cleanup( ) subroutine, passing $last_rec. Then it creates a new Scope::Guard object with the closure.

In the normal flow of operation, the subroutine will process all of the records. Then it exits the subroutine. At this point, Perl garbage collects $guard and calls the closure, which itself calls the cleanup( ) subroutine and marks the last successfully processed record.

It's possible that process_record( ) may throw an exception if it cannot process a record appropriately. It's also possible that an admin or resource limit will kill the process, or something else could stop the program before it finishes processing all of the records. Even so, $guard still goes out of scope and calls cleanup( ).

> Could you modify process_record( ) to update the record of
> the last successfully processed record? Absolutely. However,
> it's not always appropriate or efficient or possible to do so.

Hacking the Hack

Scope::Guard isn't just good for cleanup. You can perform all sorts of interesting operations when you leave a scope. For example, what if you need to chdir to various directories to run external processes that expect very specific current working directories? You could write a chdir replacement that takes a directory and return a Scope::Guard object that returns to the current working directory:

```
use Cwd;

sub change_directory
{
    my $newdir = shift;
    my $curdir = cwd( );
    chdir( $newdir );
    return Scope::Guard->new( sub { chdir $curdir } );
}
```

Of course, you could also use David Golden's File::pushd module from the CPAN.

Invoke Functions in Odd Ways

HACK #89

Hide function calls behind familiar syntax.

Everyone's familiar with the normal ways to invoke Perl functions: foo( ) or foo(*someparams*...) or, in the case of method calls, *class*->foo(...) or *$obj*-> foo(...).

The Hack

There are far stranger ways to invoke a function. All of these ways are usually too weird for normal use, but useful only on occasion. That's another way* to say that they are the perfect hack.

Make a Bareword invoke a function. If you have a function named foo, Perl will let you call it without parens as long as it has seen the function defined (or predefined) by the time it sees the call. That is, if you have:

```
sub foo
{
    ...a bunch of code....
}
```

or even just:

```
sub foo;    # predefine 'foo'
```

---

* "One of God's own prototypes. Some kind of high-powered mutant never even considered for mass production. Too weird to live, and too rare to die." —Hunter S. Thompson

then later in your code you are free to write foo($x,$y,$z) as foo $x,$y,$z. A degenerate case of this is that if you have defined foo as taking no parameters, with the prototype syntax,* like so:

```
sub foo ()
{
    ...a bunch of code...
}
```

or:

```
sub foo ();
```

then you can write foo( ) as just plain foo! Incidentally, the constant pragma prior to Perl 5.9.3 defines constants this way. The Perl time( ) function (very non-constant) also uses this approach—that's why either of these syntaxes mean the same thing:

```
my $x = time;
my $x = time();
```

You could implement a function that returns time( ) except as a figure in days instead of in seconds:

```
sub time_days ()
{
    return time() / (24 * 60 * 60);
}

my $xd = time_days;
```

If you tried calling time_days, without parens, before you defined the function, you would get an error message Bareword "time_days" not allowed while "strict subs" in use. That's assuming you're running under "use strict," which of course you are.

A further example is:

```
use Data::Format 'time2str';

sub ymd_now ()
{
    time2str( '%Y-%m-%d', time )
}

print "It is now ", ymd_now, "!!\n";
```

---

* See "Prototypes" in the Perldoc *perlsub*.

Tie a scalar variable to a function. Perl provides a mechanism, called "tying", to call a function when someone apparently accesses a particular variable. See perldoc perltie for the agonizing details.

Consider a scalar variable whose value is *really* variable—a variable that, when read, returns the current time, somewhat in the style of some old BASIC dialects' $TIME (or TIME$) variable:

```perl
{
    package TimeVar_YMDhms;

    use Tie::Scalar ();
    use base 'Tie::StdScalar';
    use Date::Format 'time2str';

    sub FETCH { time2str('%Y-%m-%dT%H:%M:%S', time) }
}

tie my $TIME, TimeVar_YMDhms;

print "It is now $TIME\n";
sleep 3;
print "It is now $TIME\n";
```

That produces output like:

```
It is now 2006-02-03T16:04:17
It is now 2006-02-03T16:04:20
```

You can even rewrite that to use a general-purpose class, which will produce the same output:

```perl
{
    package Tie::ScalarFnParams;
    sub TIESCALAR
    {
        my($class, $fn, @params) = @_;
        return bless sub { $fn->(@params) }, $class;
    }

    sub FETCH { return shift()->() }
    sub STORE { return } # called for $var = somevalue;
}

use Date::Format 'time2str';

tie my $TIME, Tie::ScalarFnParams,
 # And now any function and optional parameter(s):
    sub { time2str(shift, time) }, '%Y-%m-%dT%H:%M:%S';

print "It is now $TIME\n";
sleep 3;
print "It is now $TIME\n";
```

Tie an array variable to a function. A more sophisticated approach is to tie an array to a function, so that $somearray[123] will call that function with the parameter 123. Consider, for example, the task of giving a number an English ordinal suffix—that is, taking 2 and returning "2nd," taking 12 and returning "12th," and so on. The CPAN module Lingua::EN::Numbers::Ordinate's ordinate function can do this:

```
use Lingua::EN::Numbers::Ordinate 'ordinate';
print ordinate(4), "!\n";
```

This shows "4th!". To invoke this function on the sly, use a tied-array class:

```
{
    package Tie::Ordinalize;

    use Lingua::EN::Numbers::Ordinate 'ordinate';
    use base 'Tie::Array';

    sub TIEARRAY   { return bless {}, shift } # dummy obj
    sub FETCH      { return ordinate( $_[1] ) }
    sub FETCHSIZE  { return 0 }
}

tie my @TH, Tie::Ordinalize;
print $TH[4], "!\n";
```

which, also, shows "4th!". Perl calls the required method FETCH when reading $TH[someindex] and FETCHSIZE when reading @TH in a scalar context (like $x=2+@TH). There are other methods that you can define for accessing the tied array as $TH[123] = somevalue, push(@TH,...), or any of the various other operations you can perform on a normal Perl array. The Tie::Array documentation has all the gory details.

Tying an array to something may seem like a pretty strange idea, but Mark Jason Dominus's excellent core-Perl module Tie::File [Hack #19] puts this to good use.

Tie a hash variable to a function. One of the limitations of tying an array to a function is that the index (as FETCH sees in $somearray[*index*]) obviously has to be a number. With a tied hash, the FETCH method gets a string argument ($somehash{*index*}). In this case, you can use tying to make $NowAs{*str*} call time2str(*str*):

```
{
    package Tie::TimeFormatty;
    use Tie::Hash ();
    use base 'Tie::StdHash';
    use Date::Format 'time2str';
    sub FETCH { time2str($_[1], time) }
}
```

```
tie my %NowAs, Tie::TimeFormatty;

print "It is now $NowAs{'%Y-%m-%dT%H:%M:%S'}\n";
sleep 3;
print "It is now $NowAs{'%c'}\n";
```

That produces output like:

```
It is now 2006-02-03T18:28:06
It is now 02/03/06 18:28:09
```

An earlier example showed how to make a class Tie::ScalarFnParams which makes any scalar variable call any function with any parameters. You can more easily do the same thing for hashes—except that it already exists. It's the CPAN module called Interpolation, originally by Mark Jason Dominus. Use it to rewrite the previous code like:

```
use Date::Format 'time2str';
use Interpolation NowAs => sub { time2str($_[0],time) };

print "It is now $NowAs{'%Y-%m-%dT%H:%M:%S'}\n";
sleep 3;
print "It is now $NowAs{'%c'}\n";
```

Other hacks based on this on the CPAN include Tie::DBI, which makes $somehash{*somekey*} to query arbitrary databases (or DB_File to make it query a mere Berkeley-style database) and Tie::Ispell which makes $dict{*word*} spellcheck the word and suggest possibilities if it appears incorrect.

Of course, you can also tie a filehandle to a function **[Hack #90]**.

Add a function-calling layer to filehandles. Modern versions of Perl provide an even more powerful expansion of the idea of tied filehandles, called "PerlIO layers", where each layer between the program and the actual filehandle can call particular functions to manipulate the passing data. The non-hackish uses of this include doing encoding conversion and changing the newline format, all so that you can access them like so:

```
open $fh, '>:somelayer:someotherlayer:yetmore', 'file.dat'
```

as in:

```
open( $out, '>:utf8', 'resume.utf' ) or die "Cannot read resume: $!\n";
print {$out} "\x{2605} My R\xE9sum\xE9 \x{2605}\n";
close( $out );  # ^^-- a star character
```

The documentation for PerlIO::via, PerlIO, and Encoding describe the complex interface for writing layers. For super-simple layers, you can use a base class to reduce the interface to a single method, change. Here it is with two layer classes, Scream and Cookiemonster:

```
package Function_IO_Layer;

# A dumb base class for simple PerlIO::via::* layers.
# See PerlIO::via::dynamic for a smarter version of this.

sub PUSHED { bless {}, $_[0] } # our dumb ctor

# when reading
sub FILL
{
    my($this, $fh) = @_;
    defined(my $line = readline($fh)) or return undef;
    return $this->change($line);
}

sub WRITE
{
    my($this,$buf,$fh) = @_;
    print {$fh} $this->change($buf)   or return -1;
    return length($buf);
}

sub change { my($this,$str) = @_;   $str; } #override!

# Puts everything in allcaps.
package PerlIO::via::Scream;

use base 'Function_IO_Layer';

sub change
{
    my($this, $str) = @_;
    return uc($str);
}

# Changes "I" to "me".
package PerlIO::via::Cookiemonster;

use base 'Function_IO_Layer';

sub change
{
    my($this, $str) = @_;
    $str =~ s<\bI\b><me>g;
    return $str;
}
```

Use these layers as simply as:

```
open my $fh, '>:via(Scream):via(Cookiemonster)',
    'author_bio.txt' or die $!;
```

```
print {$fh} "I eat cookies without cease or restraint.\n",
    "I like cookies.\n";

close($fh);
```

That will make *author_bio.txt* consist of:

```
ME EAT COOKIES WITHOUT CEASE OR RESTRAINT.
ME LIKE COOKIES.
```

You can use PerlIO layers to operate on files you're reading (just change the
'>' to '<') or appending to ('>>'), or even to alter data coming to or from pro-
cesses ('-|' or '|-'). For example, this:

```
open my $ls, '-|:via(Scream)', 'ls -C /usr' or die $!;
print <$ls>;
```

shows:

```
BIN  GAMES    KERBEROS  LIBEXEC  SBIN   SRC   X11R6
ETC  INCLUDE  LIB       LOCAL    SHARE  TMP
```

where a simple `ls -C ~/.mozilla` would show just:

```
bin  games    kerberos  libexec  sbin   src   X11R6
etc  include  lib       local    share  tmp
```

Going from encoding-conversion (open `$fh`, `'>:utf8'...`) to uppercasing
(open `$fh`, `'>:via(Scream)'...`) may seem a leap from the sublime to the
ridiculous—but consider that in between the two, intrepid CPAN authors
have already written such classes as `PerlIO::via::LineNumber`, which trans-
parently adds line numbers to the start of lines, or `PerlIO::via::StripHTML`,
which strips HTML tags—all very hackish, and yet very useful.

HACK #90   Glob Those Sequences

Don't settle for counting from one to *n* by one.

Perl has a syntax for generating simple sequences of increasing integers:

```
@count_up = 0..100;
```

There's no syntax for anything more interesting, such as counting by twos or
counting down—unless you create one yourself.

The Hack

The angle brackets in Perl have two distinct purposes: as a shorthand for
calling `readline`, and as a shorthand for calling `glob`:

```
my $input = <$fh>;      # shorthand for: readline($fh)

my @files = <*.pl>;     # shorthand for: glob("*.pl")
```

Assuming you're not interested in that second rather specialized usage (and you can always use the standard File::Glob module, if you are), you can hijack non-readline angles for something much tastier: list comprehensions.

> A *list comprehension* is an expression that filters and trans-
> forms one list to create another, more interesting, list. Of
> course, Perl already has map and grep to do that:
>
> ```
> @prime_countdown = grep { is_prime($_) } map { 100-
> $_ } 0..99;
> ```
>
> but doesn't have a dedicated (and optimized) syntax for it:
>
> ```
> @prime_countdown = <100..1 : is_prime(X)>;
> ```

Running the Hack

By replacing the CORE::GLOBAL::glob( ) subroutine, you replace both the builtin glob( ) function and the angle-bracketed operator version. By rewriting CORE::GLOBAL::glob( ), you can retarget the <...> syntax to do whatever you like, for example, to build sophisticated lists.

Do so with:

```
package Glob::Lists;

use Carp;

# Regexes to parse the extended list specifications...
my $NUM    = qr{\s* [+-]? \d+ (?:\.\d*)? \s* }xms;
my $TO     = qr{\s* \.\. \s*}xms;
my $FILTER = qr{ (?: : (.*) )? }xms;
my $ABtoZ  = qr{\A ($NUM) (,) ($NUM) ,? $TO ($NUM) $FILTER \Z}xms;
my $AZxN   = qr{\A ($NUM) $TO ($NUM) (?:x ($NUM))? $FILTER \Z}xms;

# Install a new glob( ) function...
no warnings 'redefine';
*CORE::GLOBAL::glob = sub
{
    my ($listspec) = @_;

    # Does the spec match any of the acceptable forms?
    croak "Bad list specification: <$listspec>"
        if $listspec !~ $ABtoZ && $listspec !~ $AZxN;

    # Extract the range of values and any filter...
    my ($from, $to, $incr, $filter) =  $2 eq ',' ? ($1, $4, $3-$1, $5)
                                                  : ($1, $2, $3,    $4);

    # Work out the implicit increment, if no explicit one...
    $incr = $from > $to ? -1 : 1 unless defined $incr;

    # Check for nonsensical increments (zero or the wrong sign)...
    my $delta = $to - $from;
```

```
        croak sprintf "Sequence <%s, %s, %s...> will never reach %s",
            $from, $from+$incr, $from+2*$incr, $to
                if $incr == 0 || $delta * $incr < 0;

        # Generate list of values (and return it, if not filter)...
        my @vals = map { $from + $incr * $_ } 0..($delta/$incr);
        return @vals unless defined $filter;

        # Apply the filter before returning the values...
        $filter =~ s/\b[A-Z]\b/\$_/g;
        return eval "grep {package ".caller."; $filter } \@vals";
    };
```

The $ABtoZ and $AZxN regexes match two kinds of sequence specifiers:

```
<from, then,..to>
```

and:

```
<from..to x increment>
```

and both also allow you to specify a filtering expression after a colon:

```
<from, then,..to : filter>
<from..to x incr : filter>
```

The regexes capture and extract the relevant start and end values, the increment amount, and the filter. The subroutine then computes the increment in
the cases where it is implicit, and checks to see that the sequence makes
sense (that is, it isn't something like <1..10 x -1> or <1,2,..-10>).

The code then genereates the sequence using a map, and immediately returns
it if there is no filter. If there is a filter, the code evals it into a grep and
returns the filtered list instead.

Then you can write:

```
use Glob::Lists;

for ( <1..100 x 7> ) {...}           # 1, 8, 15, 22,...85, 92, 99

my @even_countdown  = <10,8..0>;     # 10, 8, 6, 4, 2, 0

my @fract_countdown = <10,9.5,..0>;  # 10, 9.5, 9,...1, 0.5, 0

my @some_primes = <1..100 x 3 : /7/ && is_prime(N)>;
                                     # 7, 37, 67, 73, 79, 97
```

Hacking the Hack

One of the neater hacks based on this idea is the CPAN module Tie::FTP,
which diverts file operations to functions that actually perform those operations on files on remote FTP servers. Another notable module is Tie::
STDERR, which provides handy options for diverting STDERR output to

email to root, an errorlog file, or an arbitrary function. For Zen-like transcendence of the very concept of "hack" or "purpose", the CPAN module IO::Null can tie to functions that do, and return, nothing at all!

HACK #91 Write Less Error-Checking Code

Identify runtime errors without writing code.

One of the less-endearing features of working with the outside world is that things can fail: you might run out of disk space, lose your network connection, or have some other sort of serious error. Robust programs check for these errors and retry or fail gracefully as necessary. Of course, checking *every* potential point of failure for every possible failure can make a lot of repetitive code.

Fortunately, Perl provides a way to fail on errors without having to check for them explicitly—the Fatal core module.

The Hack

One of the most failure-prone points of programming is IO programming, whether working with files or other computers across a network. File paths may be wrong, file permissions may change, disks can mysteriously fill up, and transitory networking problems may make remote computers temporarily invisible. If you work much with files, using Fatal can reduce the amount of code you need to write.

The Fatal module takes a list of function names to override to raise exceptions on failures. open and close are good candidates. Pass their names to the use line to avoid writing the or die( ) idiom:

```
use Fatal qw( open close );

open( my $fh, '>', '/invalid_directory/invalid_file' );
print {$fh} "Hello\n";
close $fh;
```

If you run this (and don't have a directory named *invalid_directory*), you'll receive an error message:

```
Can't open(GLOB(0x10159d74), >, /nodirectory/nofile.txt): No such file or
    directory at (eval 1) line 3
    main::__ANON__('GLOB(0x10159d74)', '>', '/nodirectory/nofile.txt') called
        at fatal_io.pl line 8
```

If it's appropriate for your program to exit with an error if this happens, this is all you need to do. To handle the error with more grace, wrap the code in an eval block and do what you need to do:

```
use Fatal qw( open close );
eval {
```

```
        open( my $fh, '>', '/invalid_directory/invalid_file' );
        print {$fh} "Hello\n";
        close $fh;
};

die "File error: $!" if $@;
```

> Of course, nothing says that your code *must* do something
> with the caught exception—but at least consider how robust
> your code should be.

Hacking the Hack

Fatal can also make your own code strict. Use it within your own modules
just as you would normally:

```
package MyCode;

sub succeed { 1 }
sub fail    { 0 }

use Fatal qw( :void succeed fail );

succeed();
fail();

1;
```

Because fail() returns false, Fatal throws an exception. This code has one
trick, in that the subroutine declarations come *before* the Fatal call. If you
use the module before Perl parses the subroutine declarations, Fatal will not
be able to find them and will throw an error.

This can be useful for your own code, but it's even more useful when you
export these functions to other code. The order of the use lines doesn't matter here, though:*

```
package MyCode;
use base 'Exporter';
our @EXPORT = qw( succeed fail );

sub succeed { 1 }
sub fail    { 0 }

use Fatal qw( :void succeed fail );

1;
```

---

* See "Understand What Happens When" [Hack #70] to learn why.

This technique even works with classes and objects; you don't have to export your methods for Fatal to work.

Return Smarter Values

#92 Choose the correct scalar for any context.

There's always one troublemaker in any bunch. When it comes to return contexts, that troublemaker is scalar.

List and void contexts are easy. In list context you just return everything. In void context, return nothing. Scalar contexts allow you to return only one thing, but there are just too many alternatives: a string, a count, a boolean value, a reference, a typeglob, or an object.

The real problem, though, isn't actually that there are too many types of possible return value in scalar context; the real problem is that Perl simply doesn't provide you with enough...well...*context* with which to decide. The only basis you have for knowing whether to return a string, number, boolean, and so on, is receiving a single uninformative defined-but-false value from wantarray.

Even then, using wantarray leads to a lot of unnecessary and self-undocumenting infrastructure:

```
if (wantarray)              # wantarray true      --> list context
{
    return @some_list;
}
elsif (defined wantarray)   # wantarray defined   --> scalar context
{
    return $some_scalar;
}
else                        # wantarray undefined --> void context
{
    do_something();
    return;
}
```

It would be much easier if you could just specify a single return statement that knew what to return in different contexts, perhaps:

```
return
    LIST   { @some_list    }
    SCALAR { $some_scalar  }
    VOID   { do_something() };
```

That's exactly what the Contextual::Return CPAN module does. It makes the previous example work like you'd expect.

Fine Distinctions

The module also allows you to be more specific about what to return in different kinds of scalar context.

For example, you might want a stopwatch( ) subroutine that returns the elapsed time in seconds in numeric contexts, but an HH:MM:SS representation in string contexts. You might also want it to return a true or false value depending on whether the stopwatch is currently running. You can do all of that with:

```perl
use Time::HiRes 'time';
use Contextual::Return;

my $elapsed     = 0;
my $started_at  = 0;
my $is_running  = 0;

# Convert elapsed seconds to HH::MM::SS string...
sub _HMS
{
    my ($elapsed) = @_;
    my $hours     = int($elapsed / 3600);
    my $mins      = int($elapsed / 60 % 60);
    my $secs      = int($elapsed) % 60;
    return sprintf "%02d:%02d:%02d", $hours, $mins, $secs;
}

sub stopwatch
{
    my ($run)     = @_;

    # Update elapsed time...
    my $now       = time();
    $elapsed      += $now - $started_at if $is_running;
    $started_at   = $now;

    # Defined arg turns stopwatch on/off, undef arg resets it...
    $is_running   = $run if @_;
    $elapsed      = 0 if @_ && !defined $run;

    # Handle different scalar contexts...
    return
        NUM { $elapsed         }
        STR { _HMS( $elapsed ) }
        BOOL { $is_running     }
}
```

With that arrangement, you can write code like:

```perl
print "The clock's already ticking\n"
    if stopwatch();                         # treat as a boolean
stopwatch(1);                               # start
do_stuff();
```

```
stopwatch(0);                                   # stop
print "Did stuff in ", stopwatch( ), "\n";      # report as string

stopwatch(undef);                               # reset
stopwatch(1);                                   # start
do_more_stuff();
print "Did more stuff in ", stopwatch(0), "\n"; # stop and report

print "Sorry for the delay\n"
    if stopwatch( ) > 5;                        # treat as number
```

Name that Return Value

The stopwatch example works well, but it still doesn't explore the full range of possibilities for a scalar return value. For example, the single piece of numeric information you want back might not be the elapsed time, but rather when the stopwatch started. You might also want to return a boolean indicating whether the stopwatch is currently running without always having to cast your call into boolean context:

```
$stopwatch_running = !!stopwatch( );      # !! --> boolean context
```

It would be handy if, in addition to all the other return options, stopwatch( ) would also return a hash reference, so you could write:

```
$stopwatch_running = stopwatch->{running};

print "Stopwatch started at ", stopwatch->{started}, "\n";
```

Returning a hash reference allows you to send back all the information you have available, from which the caller can then pick out (by name) the interesting bits. Using names to select what you want back also helps the code document what it's doing.

Contextual::Return makes it easy to add this kind of behavior to stopwatch( ). Just add a specific return value for the HASHREF context:

```
# Handle different scalar contexts...
return
        NUM { $elapsed          }
        STR { _HMS( $elapsed ) }
       BOOL { $is_running       }
    HASHREF { { elapsed => $elapsed,
                started  => $now - $elapsed,
                running  => $is_running,
              }
            }
```

Out, Out, Damn Commas!

Contextual::Return can handle other types of reference returns as well. One of the most useful is SCALARREF {...}. This block specifies what to return when the calling code uses the return value as a reference to a scalar. That is, what to return if you write:

```
${ stopwatch( ) }    # Call stopwatch( ) and treat result as scalar ref
```

The reason this particular construct is so interesting is that you can interpolate it directly into a double quoted string. For example, add a SCALARREF return block to stopwatch( ):

```
# Handle different scalar contexts...
return
        NUM { $elapsed          }
        STR { _HMS($elapsed)    }
  SCALARREF { \ _HMS($elapsed)  }
       BOOL { $is_running        }
    HASHREF { {   elapsed => $elapsed,
                  started => $now - $elapsed,
                  running => $is_running,
              }
            }
```

Then, whenever it's called in a scalar-ref context, the subroutine returns a reference to the HH:MM:SS elapsed string, which the scalar ref context then automatically dereferences. Instead of having to write:

```
print "Did stuff in ", stopwatch( ), "\n";
```

you can interpolate the call right into the string itself:

```
print "Did stuff in ${stopwatch( )}\n";
```

This turns out to be so amazingly useful that it's Contextual::Return's default behaviour. That is, any subroutine that specifies one or more of STR {...}, NUM {...}, or BOOL {...} automatically gets a SCALARREF {...} as well: one that returns a reference to the appropriate string, number, or boolean.

HACK #93 Return Active Values

Return values that automatically change as you use them.

The Contextual::Return module [Hack #92] has another very powerful trick up its sleeve. The scalar values it returns don't have to be constants; they can be "active." An active value is one that adapts itself each time it is evaluated. This is useful for performing initialization, cleanup, or error-handling code without forcing the caller to do anything special.

The Hack

For example, you can create a subroutine that returns a value that automatically tracks the elapsed time between events:

```
use Contextual::Return;
use Time::HiRes qw( sleep time );        # Allow subsecond timing

# Subroutine returns an active timer value...
sub timer
{
    my $start = time;                    # Set initial start time

    return VALUE                         # Return an active value that...
    {
        my $elapsed = time - $start;     #    1. computes elapsed time
        $start       = time;             #    2. resets start time
        return $elapsed;                 #    3. returns elapsed time
    }
}

# Create an active value...
my $process_timer = timer( );

# Use active value...
while (1)
{
    do_some_long_process( );
    print "Process took $process_timer seconds\n";
}
```

Because the timer( ) subroutine returns a contextual value that is computed within the VALUE block itself, that returned value becomes active. Each time the value of $process_timer is reevaluated (in the print statement), the value's VALUE block executes, recomputing and resetting the value stored in $process_timer.

Running the Hack

Of course, the real advantage here is that you can have the subroutine create two or more timers for you:

```
my $task_timer    = timer( );
my $subtask_timer = timer( );

for my $task (@tasks)
{
    print "Performing $task...\n";
    for my $subtask ($task->get_subtasks( ))
    {
        $subtask->perform( );
        print "\t$subtask took $subtask_timer seconds\n";
    }
    print "Finished $task in $task_timer seconds\n\n";
}
```

to produce something like:

```
$ perl do_tasks.pl

Performing set-up...
    Finding files took 0.775737047195435 seconds
    Reading files took 0.985733032226562 seconds
    Verifying data took 0.137604951858521 seconds
Finished set-up in 1.98483791351318 seconds

Performing initialization...
    Creating data structures took 0.627048969268799 seconds
    Cross-correlating took 2.756386041641235 seconds
Finished initialization in 3.45225400924683 seconds

etc.
```

Hacking the Hack

Active values can use all the other features of the `Contextual::Return` module. In particular, they can still be context-sensitive. For example, you could create a safer version of the built-in open function, where "safer" means that this version will return a filehandle that explodes catastrophically if you ever try to use the handle without first verifying that it was opened correctly.

Implement it like this:

```perl
use Contextual::Return;

sub safe_open
{
    my ($mode, $filename) = @_;
    my $user_has_tested   = 0;

    # Open a filehandle and remember where it was opened...
    open my($filehandle), $mode, $filename;
    my $where = sprintf("'%s' line %s", (caller)[1,2]);

    # Return an active value that's only usable after it's been tested...
    return (
        BOOL
        {
            $user_has_tested = 1;
            return defined $filehandle;
        }
        DEFAULT
        {
            croak "Used untested filehandle (opened at $where)"
                unless $user_has_tested;
            return $filehandle;
        }
    )
}
```

The safe_open subroutine expects two arguments: the opening mode and the name of the file to open:

```
my $fh = safe_open '<', $some_file;
```

The returned value acts like a filehandle in all contexts, but only after you have tested the value in a boolean context. Accessing the returned value in a boolean context invokes the value's BOOL block, which actively sets the $user_has_tested flag true. If you try to use the filehandle *before* you've tested it:

```
my $fh     = safe_open '<', $some_file;

my $input = <$fh>;          # Use of untested return value
                            # invokes DEFAULT block
```

the BOOL block will not have run, so the internal flag will still be false, and the value's DEFAULT block will throw an exception:

```
$ perl demo.pl
```

```
Used untested filehandle (opened at 'demo.pl' line 12) at demo.pl line 14
```

If however, the filehandle *has* been tested in any boolean context:

```
my $fh = safe_open '<', $some_file
    or croak "Couldn't open $some_file";   # the 'or' evaluates $fh in a
                                            # boolean context so it invokes
                                            # returned value's BOOL block

my $input = <$fh>;          # Invokes returned value's DEFAULT block
```

then the value's BOOL block will have set the $user_has_tested flag. Once the flag is set, the DEFAULT block will thereafter return the filehandle without detonating.

Of course, this is incompatible with the use of Fatal as shown in "Write Less Error-Checking Code" **[Hack #91]**.

Add Your Own Perl Syntax
HACK #94
Shape the language as you see fit.

Perl is a great language, but it's certainly not perfect. Sometimes bits and pieces of the implementation poke through. Sometimes the natural solution to a problem doesn't fit the existing language very well at all. Some problems are easier if you can just define them away.

Sometimes the simplest solution is just to change the syntax of Perl.

For example, it's frustrating that you can't specify a simple parameter list for a subroutine (without some gyrations, as in "Autodeclare Method Arguments" [Hack #47]):

```
my @NUMERAL_FOR    = (0..9,'A'..'Z');

sub convert_to_base($base, $number)
{
    my $converted = "";
    while ($number > 0)
    {
        $converted = $NUMERAL_FOR[$number % $base] . $converted;
        $number    = int( $number / $base);
    }
    return $converted;
}
```

Instead, you have to do it yourself:

```
sub convert_to_base
{
    my ($base, $number) = @_;    # <-- DIY parameter list

    my $converted    = ''
    while ($number > 0)
    {
        $converted    = $NUMERAL_FOR[$number % $base] . $converted;
        $number       = int( $number / $base);
    }

    return $converted;
}
```

This is why far too many people just write:

```
sub convert_to_base
{
    my $converted  = '';

    while ($_[1] > 0)
    {
        $converted = $NUMERAL_FOR[$_[1] % $_[0]] . $converted;
        $_[1]      = int( $_[1] / $_[0]);
    }

    return $converted;
}
```

buying themselves a world of future maintenance pain in the process.

The Hack

Although Perl may not be perfect, it *is* perfectable. For example, recent versions of Perl provide a way to grab your program's source code before it even reaches the compiler, change it in some useful manner, and then send it on to be compiled and executed. The easiest way to do that is to write a module that uses the standard (in version 5.8.0 and later) Filter::Simple module:

```
package My::Filter;
use Filter::Simple;

FILTER_ONLY code => sub
{
    # The code from any program that uses this module
    # is passed into this subroutine in $_.
    # Whatever is in $_ at the end of this subroutine
    # becomes the source code that the compiler eventually sees.
};

1;
```

Because the Perl compiler only sees the end result of these source filters, only that end result *has* to be valid Perl code. The original source code that the filter intercepts can be anything you like, as long as the filter can transform that anything into valid Perl.

For example, you could augment the Perl subroutine declaration syntax by creating a source filter that looks for subs with parameter lists and converts them to normal subs:

```
package Sub::With::Params;
use Filter::Simple;

# Regex that matches a valid Perl identifier (e.g. a sub name)...
my $IDENT = qr/[^\W\d]\w*/;

# Apply this filter to the code of any program
# that uses Sub::With::Params...
FILTER_ONLY code => sub
{
    s{ ( sub \s* $IDENT \s* )    # Match any named sub declaration
       (   \( .*? \)       )     # ...followed by a parameter list
       (   \s* \{          )     # ...followed by a sub body
     }
     {$1$3 my $2 = \@_;}gxs;     # Then move the param list inside the
                                 # sub, converting it to a list of
                                 # lexical variables initialized from @_
};

1;
```

By setting up this filter module so that it expects subs with parameter lists and transforms them into regular subs that unpack @_ into lexicals, now you *can* write:

```
use Sub::With::Params;

sub convert_to_base($base, $number)
{
    my $converted = '';
    while ($number > 0)
    {
        $converted = $NUMERAL_FOR[$number % $base] . $converted;
        $number    = int( $number / $base);
    }
    return $converted;
}
```

and have it work as you expect. Sub::With::Params will now intercept your source code on its way to the compiler and convert it to:

```
sub convert_to_base { my ($base, $number) = @_;
    my $converted = '';
    while ($number > 0)
    {
        $converted = $NUMERAL_FOR[$number % $base] . $converted;
        $number    = int( $number / $base);
    }
    return $converted;
}
```

HACK #95   Modify Semantics with a Source Filter

Tweak Perl's behavior at the syntactic level.

In addition to adding new syntax [Hack #94], source code filters can change the behavior of existing Perl constructs. For example, a common complaint about Perl is that you cannot indent a heredoc properly. Instead you have to write something messed-up like:

```
sub usage
{
    if ($::VERBOSE)
    {
        print <<"END_USAGE";
Usage: $0 [options] <infile> <outfile>

Options:
    -z        Zero tolerance on formatting errors
    -o        Output overview only
    -d        Debugging mode
END_USAGE
    }
}
```

rather than something tidily indented like:

```
sub usage
{
    if ($::VERBOSE)
    {
        print <<"END_USAGE";
            Usage: $0 [options] <infile> <outfile>

            Options:
                -z          Zero tolerance on formatting errors
                -o          Output overview only
                -d          Debugging mode
            END_USAGE
    }
}
```

Except, of course, you *can* have your heredoc and indent it too. You just need to filter out the unacceptable indentation before the code reaches the compiler. This is another job for source filters.

The Hack

Suppose that you could use the starting column of a heredoc's terminator to indicate the left margin of each line of the preceding heredoc content. In other words, what if you could indent every line in the heredoc by the same amount as the final terminator marker? If that were the case, then the previous example would work as expected, printing:

```
$ ksv -z filename
```

```
Usage: ksv [options] <infile> <outfile>

Options:
    -z          Zero tolerance on formatting errors
    -o          Output overview only
    -d          Debugging mode
```

with the start of each line hard against the left margin.

To make that happen in real life, you need a source filter that recognizes indented heredocs and rewrites them as unindented heredocs before they reach the compiler. Here's a module that provides just that:

```
package Heredoc::Indenting;

use Filter::Simple;

FILTER
{
    # Find all instances of...
    1 while
```

```
            s{ <<                       #     Heredoc marker
              ( ['"]             )      # $1: Quote for terminator
              ( (?:\\\1|[^\n])*? )      # $2: Terminator specification
                \1                      #     Matching closing quote
              ( [^\n]* \n        )      # $3: The rest of the statement line
              ( .*? \n           )      # $4: The heredoc contents
              ( [^\S\n]*         )      # $5: Any whitespace indent before...
                \2 \n                   #     ...the terminator itself
            }

            # ... and replace it with the same heredoc, with its terminator
            # outdented and the heredoc contents passed through a subroutine
            # that removes the indent from each line...
            {Try::outdent(q{$1$2$1}, '$5',<< $1$2$1)\n$4$2\n$3}xms;
        };

        use Carp;

        # Remove indentations from a string...
        sub outdent
        {
            my ($name, $indentation, $string) = @_;

            # Complain if any line doesn't have the specified indentation...
            if ($string =~ m/^((?:.*\n)*?)(?!$indentation)(.*\S.*)\n/m)
            {
                my ($good_lines, $bad_line) = ($1, $2);
                my $bad_line_pos = 1 + ($good_lines =~ tr/\n/\n/);
                croak "Negative indentation on line $bad_line_pos ",
                      "of <<$name heredoc specified";
            }

            # Otherwise remove the indentations from each line...
            $string =~ s/^$indentation//gm;
            return $string;
        }

        1;
```

The FILTER {...} block tells Filter::Simple how to filter any code that uses the Heredoc::Indenting module. The code comes in in the $_ variable and the block then uses a repeated regex substitution to replace each outdented heredoc with a regular left-justified heredoc.

The regex is complex because it has to break a heredoc up into: *introducer*, *quoted terminator specification*, *remainder of statement*, *heredoc contents*, *terminator indent*, and *terminator*. The replacement is complex too, as it reorders those components as: *outdenter function*, *introducer*, *quoted terminator specification*, *heredoc contents*, *terminator*, and *remainder of statement*.

This reordering also explains why the `FILTER` block uses `1 while s/.../.../` instead of `s/.../.../g`. Using the `/g` flag doesn't allow for overlapping matches, which would cause the substitution to skip over the rewritten *remainder of statement* component. The remainder of the statement might contain another indented heredoc however, which would then process incorrectly. In contrast, the `1 while...` form rematches the partially rewritten source code from the start, so it correctly handles multiple heredocs on the same line.

There's a cunning layout trick used here. Because each heredoc is rewritten as a (modified) heredoc, on the second iteration of the `1 while`, the first heredoc it will find is the one it just rewrote, so the substitution is in danger of reprocessing and re-reprocessing and re-re-reprocessing that very first heredoc ad infinitum. To avoid that, the module requires that indented heredocs have no space between their `<<` introducer and their terminator specification, like so:

```
print <<"END_USAGE";
```

Then it carefully rewrites each heredoc so that it *does* have a space between those two components:

```
{Try::outdent(q{$1$2$1}, '$5',<< $1$2$1)\n$4$2\n$3}xms;
#                             ^
#                             |
```

That way, the next time the iterated substitution matches against the source code, it will ignore any already-rewritten heredocs and move on to the first unrewritten one instead.

Each heredoc is rewritten to pass through the `Try::outdent()` subroutine at runtime. This subroutine removes the specified indentation (passed as its second argument) from the heredoc text, checking for invalid indentations as it does so.

Hacking the Hack

As an alternative, the `FILTER` block itself could run the heredoc contents through `outdent()` as it rewrites them. To do that, the second half of the substitution would look instead like:

```
{"<< $1$2$1\n" . Try::outdent($1.$2.$1, $5, $4) . "$2\n$3"}exms;
```

with the `/e` flag allowing you to specify the replacement as an expression to be evaluated, rather than as a simple string.

The advantage of this second version of the filter is that the outdenting of each heredoc now occurs only once, at compile time during the original source filtering, rather than every time `perl` encounters the heredoc at run-time. The disadvantage is that Perl will report any errors during the outdenting as occurring at the use Heredoc::Indenting line, rather than in the correct position of the heredoc in the source code. Although that's entirely accurate—they *are* occurring during the loading of the filtering module—it's not very useful to users of the module, who really want to know where their heredocs are broken, not where your module detected the breakage.

HACK #96 Use Shared Libraries Without XS

Call C code from Perl without needing a compiler.

One of the few ways in which installing Perl modules is painful is when they link to shared libraries written in other languages. The first pain is that someone has to write XS or Inline::C or Swig bindings for the shared library. The second is that installing such modules usually requires a working C development environment—and not every machine nor user has such a luxury.

For simple tasks that merely wrap a shared library, there's no reason you need that much; with a little clever coding you can use just about any shared library written in C with an idea backported from Perl 6 to Perl 5.

The Hack

Consider how Perl passes arguments to functions: in @_, on a stack. As far as the calling conventions work, any function that takes a string, an array reference, and a hash reference looks the same *for the purposes of calling the function*.

Consider how C passes arguments to functions: much the same way. Any function that takes two integers and returns a double looks the same, again as far as the calling conventions go.

Similarly, any XS code that converts between a Perl function that passes two integers (well, scalars containing integers) to a C function and expects a double (well, a scalar containing a numeric value) is the same. The only difference is the *name* of the function as Perl sees it and the actual C function it calls. Those are actually very easy to vary.

The P5NCI module builds up its own library of thunk functions (the glue between Perl and C) and allows you to bind thunks to functions in shared libraries.

Running the Hack

Suppose you want to use a good, fast library for determining the cube root of any given number. The libm shared library in the C standard library provides a nice function cbrt that takes a double and returns a double and does it fairly quickly—at least more quickly than you could do it in Perl (and certainly more easily than you could write XS code to do it).

Loading the library and creating the wrapper around cbrt is easy, once you know the name of the shared library and the function signature:

```
use P5NCI::Library;

my $lib = P5NCI::Library->new( library => 'm' );
$lib->install_function( 'cbrt', 'dd' );

print cbrt( 27 ), "\n";
print cbrt( 31 ), "\n";
```

Note that, if you have P5NCI installed, you don't need a compiler to do this, nor do you even need *math.h* installed for this to work! Just create a new P5NCI::Library object, passing the name of the library without any platform-specific prefix or suffix.* Then, call install_function( ) on that object, passing the name of the function within the shared library to wrap as well as the signature, where the first letter is the type of the returned variable and the remaining letters are the types of the arguments to the function. You probably need to read the header or at least the documentation for the shared library to find out the signature, but you don't have to have the development package or tools installed when you deploy your code.

Then call the function as if it were a normal Perl function—as far as the code cares, it is.

See the module's documentation for other call signatures.

Hacking the Hack

One drawback of the NCI approach as described here is that it requires a shared library containing the thunking layer between Perl's and C's calling conventions. Even with a few possible data types and signatures no longer than four characters, there are still many, many possible necessary thunking functions. If your project only needs a few types of signatures, building your own thunking library can be useful. If you want to distribute this thunking layer, you must compile it for the destination machines. Fortunately, you only have to compile it once.

For general use, wrapping a library such as libffi may be a better approach—it can generate the thunks on its own as needed, requiring only

---

* On a Unix system, the file is actually *libm.so*. On a Windows system, it's probably *math.dll*. Mac OS X likely refers to it as *libm.dylib*.

that you have the FFI library installed. Look for updates to P5NCI on the CPAN that do this.

It's possible to handle pointers to structures passed to and from the shared library as well. Marcus Holland-Moritz's Convert::Binary::C is a likely candidate for giving access to struct members.

HACK #97 Run Two Services on a Single TCP Port
Reuse your precious ports simultaneously.

It is a well-known trick to use the HTTP CONNECT method to politely ask a web proxy to open a specific port on a specific machine on the Internet. This is how many people manage to connect back to their SSH server at home. SSH clients such as PuTTY know how to go through web proxies using this technique.

However, your company security administrator may have configured the proxy to only allow port 443* for outgoing CONNECT requests. Well, you can easily set up your SSH server so that it listens on both 22 and 443 ports:

```
# sshd_config file
Port 22
Port 443
```

What if you also run a HTTPS server on this machine? There is no way for you to contact it outside port 443 (due to the security policy) and besides, everyone else using the service at *https://home.example.com/* uses port 443.

You have one port and two services. Do you really have to abandon one of them?

The Hack

You need some kind of proxy, or rather, reverse-proxy sitting on port 443 at home.example.com that can tell the difference between a SSL connection and a SSH connection.

Using a tool such as Ethereal, it's quite easy to notice the differences between the two protocols by looking at the first few packets of data exchanged. The SSH server packets look something like:

```
SSH-2.0-OpenSSH_3.9p1
```

while the client resembles:

```
SSH-2.0-OpenSSH_4.2p1 Debian-5
```

---

* The standard port for HTTPS.

Then they both negotiate the cyphering protocol and everything else. HTTP over SSL looks different. A common session might be:

```
Client: ....s...o......$.@]w#.U!..F.(.h..^.#y....D....[/.x.=...."..w.4..
Server: ....J...F..C.B.....y..cY.}s......h\.qo.......9..8.i.|..7..
```

Here it's unreadable garbage from the beginning—but did you notice the difference?

When using a protocol like SSH, the server always speaks first, and sends a banner to the client. When using HTTP over SSL, it's the client that speaks first.

Now you have a way to discriminate between the two services: once a client has connected to the reverse-proxy's port 443, if it immediately sends data then it's an SSL client; if it does nothing and waits for data to be sent by the server, then it's a SSH client. The reverse proxy can wait for a short timeout before deciding which of the two services to contact. With the connection established, it can start its proxy work and send data back and forth between client and server.

In 2003, Philippe "BooK" Bruhat wrote a 160-line script that did just that. Nowadays, all the necessary logic to write a network proxy is in a module aptly named Net::Proxy. Creating a reverse proxy to serve both HTTPS and SSH on port 443 of your home machine is now a handful of lines of code away:

```perl
#!/usr/bin/perl

use strict;
use warnings;

use Net::Proxy;

# show some information on STDERR
Net::Proxy->set_verbosity(1);

# run this on the server that should listen on port 443
my $proxy = Net::Proxy->new(
    {   in =>
        {
            type        => 'dual',
            host        => '0.0.0.0',
            port        => 443,
            client_first =>
            {
                type => 'tcp',
                port => 444,    # move the https server to another port
            },
            server_first =>
            {
```

```
                          type => 'tcp',
                          port => 22,      # good old SSH
                    },

                    # wait during a 2 second timeout
                    timeout      => 2,
               },
          out => { type => 'dummy' },
     }
);

$proxy->register( );

Net::Proxy->mainloop( );
```

Depending on your operating system, you may need to run the program with some administrative privileges to listen on a port below 1024.

Running the Hack

Run the program on your server. From your workstation, connect as usual. The only limitation of dual is that you have to find a pair of services with these special characteristics. HTTP and HTTPS are protocols where the client speaks first. The server speaks first with SSH, POP3, and SMTP.

Hacking the Hack

Net::Proxy is how BooK hacked the sslh hack (the 160-line Perl script). This module introduces the concept of connectors: in connectors accept incoming (client) connections and forward them toward servers via out connectors.

There is a tcp connector that handles standard TCP inbound and outbound connections, a connect connector that implements the CONNECT trick mentioned earlier, and a dummy connector that does nothing. BooK plans to add new connectors over time.

The dual connector used in this example uses the timeout trick to decide which connector (server_first or client_first) will contact the remote service. So the usual out parameter is just a dummy connector.

You can also use Net::Proxy to proxy an outgoing SSH connection through the corporate proxy:

```
#!/usr/bin/perl

use strict;
use warnings;

use Net::Proxy;
```

```
# show some information on STDERR
Net::Proxy->set_verbosity(1);

# run this on your workstation
my $proxy = Net::Proxy->new(
    {   in =>
        {
            # local port for local SSH client
            port => 2222,
            type => 'tcp',
        },
        out =>
        {
            host        => 'home.example.com',
            port        => 443,
            proxy_host  => 'proxy.company.com',
            proxy_port  => 8080,
            proxy_user  => 'id23494',
            proxy_pass  => 's3kr3t',
            proxy_agent => 'Mozilla/4.0 (compatible; MSIE 6.0; Windows XP)',
        },
    }
);

$proxy->register();

Net::Proxy->mainloop();
```

To reach the https server, use your browser as usual—you've already configured it to use the corporate proxy!

Two scripts included in the Net::Proxy distribution support both of these uses. sslh lets you run two services on a single port on the server side and connect-tunnel helps you get through the corporate proxy on the client side.

HACK #98 Improve Your Dispatch Tables

Run code based on regex matches.

A dispatch table, in the form of a hash, is a useful technique for associating code with keys:

```
my %dispatch =
(
    red   => sub { return qq{<font color="#ff0000">$_[0]</font>} },
    green => sub { return qq{<font color="#00ff00">$_[0]</font>} },
    blue  => sub { return qq{<font color="#0000ff">$_[0]</font>} },
    black => sub { return qq{<font color="#000000">$_[0]</font>} },
    white => sub { return qq{<font color="#ffffff">$_[0]</font>} },
);
```

This approach lets you print out pretty HTML:

```
print $dispatch{black}->('knight');
```

Of course, this only works as long as the keys you use are fixed strings, because the hash lookup relies on string equality.

A regular expression that contains meta-characters (such as \d or [abc]) can match strings, but the string matched is not equal (in the sense of string equality) to the regular expression. In other words, this reasonable-looking code just does not work:

```
my %dispatch =
(
  # note that backslashes need to be "doubled up"
  '\\d'   => sub { return "saw a digit" },
  '[a-z]' => sub { return "saw a lowercase letter" },
);
```

Looking up $dispatch{5} won't find anything. Being able to make it work would be very useful; Regexp::Assemble will let you do just that.

The hack

The idea is to gather all the different keys of the dispatch table and assemble them into a single regular expression. Given such an expression, you can then apply it to a target string and see what matches.

Even better, specifying a tracked pattern lets you find out after the match which pattern from the dispatch triggered the match. Once you have this, use it as a key into the dispatch table and call the corresponding code block. The more keys there are, the better the situation becomes, because instead of running down a long chain of regular expression matches in an if/elsif/ elsif chain sequentially, you need only one match to try them all at once.

At the simplest, assemble the keys in the above dispatch table into a single tracked regular expression with:

```
my $re = Regexp::Assemble->new->track->add(keys %dispatch);
```

You can then use this to process a file with a loop as simple as:

```
while (<>)
{
    $re->match($_) and print $dispatch{$re->matched}->();
}
```

Running the Code

As an example, consider an IRC bot. You may wish to program a bot to react to many different messages observed on a channel. Ordinarily, you might do this with a mini-parser running through a list of regular expressions. Regexp::Assemble allows you to use a dispatch table instead.

All that you need is a hash whose keys are regular expressions (or to be precise, scalars usable as regexps), and whose values are code references.

First assemble the hash keys, and then match the resulting expression against incoming messages on an IRC channel. When a match occurs, recover the original regexp and use it to look up the code reference in the dispatch table and call that, passing in the captured variables that the pattern specified.

Here's a bare-bones IRC bot that has just enough smarts to keep track of karma (foo++, bar--) and factoids (for instance, the association that TPF is The Perl Foundation, so when someone asks "TPF?", the bot responds with the definition).

The instantiating code is very short, thanks to Bot::BasicBot:

```
use DispatchBot;

my $bot = DispatchBot->new(
    server   => "irc.perl.org",
    port     => "6667",
    channels => ["#bottest"],
    nick     => 'rebot',
);
$bot->run( );
```

The package DispatchBot is where everything all happens:

```
package DispatchBot;

use strict;
use Regexp::Assemble;
use Bot::BasicBot;
use YAML qw(LoadFile DumpFile);

use vars qw( $VERSION @ISA );
$VERSION     = '0.03';
@ISA         = 'Bot::BasicBot';

my $factoid = _load( 'factoid.dat' ); # "foo" is "bar" factoids
my $karma   = _load( 'karma.dat' );   # keep track of foo++ and foo--

sub _load
{
    my $file = shift;
    return -e $file ? LoadFile($file) : {};
}

sub _save
{
    my ($dictionary, $file) = @_;
    DumpFile( $file, $dictionary );
}
```

```
sub _flush
{
    _save( $factoid, 'factoid.dat' );
    _save( $karma,   'karma.dat' );
}

END { _flush }

my %dispatch =
(
    # define a factoid
    '(\\S+) is (.*)$' => sub { $factoid->{$_[0]} = $_[1]; _flush; return },

    # query a factoid
    '(\\S+)\s*\\?$' => sub
    {
        exists $factoid->{$_[0]}
            and return "I believe that $_[0] is $factoid->{$_[0]}"
    },

    # drop a factoid
    'forget (\\S+)$'=> sub
    {
        if (exists $factoid->{$_[0]})
        {
            my $message = "I forgot $_[0]";
            delete $factoid->{$_[0]};
            _flush;
            return $message;
        }
    },

    # karma shifts
    '(\\S+)\\+\\+' => sub { $karma->{$_[0]}++; _flush; return },
    '(\\S+)--'     => sub { $karma->{$_[0]}--; _flush; return },

    # karma query
    '^karma (\\S+)$' => sub
    {
        return exists $karma->{$_[0]}
            ? "$_[0] has karma of $karma->{$_[0]}"
            : "$_[0] has neutral karma"
    },

    # time... to die
    '^!quit$' => sub { exit },
);

my $re = Regexp::Assemble->new->track->add(keys %dispatch);

sub said
{
    my ($self, $arg) = @_;
```

```
$re->match($arg->{body})
    and return $dispatch{$re->matched}->($re->capture);
return;
}
```

Track Your Approximations

HACK #99

Avoid rounding errors; get the right results.

Floating-point numbers are inherently approximate. Perl represents numbers in the most accurate way it can on your hardware, but typically it can't do better than about 16 significant digits. That means that a calculation you think is accurate:

```
my $dx    = 2112300000000000000000000000000000000000000000000000000000;
my $rate = 1.23e12;

my $end  = ( 23 * $dx - $rate * 230 - 2.34562516 ** 2 - 0.5 ) ** 0.33;
```

may in fact not be precise.

On a 32-bit machine, the various floating-point approximations introduced along the way may mean the final value of $end is inaccurate by about 937. Of course, the correct value of $end is approximately 520642400412471062. 6461124479995125761153. If $end is your annual profit margin, you may not really care if it's off by a thousand dollars or so. On the other hand, if the same calculation were a trajectory for a lunar lander, turning off the retro-rockets 937 meters too high might matter a great deal.

How can you make sure your calculations aren't fatally inaccurate? The easiest way is to let Perl do it for you. To accomplish that, you need to change the way floating-point numbers work. Easy.

Interval interlude

Interval arithmetic is a simple technique for tracking the accuracy of numeric computations. Instead of representing each value as a single number, encode it as a range: minimum possible value to maximum possible value.

For example, most platforms can't represent the number 1. 2345678901234567890 exactly. Interval arithmetic would encode it as the range [1.23456789012345, 1.23456789012346], assuming those two values are the closest lower and upper bounds that your machine *can* represent. On the other hand, if your machine could represent the number 1.23456, then it would encode it as [1.23456, 1.23456], with identical lower and upper bounds as there is no uncertainty about the actual value.

Once every number is properly encoded, any unary operations on the number are applied to both the minimal and maximal values, producing a new range that encodes the result. For example, the operation:

```
sqrt( [1.2, 1.3] )
```

yields:

```
[1.095445, 1.140175]
```

being the square roots of the minimal and maximal values. Logically, the true square root of the true value must lie somewhere in that new range.

Binary operations are more complex. They have to be performed on every possible combination of the minimal and maximal values of each operand. Then the minimal and maximal outcomes are used as the encoding of the result. For example, the multiplication:

```
[1.2, 1.3] * [-1, 0.9]
```

produces the result:

```
[-1.3, 1.17]
```

because:

```
1.2 *  -1 → -1.2
1.3 *  -1 → -1.3    (minimal value)
1.2 * 0.9 →  1.08
1.3 * 0.9 →  1.17   (maximal value)
```

The advantage of interval arithmetic is that, provided you're careful about rounding errors, the exact result is always *guaranteed* to lie somewhere in the interval you produce. Intervals also make it easy to estimate how accurate your computation is: the smaller the interval, the more precise the answer.

You can also think of intervals as: *average value(±half-interval)*. So you could also write the operation:

```
[1.2, 1.3] * [-1, 0.9]  →  [-1.3, 1.17]
```

as:

```
1.25(±0.05) * -0.05(±0.95)  →  -0.065(±1.235)
```

This representation gives a clear indication of how the accuracy of the approximation changes under different operations, and how the uncertainty in the result grows over time.

Teaching Perl to think in intervals

To make Perl track the accuracy of your floating-point calculations, you first have to convince it to represent every floating point number as an interval:

```
package Number::Intervals;

# Compute maximal error in the representation of a given number...
sub _eps_for
{
    my ($num, $epsilon) = (shift) x 2;          # copy arg to both vars
    $epsilon /= 2 while $num + $epsilon/2 != $num;  # whittle epsilon down
    return $epsilon;
}

# Create an interval object, allowing for representation errors...
sub _interval
{
    use List::Util qw( min max );
    my ($min, $max) = ( min(@_), max(@_) );
    return bless [$min - _eps_for($min), $max + _eps_for($max)], __PACKAGE__
;
}

# Convert all floating-point constants to interval objects...
sub import
{
    use overload;

    overload::constant(
        float => sub
        {
            my ($raw, $cooked) = @_;
            return _interval($cooked);
        },
    );
}
```

When your code uses Number::Intervals, its import() will call the
constant() subroutine from the standard overload module. That subroutine does exactly what its name suggests: it overloads the standard handling of constants with new behaviors. In this case, you're overloading the
handling of floating-point constants by providing a subroutine that will be
called every time a literal floating-point value appears in your program.

That handler subroutine receives two arguments: a string containing the raw
source code that defined the constant ($raw), and a numeric value that is
how Perl would normally interpret that source code definition ($cooked).
The subroutine should return an object to use instead of the constant value.

In this instance, the handler just returns the corresponding interval object
for the cooked value, as provided by _interval($cooked). That function
determines the minimal and maximal values it receives and uses them as the
lower and upper bounds of the resulting range. Note that it also subtracts
the smallest possible amount (_eps_for($min)) from the lower bound and
adds the smallest possible amount (_eps_for($max)) to the upper bound.

Adding and subtracting these epsilon values doesn't produce the smallest possible interval representing the original value, but the interval it does produce has three essential advantages: it's trivial to compute, it's guaranteed to correctly bound any number passed to _interval() (regardless of the rounding scheme your floating-point implementation uses), and it still produces the second-smallest possible interval representing the original number.

Of course, this isn't the end of the story. Depending on how you use Number::Intervals objects, you may get the wrong results. You can fix that too, though, in "Overload Your Operators" [Hack #100].

Overload Your Operators
Make your objects look like numbers, strings, and booleans sensibly.

Few people realize that Perl is an operator-oriented language, where the behavior of data depends on the operations you perform on it. You've probably had the experience of inadvertently stringifying an object or reference and wondering where and why you suddenly see memory addresses.

Fortunately, you can control what happens to your objects in various contexts.

Consider the Number::Intervals module from "Track Your Approximations" [Hack #99]. It's useful, but as shown there it has a few drawbacks.

The effect of the import() subroutine is that any code that declares:

```
use Number::Intervals;
```

will thereafter have every floating-point constant replaced by a Number::Intervals object that encodes upper and lower bounds on the original constant. That impressive achievement (utterly impossible in most other programming languages) will, sadly, be somewhat undermined when you then write:

```
use Number::Intervals;

my $avogadro    = 6.02214199e23;    # standard physical constant
my $atomic_mass = 55.847;           # atomic mass of iron
my $mass        = 100;              # mass in grams

my $count       = int( $mass * $avogadro/$atomic_mass );

print "Number of atoms in $mass grams of iron = $count\n";
```

The unfortunate result is:

```
$ perl count_atoms.pl

Number of atoms in 100 grams of iron = 99
```

Iron atoms are heavy, but they're not *that* heavy. The correct answer is just a little over 1 million billion billion, so converting to intervals appears to have made the calculation noticably *less* accurate.

The problem is that the import( ) code you implemented to reinterpret Perl's floating-point constants did just that. It converted those constants into interval objects; that is, into references to blessed arrays. When you multiply and divide those interval objects, Perl converts the corresponding array references to integer addresses, which it then multiplies and divides. The calculation:

```
$mass * $avogadro / $atomic_mass
```

becomes something like:

```
100 * 0x1808248 / 0x182dc10
```

which is:

```
100 * 25199176 / 25353232
```

which is where the spurious 99 came from.

Somehow, you need to teach Perl not only how to convert floating-point numbers to interval objects, but also how to compute sensibly with those objects.

The Hack

The trick, of course, is to overload the arithmetic operators that will apply to Number::Intervals objects by using the overload pragma:

```perl
# Overload operators for Number::Intervals objects...
use overload
(
    # Add two intervals by independently adding minima and maxima...
    q{+} => sub
    {
        my ($x, $y) = _check_args(@_);
        return _interval($x->[0] + $y->[0], $x->[1] + $y->[1]);
    },

    # Subtract intervals by subtracting maxima from minima and vice versa...
    q{-} => sub
    {
        my ($x, $y) = _check_args(@_);
        return _interval($x->[0] - $y->[1], $x->[1] - $y->[0]);
    },

    # Multiply intervals by taking least and greatest products...
    q{*} => sub
    {
        my ($x, $y) = _check_args(@_);
        return _interval($x->[0] * $y->[0], $x->[1] * $y->[0],
```

```
                          $x->[1] * $y->[1], $x->[0] * $y->[1],
                      );
    },

    # Divide intervals by taking least and greatest quotients...
    q{/} => sub
    {
        my ($x, $y) = _check_args(@_);
        return _interval($x->[0] / $y->[0], $x->[1] / $y->[0],
                         $x->[1] / $y->[1], $x->[0] / $y->[1],
                      );
    },

    # Exponentiate intervals by taking least and greatest powers...
    q{**} => sub
    {
        my ($x, $y) = _check_args(@_);
        return _interval($x->[0] ** $y->[0], $x->[1] ** $y->[0],
                         $x->[1] ** $y->[1], $x->[0] ** $y->[1],
                      );
    },

    # Integer value of an interval is integer value of bounds...
    q{int} => sub
    {
        my ($x) = @_;
        return _interval(int $x->[0], int $x->[1]);
    },

    # Square root of interval is square roots of bounds...
    q{sqrt} => sub
    {
        my ($x) = @_;
        return _interval(sqrt $x->[0], sqrt $x->[1]);
    },

    # Unary minus: negate bounds and swap upper/lower:
    q{neg} => sub
    {
        my ($x) = @_;
        return _interval(-$x->[1], -$x->[0]);
    },

    # etc. etc. for the other arithmetic operators...
);
```

The overload module expects a list of key/value pairs, where each key is the name of an operator and each value is a subroutine that implements that operator. Once they're installed, each of the implementation subroutines will be called whenever an object of the class is an argument to the corresponding operator.

Unary operators (including int, neg, and sqrt) receive the operand object as their only argument; binary operators (like +, *, and **) receive three arguments: their two operands and an extra flag indicating whether the operands appear in reversed order (because the first operand wasn't an object). Binary operators therefore need to check, and sometimes unreverse, their arguments, which the _check_args( ) subroutine does for them:

```
# Flip args if necessary, converting to an interval if not already...
sub _check_args
{
    my ($x, $y, $reversed) = @_;

    return $reversed              ? ( _interval($y), $x             )
         : ref $y ne __PACKAGE__  ? ( $x,            _interval($y) )
         :                          ( $x,            $y            );
}
```

Note that this utility subroutine also converts any non-interval arguments (integers, for example) to interval ranges. This means that, after calling _check_args( ), all of the binary handlers can be certain that their operands are in the correct order and that both operands are proper interval objects. This greatly simplifies the implementation of the overloaded operators. In particular, they don't need to implement three separate sets of logic for handling interval/number, number/interval, and interval/interval interactions.

Saying what you mean. Reimplementing the necessary operators enables you to add, subtract, multiply, divide, and so on, interval representations correctly. However, even with the overloading in place, the results of counting the atoms are still more ironic than ferric:

```
$ perl count_atoms_v2.pl

Number of atoms = Number::Intervals=ARRAY(0x182f89c)
```

The problem is that, although Perl now knows how to do operations on interval objects, it still has no idea how to convert those interval objects back to simple numbers, or to strings. When you try to print a floating-point interval object, it prints the string representation of the object reference, rather than the string representation of the *value* that the object represents.

Fortunately, it's easy to tell the interpreter how to convert intervals back to sensible numbers and strings. Just give the Number::Intervals class two extra handlers for stringification and numerification, like this:

```
use overload
(
    # Stringify intervals as: VALUE (±UNCERTAINTY)...
```

```
q{""} => sub
{
    my ($self) = @_;

    my $uncert = ($self->[1] - $self->[0]) / 2;

    use charnames qw( :full );
    return $self->[0]+$uncert . " (\N{PLUS-MINUS SIGN}$uncert)";
},

# Numerify intervals by averaging their bounds (with warning)...
q{0+} => sub
{
    my ($self) = @_;
    carp "Approximating interval by a single (averaged) number";
    return ($self->[0] + $self->[1]) /2;
},
);
```

With that back-translation in place, the floating point calculations can finally proceed correctly, with their accuracy being automatically tracked and reported as well:

```
$ perl count_atoms_v3.pl
```

```
Number of atoms = 1.07832864612244e+24 (±805306368)
```

HACK 101   Learn from Obfuscations

Learn more about Perl from the play of others.

Perl has a reputation for serious play. Think of Perl golf (solving problems in the fewest characters possible), JAPHS (printing a simple message in creative ways), and obfuscation (writing odd code that does surprising things). Though you'd never use these tricks in production code, producing such creative programs requires careful study and exploration—both tricks of good hackers.

Exploring obfuscation can also expand your Perl skills.

Consider an obfuscation I posted at Perl Monks (*http://www.perlmonks.org/index.pl?node_id=77619*; the link includes a deconstruction and explanation by Guildenstern). It is a non-traditional JAPH that is self-referential. Sort of. The use of a variable called pi, the use of the sin function, and the visual layout of the code all hint at what the output will be. The irony of course is that while the layout helps you know what to expect, it actually hinders understanding.

```
#!/usr/bin/perl                              # how to (ab)use substr
use warnings;
use strict;

my $pi='3.141592105351526233464752403750621637504462403335433750 62';
```

```
      substr    ($^X,0)=
        substr    ($pi,-6);map{
          substr    ($^X,$.++,1)=chr(
            substr ($pi,21,2)+
            substr ($pi,$_,2))}(12,28,-18,-6,-10,14);map{$^O=$"x(
          substr    ($pi,-5,2));
        substr    ($^O,sin(++$a/8)*32+
      substr    ($pi,-2)/2+1,1)=$_;
    substr    ($^O,sin($a/4)*(
  substr    ($pi,2,2))+
substr    ($pi,-7,-5)-1,1)=$_;print"$^O$/";eval{$^X.('$b','x3).
substr    ($pi,-3,1).'.'.
  substr    ($pi,9,2));}(map{chr($_+
    substr    ($pi,21,2))}(
      substr    ($pi,8)x6)=~/../g);
```

"So", you may think, "what could be the pedagogical value of this rather ridiculous piece of code?". I believe its value lies in its ability to raise questions that cause the curious to seek out answers.

Complete beginners might inquire:

- l00k5 k3w1 d00d!!! Wh4t l4ngu4g3 15 th4t?
- Is this really a computer program that runs and does something?

Those with a little exposure to Perl may ask:

- Does Perl allow such bizarre formatting without throwing errors?
- Can you really create a number with that many digits of accuracy?
- What does substr do? Is it like the C function?

More experienced programmers may wonder:

- How does the animation work with only one print statement and no for or while loops?
- You can put substr on the left hand side?
- Are there both two and three argument forms of substr?
- I've figured out that there's a select call in the program, but what's it doing?
- How come use strict; and use warnings; don't complain? Aren't they supposed to ensure the quality of your code?
- Why didn't he have to declare $a and $b using my?

As for myself, the value of this obfu was in the enjoyment I received from creating and sharing it with the Perl community, and in the comments and feedback I received because of it. I consider the few hours that it took to write it time well spent.

When you come across Perl play in your travels, certainly do take apart the code with B::Deparse and pore through perldoc perlfunc and perldoc perlvar to find out what's going on. Then take a step back to ask the deeper questions and ponder how you too can assemble your own creations from Perl's rich vocabulary.

Happy coding!

Index

We'd like to hear your suggestions for improving our indexes. Send email to *index@oreilly.com*.

invisible characters, debugging
      and, 130–133
invoking functions, 224–230
IO::Scalar module, 183
iteration, 66
      multiple values from iterators, 68–70

L

lib pragma, 73
libraries, shared, XS and, 248–250
list comprehension, 231
List::UtilTerm::ReadKey module, 221
live code, testing, 162–164
locked hashes, 221–222

M

Mac::Growl module, 37
memory, program size, 204–206
methods
      accessor, autogenerating, 125–128
      encapsulation, 113–116
mod_perl, 168, 183
module, 224
      Test::Harness, 159
Module::Build module, 45, 150, 156,
      173
Module::CoreList module, 186
Module::Reloader module, 75
modules
      aliased, 71
            importing and, 72
      Attribute::Docstring, 111
      Attribute::Handlers, 112, 120
      B::Concise, 196, 210
      B::Deparse, 117, 142, 266
      B::Generate, 119
      B::Keywords, 211
      B::Lint, 211
      B::Lint::Pluggable, 212
      B::Lint::VoidSyscalls, 212
      Bot::BasicBot, 255
      B::Terse, 210
      B::TerseSize, 204
      bundles, 76–78
      B::XPath, 197
      Class::BuildMethods, 127
      classes, name shortening, 71–72
      Class::HideMethods, 113
      Class::InsideOut, 108
      Class::MethodMaker, 126

Class::Roles, 184
Class::Std, 108
Class:Std, 108
Class::Trait, 184
Contextual::Return, 238
Convert::Binary::C, 250
core, tracking, 186–187
CPAN, 93–96
Data::Dump::Streamer, 142, 195
debugging, 101–105
Devel::Command, 146
Devel::Peek, 199
Devel::Symdump, 202
Devel::TraceUse, 189
DumpValue, 182
Exception::Class, 91
Export, 60
ExtUtils::MakeMaker, 45, 150
Fatal, 233
File::Glob, 231
File::ReadBackwards, 54
File::Slurp, 221
Filter::Macro, 84
Filter::Simple, 243
Firefox
      comments, 3
      documentation, 2
      search for, 2
Hash::Util, 221
HTTP::Proxy, 49
Inline::C, 248
installations and, 78–80
IO::Interactive, 32
IO::Prompt, 33
IO::Scalar, 183
IO::Zlib, 93, 95
List::UtilTerm::ReadKey, 221
Module::Build, 47, 150, 156, 173
Module::CoreList, 186
Module::Reloader, 75, 172
Net::Netmask, 67
Net::Proxy, 251
Object::InsideOut, 108
overloading, 257
P5NCI, 248
PadWalker, 193
PAR, 97
Parse::CPAN::Modlist, 95
patching, 87–89
paths and, 72–74
      presolving, 81–82

Colophon

The tool on the cover of *Perl Hacks* is a pair of work boots. Work boots are often worn for protection from the elements while hiking or fishing, or by any number of laborers—such as contractors and steel workers—to protect their feet from injury. Work boots come in many different sizes, materials, and colors.

The cover image is from The Creatas Images division of JupiterImages Corp. The cover font is Adobe ITC Garamond. The text font is Linotype Birka; the heading font is Adobe Helvetica Neue Condensed; and the code font is LucasFont's TheSans Mono Condensed.

Better than e-books

Buy *Perl Hacks* and access the digital
edition FREE on Safari for 45 days.

Go to www.oreilly.com/go/safarienabled
and type in coupon code SKHQ-2SWI-NM7S-GDHC-5ZB9

Search
thousands of
top tech books

Download
whole chapters

Cut and Paste
code examples

Find
answers fast

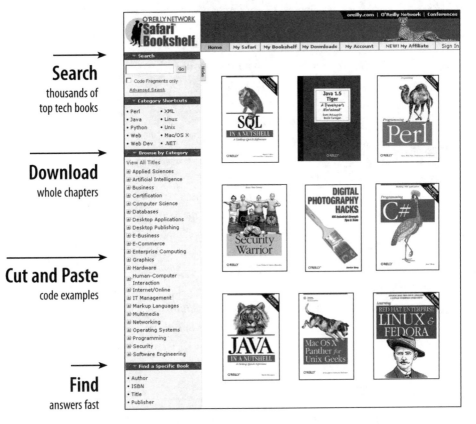

Search Safari! The premier electronic reference
library for programmers and IT professionals.

Related Titles from O'Reilly

Perl

Advanced Perl Programming, *2nd Edition*

CGI Programming with Perl, *2nd Edition*

Computer Science & Perl Programming:
 The Best of the Perl Journal

Embedding Perl in HTML with Mason

Games, Diversions, & Perl Culture: The Best of the Perl Journal

Intermediate Perl

Learning Perl, *4th Edition*

Mastering Algorithms with Perl

Mastering Perl/Tk

Mastering Regular Expressions, *2nd Edition*

Perl & LWP

Perl & XML

Perl 6 and Parrot Essentials, *2nd Edition*

Perl Best Practices

Perl CD Bookshelf, *Version 4.0*

Perl Cookbook, *2nd Edition*

Perl Debugger Pocket Reference

Perl for System Administration

Perl Graphics Programming

Perl Hacks

Perl in a Nutshell, *2nd Edition*

Perl Pocket Reference, *4th Edition*

Perl Template Toolkit

Perl Testing: A Developer's Notebook

Practical mod_perl

Programming the Perl DBI

Programming Perl, *3rd Edition*

Programming Web Services with Perl

Regular Expression Pocket Guide

RT Essentials

Web, Graphics & Perl/Tk: The Best of the Perl Journal

XML Publishing with AxKit

O'REILLY®

Our books are available at most retail and online bookstores.
To order direct: 1-800-998-9938 • *order@oreilly.com* • *www.oreilly.com*
Online editions of most O'Reilly titles are available by subscription at *safari.oreilly.com*